CLONDALKIN

MEMORIES OF A
NEIGHBOURHOOD

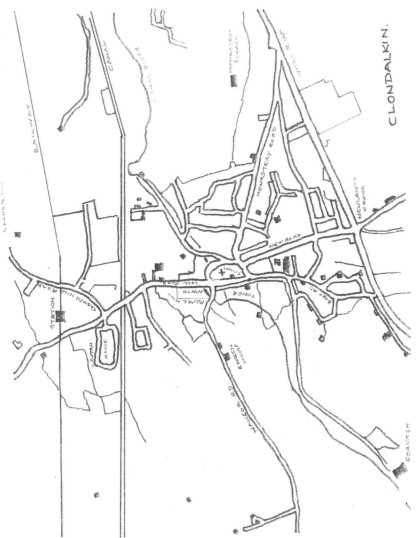

Credit for hand-drawn map to my late brother-in-law, Brendan O'Byrne.

CLONDALKIN

MEMORIES OF A
NEIGHBOURHOOD

GERTRUDE REYNOLDS

Raheen Cottage and, below, Raheen Cottage garden..

PROLOGUE

The history of Clondalkin and surrounding areas has been well-documented but my aim is to give a flavour of what it was like growing up in the area from the 1930s to the 1970s. I hope to give an insight into peoples' lives, the conditions in which they lived and to reflect on how things meshed together for good or for ill.

Aerial view of Clondalkin c. 1960s.

My family lived at the beating heart of Clondalkin, up the Nangor Road, as people used to say, although it is now known as 'Old Nangor Road.' Our home, Raheen Cottage, stood within an enclosed farmyard.

Bringing the reader out from town to our home, I propose to meander around different roads and outline the social map; who lived where, who was related to whom, and how the community intermingled, thus blurring lines between memoir and social history.

I want to emphasise that these are my personal memories which might differ from those of other family members or neighbours. Like everybody else, my memory rests with certain people and events often involving people of my own age - people that others might not consider memorable at all. As in every community, houses and places harbour secrets beneath the placid surface. I have no wish to cause offence in recording events on paper, nor do I wish to offend either by inclusion or omission of people or events. Before embarking on the journey, I want to highlight some important features that underpinned most communities, as Ireland was a very different place up to the 1970s and the book has to be read in context with the times.

The Irish Constitution of 1937 envisaged the 'family' as one based on marriage alone. Until 1973, women were forced to resign their job on marriage based on the 'marriage bar,' which existed in banks and the Public Service. The idea of equal pay and equal opportunity was only getting an airing in the early 1970s with the Commission on the Status of Women in 1972 setting off campaigns for womens' rights. Legislation on equal pay was introduced in 1974 and employment equality legislation followed in 1977, both as a result of European directives. Contraception for all had not been legalised and children born out of wedlock had an 'illegitimate' status until 1987. Divorce was rejected by a substantial margin of voters in the first divorce referendum and it took ten more years before divorce was finally signed into law in 1996. The power of the clergy was largely unchallenged; people bowed to them as they did with other pillars of the community.

Religion permeated most aspects of life in Ireland and there were essentially two religions, Catholic and Protestant. Not alone did your persuasion tie you together by invisible threads, it also governed your church attendances and spilled over into education and social life. This caused a natural divide in the community, which was innately recognised by all, a case of 'us' and 'them.'

One might presume that this worked in reverse too, especially where religious groups were outnumbered. One must also take into consideration that many Catholics referred to certain families as 'Protestant' despite the fact that some were Presbyterian, Methodist, Anglican or of other persuasions.

Another feature of the 1930s was the influence of the local grandee families who provided employment and in many cases, housing. Practically every household had family members that worked either at grand houses, on the farm or engaged as servants. In the 1911 census, occupations shown include steward, housekeeper, cook, dairyman, herdsman, butler, footman, underservant, valet, maid, coachman, chauffeur, stable hand, gardener or labourer. Notably, most were documented as literate, but some are shown as illiterate. As dwelling places often came with a livelihood, many roles were passed down through generations. Others made a living indirectly from these establishments, providing local produce, provisions and services such as horse and cart hire, taxi hire, farm machinery repairs, farrier and veterinary services. It might be said that with this measure of dependency, a certain deference was expected.

Large families and overcrowding were commonplace, especially among Catholics to whom contraception was against the teaching of the church, the Humanitae Vitae having decreed in 1968 that artificial contraception in all forms was immoral. Vigorous campaigns resulted in limited availability of contraception in 1980. It was finally made available to all in 1985. Large families meant people were poorer and frequently lived hand-to-mouth, in tied cottages or tenanted accommodation. Families often took in lodgers or 'nurse' children to supplement the household income, even those who had insufficient accommodation for themselves. Thus, the census indicates people of different surnames living at the same address, variously described as 'boarder,' 'lodger,' or 'nurse child.'

Tuberculosis was a scourge on many families until its decline following an eradication programme in the 1950s. By the 1970s, it had all but vanished from our shores. Mortgages or loans were not a feature in the lives of ordinary folk who were paid low wages in cash and who invariably had no bank account and no prospect of ever having one, much less owning their own home. Despite being engaged in low-skilled jobs and the fact that most children only attended school until the age of fourteen, it would be foolish, however, to underestimate their untapped abilities.

The Shannon Scheme was set up in 1927 and following the erection of electricity poles all over the country, electrification arrived in 1939. After that, there was no more feeling around for a candle or messing about with oil and paraffin lamps. A measure of public street lighting made it easier to find your way home in the dark. Out went the 'wireless' too and when gadgets arrived by degrees - electric kettle, cooker, fridge, toaster – people wondered how they'd managed before. However, not everybody signed up for electricity, some were terrified at the prospect of ESB bills. My family were unusual in that we always had mains water but when mains water arrived for all, it changed peoples' lives. Another new development was the telephone and we are talking public telephone box here, not the private telephone in the home which came much later. Although convenient back then, telephone kiosks are mostly gone from streetscapes but not forgotten. Many queueing outside in the rain cursed when a caller pushed extra coins into the slot to extend a telephone conversation.

Back in the 1930s, life in the village of Clondalkin revolved around the Clondalkin Paper Mill, known locally as simply 'the Mill.' Being a small community, there was a certain cosiness and sense of belonging. People had friends from all walks of life and there was less snobbery. The village had a library, a cinema and playing fields and several sports clubs – golf, tennis, camogie and football. Evening classes, plays and concerts were held from time to time and the circus came once a year. There were four butchers in the village – Murphy's, Kelly's, Cruise's and Leahy's. Emmy and Maisie Jacobs kept a grocery shop and the telephone exchange. The Healy family had a newsagents and a sweetshop and owned the Black Lion bar and the Hart family ran a public house and a general store. Myles Sullivan sold cigarettes and sweets in his shop, where you could buy eight NKM toffees for a halfpenny, sixteen Nancy Balls for a penny or a stick of liquorice for a penny.

The doctor was Doctor Ryan and the fee for a callout to the house was two shillings and sixpence. The Jubilee Nurse did her rounds calling on sick people and the village had a dispensary, but no chemist. In the past, doctors made and dispensed their own formulations and thus, the term dispensary applied within a hospital setting or a doctor's clinic. Nowadays, medicines are manufactured by pharmaceutical companies and sold in individual pharmacies either upon prescription or with drugs that do not need to be prescribed, over the counter.

Some affluent families owned properties in Clondalkin and surrounding areas, ranging from landed gentry estates to tenanted cottages. Often, the views from these homes extended across the rural landscape and as far as the mountains on the Dublin/Wicklow border. The aftermath of World War II heralded changes to a familiar social landscape with evidence of a fall-off in numbers returning to work the land and serve the big houses, which had many repercussions.

Factors which contributed to Clondalkin's healthy rate of employment included the surrounding waterways - the Camac River and the Grand Canal - which lent to the establishment of factories, as well as its proximity to the railway and to the centre of Dublin, all within cycling distance. As well as having a hive of industry and small businesses, Clondalkin had an agricultural backdrop which was still there, right up to the 1970's. It was not unusual to see a dairy herd crossing the public road towards the milking parlour, or to pass steel milk churns left on raised wooden platforms outside a farm gate, for easy collection. In time, the milk truck ended the needs for churns.

In the 1930s, pockets of houses were built in Clondalkin, for example, fourteen local authority houses were built further up the Old Nangor Road, then Ledwidge's farm up the Boot Road was built upon. However, the village's relatively pastoral setting started to change when builders bought up more farmland for development. Expansion escalated over the years with housing estates going up at Moyle Park, St. Patrick's Park, St. Bridget's Road, Newlands, Laurel Park, Monastery Road, Cappaghmore and many more places. Bit by bit, the builders inched their way until the village was finally subsumed into the suburban fabric of Dublin. I know of a couple living in the area all their lives who got lost around the Red Cow roundabout and found their way home by following a number 51 bus. Once Clondalkin was designated a 'satellite town,' it changed almost beyond recognition. The Naas Road, once a highway to Limerick, became the first dual-carriageway in Ireland, later the N7 and later still, the M7 motorway.

In the late 1980s, the M50 motorway went up and not too far away, the 'New' Nangor Road was built. By that stage, the rumble of traffic could be heard from our old home and the fields where I once played were built upon. The Old Nangor Road now bears no resemblance to the road I once knew, crisscrossed as it is by new roads, junctions and dead ends, to the detriment of the local character and integrity of the village.

Clondalkin's newer inhabitants cannot be expected to know the one-time importance of landmarks such as the 'Sandy Hole,' a favourite swimming spot for kids, or the 'Towers Field,' a sports field with its entrance beside the Presbytery on the New Road, 'Ging's shop,' which was on the corner of Old Nangor Road or indeed, places that inspired fear into children, due to their ghostly connections, such as Moore's Lane, Sally Park and Lover's Lane at Collinstown House – more about them later. They are probably not aware either that nicknames abounded to such a degree that people were often known only by nickname and you might never learn their real name at all. The local barber, 'Snip-Snap-the-Enchanter,' the bicycle man, 'Soluice Bonk,' a skinny policeman, 'Chain Breaker' and others - I have deliberately omitted the surnames of a few that come to mind: 'Bunty,' 'Skinner,' 'Bumpy,' 'Pop,' 'Bogey,' 'Dykes,' 'Legs', 'Salty,' 'Snowball,' because of his blonde hair and 'Tombstone,' because he never smiled. How most of them got their names I do not know, but I believe my older brother 'Son' was part of the group who came up with nick-names.

It is part of life that people break away and although they might end up living not too far away, you may not see them for years. When you bump into them, you can easily re-connect, despite how far you have travelled, as there is mutual understanding and that same upbringing is in the very marrow of your bones. I felt the need to reach into the past, put pen to paper and record for posterity a way of life around Clondalkin that is gone forever. My wish is to record my memories of a particular time and the characters and habits that made the village of Clondalkin what it was and moulded it for the future.

Tower Road, Clondalkin c. 1890. St. John's schoolhouse and schoolteacher's house on the right.

Tower Road, Clondalkin c. 1960. St. John's schoolhouse and schoolteacher's house on the right.

ACKNOWLEDGEMENTS

With very special thanks to South Dublin County Libraries and Dublin City Council for their kind sponsorship of this book.

Carrowmore Publishing, The History Press, Dublin 2, also deserves a special thanks and in particular, Ronan Colgan, Publishing Director, whose calm and practical approach is much appreciated, also the very patient Sam Tranum.

Many thanks also to Gerard Byrne of Old Clondalkin and Surrounding Districts. Gerard's generosity in posting photos and information brings much pleasure to people at home and abroad with an interest in Clondalkin and engenders a sharing environment that brings forth further memories and records.

A further thankyou to Patrick Ging and the Clondalkin History Society who maintain a great archive on Clondalkin that reaches all by way of blogposts - a mine of interesting photos and information.

A great debt is owed to my late brother-in-law, Brendan O'Byrne, and my sister, Gwen, for the fruit of years of prolific family research and an invaluable photographic record which they kindly shared.

Many thanks also to Paul Murray, prize-winning poet and former Killeen Paper Mills employee for sharing his wonderful poem, 'Camac Maiden.'

The author gratefully acknowledges the following people and institutions who assisted, pointed me in the right direction and generously shared information, photographs and permission to reproduce them.

Artwork – Monica Sproule, Mary Reynolds and Josephine Byrne for sharing Laetitia Hamilton's print.

Clondalkin History Society.

Dublin City Council – Mary-Liz Walshe.

Editorial assistants – Mary Reynolds, Mairead Rooney and Laura McKenna.

Keogh family – Tommy Keogh and Kevin Keogh.

National Folklore Collection, Folklore Department, UCD and dúchas.ie. (The Schools Collection).

National Inventory of Architectural Heritage – Willie Cumming, Senior Architectural Advisor,

Department of Arts, Heritage, Regional, Rural and Gaeltacht Affairs.

Old Clondalkin and Surrounding Districts (Facebook site)

South Dublin County Libraries - Ann Dunne.

I wish to extend my appreciation to all others who advised and helped as I would like them to feel included in this acknowledgement. I also wish to thank at this stage any photographer and those who shared photographs, with whom I was unable to establish contact in time for this publication.

Photographs and art

Front cover: The watercolour painting of Clondalkin's Round Tower, which has been much painted and photographed over the years, is by my daughter, Mary.

Back cover: The painting of Clondalkin village is by Letitia M. Hamilton. Many thanks to Josephine Byrne for permission to include it in this book.

Inside covers: The photographs of Raheen Cottage on the inside cover were taken by my late brother-in-law, Brendan O'Byrne. The painting of the barns in our yard, now demolished, is by my daughter, Mary.

Other artwork: The paintings featured throughout the book are family creations; either by the hand of my late uncle, Harold Small, my sister, Monica Sproule, my daughter, Mary, or myself.

Disclaimer

The author acknowledges that there may be errors in this publication. Every effort has been made to verify the contents within the book and the author accepts no responsibility for any inaccuracies that were inadvertent and may have slipped through.

The author has made all reasonable efforts to identify and contact the original owners of documents and photographs reproduced in this book, to acknowledge copyright holders and to credit those who took or shared the photographs. Apologies if contact was not established with the individuals concerned or if credit was not given or misplaced.

CONTENTS INDEX

Introduction   5

1.   The History of Clondalkin village   15

2.   Connection of the Small family with Clondalkin   21

3.   Journey from the city centre to the fringes of Clondalkin   36

4.   Our home on the Nangor Road and our parents   50

5.   Red Cow and up the Belgard Road   59

6.   Small's Yard   69

7.   Naas Road towards Kingswood   76

8.   Extended family   84

9.   Along Monastery Road into Clondalkin village   91

10.   Domestic life at Raheen Cottage   103

11.   A circular tour around the core of Clondalkin village   112

12.   Clondalkin National School   128

13.   Up the New Road   135

14.   Extra-curricular activities   143

15.   Up the Boot Road and to Corkagh   156

16.   Outings   167

17.   Left side of Nangor Road from Ging's shop   173

18.   Food, Newspapers and Cigarettes   184

19.   Right side of Nangor Road from Ging's shop   191

20. Hallow 'Een and Christmas 202

21. 9th Lock Road to Lucan and Cloverhill 209

22. The War Years 233

23. The Camac River and its mills 239

24. Grown-up pursuits 263

25. Religion 271

26. Life after National School 285

27. Politics 297

28. Night life 301

29. Ghostly tales 307

Epilogue 313

1.
THE HISTORY OF CLONDALKIN VILLAGE

Clondalkin is a suburban town situated 10km west of Dublin city centre, under the administrative jurisdiction of South Dublin County Council local authority area. The town is a civil parish in the ancient barony of Uppercross, a name also used in relation to some local religious parishes. In Irish, 'Cluain Dolcáin,' means 'Dolcan's meadow.' Clondalkin forms part of the Dublin Mid-West Dáil political constituency. Its postal code is Dublin 22.

The River Camac, 24km in length, played an important part in the establishment of a settlement at Clondalkin. It is believed that Neolithic tribes first settled in the area around 7,600 years ago, taking advantage of the favourable location on the Camac River and the inland pass between the mountains and the river. Evidence of the presence of the Cualann Celtic tribespeople can be found in various mounds and raths.

Around the 6th century, it is believed that Saint Crónán Mochua, a reputed healer from Connaught, founded Clondalkin as a monastic settlement and became its first Abbott. The Annals, or records from the year, report that in 790, relics of St. Chrónáin and St. Kevin of Glendalough were displayed in the Tower. It is uncertain whether the relics were the bones of the saints or perhaps some of their possessions.

The round tower dates back to around 790 A.D., when it was built as part of the monastery, its main functions being the safety and veneration of the monastery's relics. At approximately 26 metres in height, the tower dominates the Clondalkin area and acts as a focal point. It is one of four remaining round towers in County Dublin and acknowledged as one of the oldest and best preserved in the country, still with its original conical cap.

Constructed of rough calp limestone, its door and window openings are framed with granite. It has a very shallow foundation, approximately 1 metre deep, and stands directly on a bed of calp limestone. Its circumference ranges between 15 and 17 metres with the circumference immediately above the buttress at 12.7 metres, making it the most slender of the remaining measurable examples of a round tower. An unusual feature is the buttress around the base of the tower which is one metre thick. As this does not appear to have been bound into the original structure, nor is it a feature of any other round tower, it appears that the buttress was a later addition. There are six windows in the tower. The stone corbels that held the wooden floors in place inside the tower show evidence of six floors, although there are only four floors now, so two floors must have been removed. A flight of stone steps ascends to a door which stands 4.20 metres above the pavement.

The Tower would have housed a scriptorium, a place where monks produced manuscripts. In the eighth century, during the time of Saint Fugillus, the first Bishop of Clondalkin, monks created famous artistic manuscripts of the Gospels on animal skin better known as 'vellum.' A portion of one of these manuscripts produced in Clondalkin, known as 'The Clondalkin Mass Book,' survives today in Karlsruhe Library in Germany.

In 833 A.D., when the Round Tower was attacked by Vikings, the monastery was plundered and burned to the ground and one of the early Norse kings of Dublin, Amlaíb Conung, built a fortress on the site. In 867 A.D., a force led by Cennétis Mac Gaíthéne, King of Loígis, burned the fortress at Clondalkin and killed many of Amlaíb's followers. The monastery was later restored and, with help from other surrounding monasteries, influenced the Viking settlers in their conversion to Christianity. The district remained under Danish control until 1014 A.D., prior to the Battle of Clontarf, when Brian Boru's troops ransacked the town and defeated the Vikings.

In the 12th century, when Clondalkin diocese was united with Dublin, it became an even more significant village of both prayer and learning. Clondalkin witnessed another historic event during the Norman invasion in 1171 when there was a battle there between Richard de Clare (known as 'Strongbow') and the last High King of Ireland, Ruairi O'Conchúir.

By 1547, Clondalkin was 'among the walled and good towns of this country' consisting of five streets, Mill Street, Steeple Street, Mahon Street, New Street and Pope Lane. One hundred years later, the village was the scene of fighting during the 1641 rebellion (also called the Eleven Years War), when a troop completely destroyed the village. In 1649, St. John's medieval church closed.

In the 18th and 19th centuries, when aristocratic gentlemen undertook tours of Ireland, they often visited the Clondalkin Round Tower. Many paintings and illustrations of the tower were completed by artists such as Samuel Molyneux in 1725, Gabriel Beranger, the Huguenot artist, in 1767, T. Archdeacon in 1770, George Petrie and Wakeman in 1843.

Photographer on Tower Road taking a picture of the Round Tower, c. 1901. St. John's School on the right. Kindly shared by Theresa Phelan.

St. John's Church and graveyard stand on the site of the former monastery. St. John's Church was built on the site of a previous church and dates back to about 1787. All that now remains of the monastic settlement is the round tower, medieval crosses in the grounds of St. John's Church and a recently discovered fosse, a type of medieval moat fortification, which could be traced along Orchard Road. The record in Thom's Almanac 1858 shows, 'Clondalkin Church, Rev. David Reade, Rector, Glebe House,' while Thom's Almanac 1882 shows, 'Clondalkin Church, Rev. Winslow Berry, Rector, Glebe House.' Porter's Guide and Directory for County Dublin 1912, records for Clondalkin Church of Ireland, 'Rev. Good, the Glebe.'

The old schoolhouse was built in 1870 alongside St. John's Church and in 1879, Church Terrace was built, com-

Repairs to Round Tower, Clondalkin in 1932, following a thunderstorm. Lightening conductor added. Photo courtesy Gerard Byrne.

Church Terrace (also known as 'The Almshouses'), Tower Road.

prising four houses known as 'The Alms Houses,' in memory of a former incumbent, Rev. David John Reade.

The Feast Day for the founder of the monastery in Clondalkin, is celebrated on the 6th of August. It was traditional to walk from the Round Tower in Clondalkin to Tobair Mochua in Celbridge on the eve of this feast day. In commemoration of this, the Round Tower Heritage Group now have an annual event known as Slí Chrónáin, where people from Clondalkin walk along the Grand Canal in the direction of Celbridge and meet walkers from Celbridge at Gollierstown Bridge. A Clondalkin Heritage umbrella group, Rally Round the Round Tower, was set up in 2004 to prevent potentially destructive commercial development in the vicinity of the ancient tower, in favour of a visitor centre, a campaign which luckily succeeded. The new visitor centre opened in 2017.

Clondalkin is also home to St. Brigid's Well, said to have been established as a well for baptising pagans. Legend has it that St. Brigid came to the site of the monastery at Clondalkin in the 5th century and baptised pagans at the well on Boot Road. The structure around it dates from 1761. The original railings were donated by Mill workers in the 1940s and the statue was given by Mary O'Toole. Back then, there were processions to the well on the 1st February each year, the feast day of St. Bridget. The well is believed to have curative powers. It was said that a piece of rag dipped in the water and used to wipe the face, particularly of young girls, cured eye complaints. After use, the rag was hung on an adjoining tree. The well was restored by South Dublin County Council in 1995.

Clondalkin Castle - view from 1830

In Lewis's Topographical Dictionary of Ireland, 1837, he describes how 'the greater portion of the parish of Clondalkin is arable land with fertile soil and the system of agriculture very much improved under the auspices of many resident gentlemen who farm their own estates and have established ploughing matches for prizes.'

Brown's Barn, formerly the Bianconi Coach House. Photo courtesy niah.ie.

Other important features on the outskirts of Clondalkin were the Grand Canal, with twelve miles of canal officially opening to traffic in 1779, and Charles Bianconi's Royal Garter Stables on the Naas Road, his principal depot to house his fleet of vehicles, more commonly known back then as the Bianconi Coach House but now known as Brown's Barn.

Painting by Monica Sproul (nee Small)

2.
CONNECTION OF
THE SMALL FAMILY
WITH CLONDALKIN

First off, I'll tell you a bit about the Small family and how they fit into the scheme of things in Clondalkin.

The Smalls are a sept of the Scottish Clan Murray of Atholl. My predecessors can be traced back to a Scottish charter of 1588 wherein John, the 5th Stewart Earl of Atholl, granted lands at Dirnanean in Strathardle to the Small family.

SMALL AND RELATED FAMILIES. 165

Seat—Kindrogan, County Perth.—Burke's Landed Gentry. Vol. 1, p. 665. 1852.

WILLIAM SMALL OF KINDROGAN, married ANNE
STEWART

The Small family motto is "*Ratione non ira*," which translates to "*By reason not rage.*" The Small family crest is an erect branch of palm. A gold button bearing an erect palm surrounded by the Small family motto was recently dug up in a garden plot on the Dirnanean estate.

By the time James Small (1835–1900) inherited the estate in 1859 on the death of his father, Patrick Small, the Dirnanean estate had been passed from father to son for nine generations. In 1867, James married Janet, daughter of Sir Jervoise Clarke-Jervoise.

James Small, Laird of Dirnanean (1835-1900), at Dirnanean in 1884, and James Small Memorial Stone, Kirkmichael, Perthshire, Scotland.

James was a major landowner and Strathardle Gathering Chieftain who served on local bodies which shaped the area and improved the roads. In honour of James's service to Perthshire, the community erected the James Small of Dirneanan monument, a Celtic cross which stands on the outskirts of the village which bears the following inscription:-

To the memory
of
James Small

of Dirnanean and Kirkhillocks
Justice of the Peace and Deputy Lieutenant
for the county of Perth.

Born 28th May 1835. Died 25th June 1900.
This cross was erected by 350 of his friends who loved and trusted him.

Dirnanean, in Gaelic, *Dior-na-nEan*, translates as 'The Bird's Grove,' an estate in the Parish of Kirkmichael. The following ditty appears in an article written in 1886.

Near-by the lodge of Dirnanean
There sleeps a warrior young and brave,
Who met with death in ancient days.
And here a mound marks his grave-
The plain fact is, a horse bones
Lie 'neath the mound between the stones,

About sixty years ago, when in his prime
The old laird Small spent a jovial time,
A favourite horse died on the hill,
Close by Dalreoch's gurgling rill
T'was here they buried it, and laid the bier,
Wi' many a sigh and many a tear!

When James Small died without a direct heir, the ownership of Dirnanean transitioned to a series of his nephews, but continued until the 1970s, having been purchased in 1926 by a distant Small family cousin, Francis Keir Balfour. Dirnanean is no longer in the ownership of the Small family but there are still Smalls living in Kirkmichael in Perthshire and memorial stones in the graveyard bear the name Small.

My own branch of the Small family had moved from Kirkmichael to Dundee before 1800. My paternal great-grandfather, Robert Small, was born in Dundee in 1809, but later moved to London where he worked as a mercantile clerk. My paternal grandparents were William Wilson Small and Margaret Semple.

William Wilson Small was born in 1830 in Dundee and trained as a scenic artist in the theatre. Married twice, he had twenty children in all, many whom did not survive childhood.

He had twelve children with his first wife, Georgina (nee Loch-Mitchell), who died in Islington in 1873 following childbirth and eight children with his second wife, my grandmother Margaret Semple. His occupation is shown variously on birth certificates as 'painter,' 'artist' and 'scene painter,' the latter being the first reference to any theatrical association.

The family moved to accommodate my grandfather's work as a scenic artist at the Royal Theatre in Edinburgh and the Britannia and Drury Lane Theatres, in London. We know of the family having lived at Elgin in Edinburgh, Glasgow, Sheffield, Liverpool and London. The name 'W. Small' appears on playbills for pantomime, drama and comedy at the Britannia Theatre; some are preserved in the Enthoven Collection housed at the Victoria and Albert Museum, London. In 1878, the name 'W.W. Small' appears on playbills as a scenic

William Wilson Small.

Margaret Small (nee Semple) with daughter Geraldine on the day her husband died 1914.

artist at a new theatre in Glasgow, 'The Princesses.' One hundred and twenty-nine descendants of his first marriage are now widely dispersed and living in the U.K., Australia, New Zealand, Canada, Spain and Germany.

In 1881, my grandmother, Margaret Semple, married my grandfather, William Wilson Small, in Glasgow, according to the 'forms of the Presbyterian Church.' She was twenty-seven and he was fifty-one. Born in Glasgow in 1854, she worked until marriage in an upholsterer's warehouse where her father was the foreman. They went on to have eight children. The birth and death certificates of their eight children indicate that his work took the family to various places in England and Scotland. The names of both William and Margaret appear on an advertisement in the Newcastle Daily Chronicle on the 21st of December 1883 for the Christmas Pantomime at the Theatre Royal in Newcastle-upon-Tyne. Margaret was the seamstress who made the costumes. On the 26th of December 1885, a local newspaper, the Blackburn Standard, commented on 'the magnificent scenery painted by Mr. Small for Sinbad the Sailor,' at the Royal Theatre in Blackburn, Lancashire.

In 1886, William Wilson Small moved with his family to Ireland at the invitation of Mr. Whitbread, a philanthropist and passionate theatregoer, who was anxious to ensure the survival of theatre in Ireland. William took up employment as a scenic artist at the Old Queen's Theatre in Dublin and remained there for the next twenty-one years. Queen's Theatre was known as the home of Irish drama and celebrated Ireland's heroes and historical characters like Saint Patrick, Wolfe Tone, Lord Edward FitzGerald, Robert Emmet and Father Murphy.

As up to fifteen canvases were required for each play, family

Queen's Theatre. Courtesy Cecil Allen.

members used to help him to stretch the huge backdrop canvases. When the theatre was closed for demolition in 1907, William Wilson Small's career as a scenic artist came to an end. He was aged seventy-seven.

His poem on the demolition of the Queen's Theatre appeared in a Dublin newspaper:

The Old Queen's Theatre, Great Brunswick Street, Dublin, is in the process of demolition. Before long, not a stone of the Temple of Thespis where so many thousands of our good citizens and enjoyed themselves thoroughly, year in, year out, for many, many years, will stand. Thoughts of pleasurable regret fill the mind as we see the 'front' coming down bit by bit, just as if the place were any old tenement. The lines appended are written by one who for twenty golden years was associated with the 'Queen's' and therefore, we not only print them with pleasure, but we give them without the disturbance of so much as a single comma:-

The Old Queen's Theatre

Farewell historic fane, thy creaky stage,
Long predestined, at length must meet it's doom;
The hoary walls and rafters, grim with age,
Must to the pickaxe and spade succumb.
As the full harvest crop, in ripest bloom,
Must to the sickle of the mower yield,
Leaving behind a barren vacuum
The desolation of a stubble field
Its treasures reaped, its glories shorn away,
Wrap'd in a record of a bygone day.

And yet how often from those crazy boards
Has young Ambition to the ladder clung,
Lisped his first essay in melodious words,
And tuned to elegance his amorous tongue.
With foot suspended on the lower rung,
Until the sage divinities applaud;

And Mother Fame, her magic garland flung,
The icy critic into kindness thawed.
And warm approval would at length confess
The piece a hit - the effort a success.

But fame no longer on the author calls,
The actor's triumphs, too, have died away;
Applause no longer echoes from the walls,
That rent and shattered tumble to decay.
But from their ashes on some future day
That fabled Bird of Promise will arise;
Its newer plumage to the world display,
And spread its pinions to admiring eyes.
Talent will then, and Genius may once more,
Adorn its boards and pace its new laid floor,

William Wilson Small 1907

The Small family lived on the north of Dublin city, initially at No. 8 Leinster Street, Strandville Avenue and later, at No. 6 Talbot Place between 1890 and 1905. Their neighbours at Talbot Place included the Toft family, of Toft Amusements renown and the Frame family, who ran the Hammond Lane Foundry. Later on, the Small family moved to Millbourne Avenue in Drumcondra.

In addition to his talents as a painter, William Wilson Small wrote verse and stories and took pleasure in writing plays that his children performed. In 1905, the Northern Scot and Moray and Nairn Express printed his story, 'A Romance at Fochaber's Wood.' With a thirst for education, he was known to take up to six night classes a week and one can only surmise that this must have been during his bachelor days. The following is a poem he wrote after the death of his daughter, Annie Elizabeth Helen Mary Small in 1904:

Say Little Star, the Reason Why
you gleam so Brightly in the Sky
Were't Thou a Spirit wrap't in Clay
that dwelt among us for a Day.

And would some kindly Message Post
To friends who mourn a loved one lost.
Ah, fain, would I that message hear
Could'st thou unto the earth draw near
A little from thy orbit stray
And for a time - the truant play
And vain the thought. Dear Little Star
No phone we hear - thou art so far
But we behold thy Sparkling Ray
'I loved you all it seemed to say
And when that little star you see
Remember this and think of me'
These were the words our Darling said
While yet on earth with us she stayed
Such was the wish which she express'd
Ere yet the spirit sought its rest
In Bethel once, a star did shine,
Of Good Portent, a Heavenly Sign
So may our star a Token be
Of love throughout eternity.
The sculptured Stone may waste away
In mouldering ruin and decay
The Mausoleum and Pyramids
beneath the level dust be hid
Out Little Star, may shine above
An emblem of undying love.

The following obituary appeared in an Irish newspaper when William Wilson Small died in 1914:

Death of a Veteran Scenic Artist

We regret to announce the death of Mr. W. W. Small at his residence, 11 Millbourne Avenue, Drumcondra. Mr. Small, who had attained a ripe old age, was connected with the Dublin stage for very many years. He was a native of Scotland, and one of the most accomplished scenic artists of his time. His prime was passed during a period when the stock company was in vogue, and when to each considerable theatre was attached a resident scene painter.

Mr. Small in those days acquired a vast experience and a versatility and adaptability in his profession rare in these modern times. The last position he occupied was scenic artist the Queen's Theatre, which he filled for twenty-seven years uninterruptedly, and where he did a great deal of the most excellent and varied scene painting. Such a consummate master of stage craft as Mr. Whitbread, the stage manager and dramatic author, had the very highest opinion of Mr. Small's qualifications as a designer and executant of sets and scenery of all kinds. In the pantomime's produced at the Queen's, his work was a brilliant feature of his productions, and contributed greatly to their popularity and success.

Since the closing of the old Queen's, Mr. Small has been in retirement and in the last few years, failing health and eyesight kept him almost entirely within his home. He was a man of considerable reading and literary attainments, and some verses he wrote on the closing of the old theatre in Great Brunswick Street, with which so much of his life had been identified, were marked with touching pathos and feeling. His son, Mr. Robert Small, inherits his father's genius as a scenic artist. He succeeded him at the Queen's Theatre, of which house he is now stage manager, discharging his responsible duties with conspicuous talent and skill. The interment of the late Mr. Small will take place tomorrow, Saturday morning at 10 o'clock from Millbourne Avenue, for the burial ground, Drumcondra.

William Wilson Small is buried in Drumcondra Churchyard, together with my grandmother and two bachelor uncles, Harold and Eddie. The architect, James Gandon, and the antiquarian, Francis Grose, (*Grose's Antiquities*) are also buried there.

As for William's sons, Bob Small became manager of the Empire Theatre in Dublin and John Whittin Small became stage manager and scene painter at Her Majesty's Theatre in Aberdeen. His other sons went into the painting and decorating business.

My father, George Sinclair Small, was born in 1892, the sixth child of the second family of William Wilson Small and Margaret Semple, while they were living at No. 6 Talbot Place in Dublin. As a boy, he assisted his father at the Queen's Theatre. His birth certificate was among those destroyed in 1922 by a fire in the Public Records Office at the Four Courts, but his baptism is recorded at Trinity Church, S. Thomas in Dublin on 18th of September 1892. He attended St. Mark's Protestant school in Pearse Street until the family moved to Drumcondra.

The Small family had a tradition of christening children with middle names attributable to maternal family surnames. With Harold 'Peebles'

George Sinclair Small.

Small, the 'Peebles' is attributable to Harold's paternal great-grandmother, Helen Peebles, and with my own father, George 'Sinclair' Small, the 'Sinclair' is attributable to his maternal grandmother, Ann Sinclair.

My maternal grandparents were James Walsh and Margaret Brien, born in 1872 and 1873, respectively, both of Kildare farming stock. They married in 1898 at St. Peter's Church, Phibsboro. James Walsh (Jim) worked as a tram driver in Dublin. Married twice, he had four children in all, three of the first marriage to my grandmother, Margaret Brien, and a son, Louis, of his second marriage to Agnes Foley.

My mother, Mary ('Molly') Walsh, born in 1898, was the eldest child of the first family. Birth certificates show the family had lived at No. 30 Blackhall Place, Dublin, however, they were living at No. 6 Francis Street when my grandmother, Margaret Brien, died at the age of thirty. She is buried in Bodenstown Cemetery where Wolfe Tone is also buried.

My mother was aged eight when her mother died and this event completely

Mary Walsh.

changed her circumstances. She was sent to Tipperary to live with her mother's brother, Richard ('Dick') O'Brien and her aunt by marriage, Mary, who had no children of their own. Her brother, John, went to live with my grandmother's people at Daars, near Sallins, Co. Kildare and her infant brother, Laurence ('Larry'), aged two, remained with her father.

As a result of the premature death of my grandmother and the early death of my mother when I was aged nineteen, there is a gap in knowledge as regards my mother's side of the family. A debt is owed to my sister, Gwen, and her husband, Brendan O'Byrne, who carried out extensive family research, thus providing the family with all the knowledge we now have to hand.

Dick O'Brien worked as a steward at Loughton House, located about half way between Toomevara, Co. Tipperary and Moneygall, Co. Offaly, and lived in Loughton's gate lodge. (Richard had added an 'O' to his surname by then, changing it from 'Brien' to 'O'Brien'). The estate was more recently owned by the former Minister for Health, Dr. James O'Reilly. Jack Tracey, who in his youth worked under Dick, described him as 'a lovely man.' As the workers assembled each morning to receive instructions on the day's tasks, Dick used to come through the trees whistling a tune. Dick's nephew, Paddy Murphy, described him as a 'marvellous character.' From all accounts, he appears to have been a man of firm conviction and a loyal family man, dependable and trustworthy, respected by both employer and employees. Dick had a huge interest in Gaelic football and hurling and his house at Loughton was festooned with G.A.A. photographs. He had once captained a winning Clane team in a Kildare championship.

School records show that my mother first attended Clash National School in Toomevara before enrolling at Moneygall National School in 1906. Back then, Moneygall was a one-roomed school which closed when a new school was built. The old school was renovated in 1986 and is now in use as a community hall.

Loughton House on 226 acres on the Tipperary-Offaly border near Lough Derg Courtesy O'Byrne private collection.

Loughton Gate Lodge. Courtesy O'Byrne private collection.

As well as concentrating on what was known as the three 'R's - reading, writing and arithmetic - a young seamstress, Margaret Nolan, taught the girls needlework in the afternoons. My mother made her First Holy Communion and Confirmation in the local parish church, St. Joseph's. The Census of 1911 shows Mary Walsh, aged twelve, described as 'scholar,' still living with her aunt and uncle at Laughton. My grandfather had by then re-married and like many tram drivers, lived at Pembroke Cottages, Donnybrook.

Dick's wife, Mary, was known to help out at Loughton House on occasion and apparently, was a very strict woman. Presumably, my mother would also have gone along to give a hand, thus learning about household management. In her teens, my mother left Tipperary for a live-in job with the O'Brien family in Dublin, where she looked after the children, especially one of the boys who was unable to walk until about the age of six. She also sewed for the family and made all the children's clothes. She more or less became part of the family so that when the O'Briens' went on outings, they always took my mother along. As a result, my mother was familiar with the Dublin mountains and many day trip locations.

John O'Brien, generally known as 'John O' (or 'Johnno'), was a wealthy farmer with extensive lands around the village of Clondalkin. He never lived in Clondalkin; he lived at Tritonville Road in Sandymount, which back then

Outdoor staff at Loughton House. Dick O'Brien with moustache, 4th from left. Courtesy O'Byrne private collection.

was a much less built-up area. This meant there was constant horse and cart traffic between his properties in Sandymount and Clondalkin until lorries took over the run. The milk yield from Johnno's dairy herd in Clondalkin was transported daily to Sandymount to be sold and in winter, a constant supply of hay was needed for the herd who were sheltered in the yard behind the O'Brien's house in Sandymount.

My father, George Small, progressed from helping his father with his work as a scenic artist in the theatre to becoming involved with Tofts Amusements, his interest stemming from his association with the Toft family, who lived next door. Abby Toft and his wife Florence, ran their amusement business throughout the country. Their association with Eyre Square in Galway goes back to 1883, when they first brought a carnival there. The family are commemorated in the place name, Toft Park, at the back of Seapoint in Galway.

My father ran a business renting out and setting up marquees, tents,

Photo Toft's Amusements

Railway poster advertising trips to the Spring Cattle Show, Clondalkin. Accessed from Donnellys of Bearna. Photo credit David O Muineachain.

dancefloors, swinging boats and a mountain slide. Later on, we used some of the mats from the mountain slide at home. The job took him as far afield as Sligo and Mayo in summertime and he also did work at the Spring Show and the Horse Show at the R.D.S. Ballsbridge. When not engaged in these activities, he did painting and decorating as well as small building jobs. He rented a yard with sheds near the O'Brien's place in Sandymount to store tools and equipment.

My parents met in Sandymount. I never got to hear the story but with my mother working for the O'Brien's and my father renting sheds nearby, it's easy to join the dots. When they decided to marry, 'Johnno' offered my parents a place on Old Nangor Road in Clondalkin. It was a small one-storey building, 'Raheen Cottage,' located within an enclosed farmyard. A gated entrance between tall pillars led past the gabled end of outbuildings into the farmyard. It consisted of a harness room with bare rafters and two other rooms with a cloakroom at one end, which I believe was as a dancehall around the 1850s.

Pastoral scene - Painting by Harold Small

3.
THE OLD NO. 51 BUS JOURNEY FROM THE CITY TO THE OUTER REACHES OF CLONDALKIN

Let me take you on the old number 51 bus route from the city centre out to the fringes of Clondalkin. The bus left from Aston Quay, beside O'Connell Bridge and went down the Quays, through Islandbridge, Kilmainham and Inchicore and travelled along the Naas Road, until the turn-off for Monastery Road into Clondalkin. The nine-mile distance with fields and farms aplenty in between gave Clondalkin a breathing space away from the encroaching metropolis, such that the village remained relatively rural, even after the earliest housing estates were built.

The bus service was run by private operators - all single decker - Excelsior used green buses and IOC buses were red and white, 'IOC' being short for 'Irish Omnibus Company.' The IOC bus travelled along the Naas Road but did not go through Clondalkin village; instead it ran straight up to Rathcoole. Some Rathcoole children who were at school with me had to make their way to the Naas Road to catch the bus – I remember the Minogue, Holland and Hernon children going for the IOC bus. Around 1943, at a time when trucks were being used more frequently to transport goods and the railways were shutting down, transport in Ireland came to a crossroads. The Government stepped in and nationalised private bus companies and the railways and Coras Iompar Eireann (CIE) was formed.

In sixty years, the bus numbers for buses from the city to Clondalkin never changed – routes 51, 68 and 69 got you to Clondalkin, the number 51 being its main and most frequent bus route. The number 68 ('Newcastle bus')

Photo of bus. Attribution: Kieran Swords

McBirney's, Aston Quay, starting point for No. 51 bus, and mosaic entrance at McBirney's

went through Clondalkin village and on to Milltown, Peamount, Baldonnel and Newcastle and later, Greenogue Business Park. The number 69 ('Rathcoole bus') skirted Clondalkin at the Naas Road and went on to Kingswood, Saggart and Rathcoole. The numbers 68 and 69 still run, alongside some speedier express buses, but the plain 51 was discontinued years ago, now replaced by a myriad of routes that traverse Clondalkin, reflecting its expansion in several directions.

The bus stop was outside McBirney's department store on Aston Quay, which has long since closed. However, the building still stands with McBirney's name imprinted in a brass plate above the entrance and in mosaic under foot. Virgin Megastore, Supervalu and other businesses have since occupied the premises.

Off we go, past some of the old Georgian four and five storey buildings that remain along the quays, touching on some of the River Liffey's bridges, like the Ha'penny Bridge (1816) and Grattan Bridge (1875). Unlike our European counterparts, many of these tall buildings are only in use at ground floor and first floor level; they used to house shops, antique sellers, book sellers and offices. Sadly, many were demolished, especially those along Essex Quay but luckily, Sunlight Chambers on the corner of Parliament Street and Essex Quay was saved.

(L) Sunlight Chambers, Essex Quay. The building once came close to demolition. Reynolds Collection. (R) The Four Courts. Courtesy Dublin Port Company.

This building was designed for Lever Brothers, English soap manufacturers. Its two panel friezes with colourful washerwoman figurines tell their own story. Next we pass Sam Stephenson's modern office blocks at Wood Quay, which house Dublin City Council. Despite a lengthy battle with the Council in the 1970's, development went ahead on a Viking settlement back to the year 841 A.D. Next, O'Donovan Rossa Bridge (1816) from Winetavern Street to Chancery Place and Father Mathew Bridge (1818) from Merchant's Quay to Church Street.

Across the river is the Four Courts at Inn's Quay, designed by the architect James Gandon between 1786 and 1802 with a green copper dome setting it off. The dome is enriched with the stucco work of the sculptor Edward Smyth whose five roofline statues survived – these are identified as Moses, Justice, Mercy, Authority and Wisdom. The building was badly damaged during the Civil War in 1922 and the adjoining Public Records Office was completely destroyed, with the loss of invaluable legal and historical records, including the complete records of the Irish Parliament, the original wills of every Irish testator from the 16th century and the registers of hundreds of Irish parishes. Following re-building, the hall and domes are now largely as Gandon intended. The Four Courts formed a 'legal triangle' with the King's Inn's on Constitution Hill and the Law Society in Blackhall Place.

Cattle on North Circular Road

Next, a mere glimpse of Smithfield up a laneway. Laid out in the mid-17th century as a marketplace on the outskirts of medieval Dublin City, this square, also known as 'the Haymarket,' was used as an agricultural trading post, primarily for cattle-trading. Not too long ago, the square was lined with inner city 'farm yards' to house livestock and it was populated by cattle dealers.

A short distance beyond Smithfield, cattle auctions were held at Gavin Lowe's market beside Hanlon's Corner until 1974. Those riding on the top of a double decker bus could see the animals held in steel pens inside the mart. The animals either arrived at the city by cattle truck or they were manoeuvred by drovers who kept them overnight in holding fields or penned into yards around Prussia Street. Passers-by bore witness to the roars of the animals and bales of hay stacked up as feed. After auction, the cattle were herded into small slaughterhouses close to the mart to meet their fate or otherwise, drovers ran them along the North Circular Road right down to the docks and onto the ferry to England as 'live' cattle exports. The Horse Fair is still held in Smithfield twice a year, despite being surrounded by modern apartment blocks. Following the establishment of the Old Jameson Distillery in the late 1700's, the square was bestowed with a chimney 185 feet tall in 1895, an immediately recognisable landmark.

Back to the Quays and on past Rory O'Moore Bridge (1861), which straddles the Liffey between Watling Street and Ellis Street, and Mellows Bridge

'House of the Dead,' Usher's Quay

(1768), between Bridgefoot Street and Queen Street. New bridges built in the last twenty years include the Millenium footbridge (1999), James Joyce Bridge from Usher's Island to Ellis Quay (2003) and Frank Sherwin Bridge (1982), which took the traffic from Sean Heuston Bridge (1828), latter which is now confined to the Luas tram and pedestrians.

Towards the Guinness brewery, a tall Georgian house on Usher's Quay is colloquially known as the *"House of the Dead,"* as James

Guinness barges

Joyce's story, 'The Dead' was set there. Joyce is reputed to have spent Christmases there with his aunt. Thankfully, it is a protected structure

The Guinness Brewery originally covered a four acre site leased in 1759 to Arthur Guinness at IR£45 per year for 9,000 years. In the 1870's the Guinness site expanded to surrounding streets which housed brewery employees and offices as well as extending towards the river Liffey where a jetty was built at Victoria Quay in 1873. As a child I used to sit on the left hand side of the bus from town to watch the barges and the horse-drawn drays, drawn by beautiful Clydesdale horses with their brasses shining. The Guinness barges (otherwise called Steam Lighters) carried wooden casks of Guinness from the brewery to Dublin Port for loading on to Guinness seagoing vessels with names such as Lady Gwendoleyn, Lady Brigid, Lady Maud and Lady Miranda. The last Guinness barge sailed down the Liffey from Victoria Quay to the Custom House in 1961 and a colourful chapter in history drew to a close. Victoria Quay has since been demolished.

On the opposite side of the river is the Esplanade, where the Croppy Boys are buried. Behind that is Collins Barracks, once an active army base, now a museum. At this point, we have reached Heuston railway station, which stands proud, lit up with good effect at night. Older people remember it as Kingsbridge Station.

Of the four churches along the quays, one a Presbyterian and three Catholic, only one Catholic church functions today. However, the Blessed Sacrament Chapel built in latter years along Batchelor's Walk is much frequented. Hard to believe, but here we are pages on and we haven't even left the quays – at this rate we will never reach Clondalkin.

Crossing the river, we swing left into Parkgate Street, past a circular newsagent's kiosk and Hickey's Fabrics bordering the Liffey wall, on past the iconic Ryan's pub on the right. The focal point of this street used to be the entrance to the Phoenix Park, but more recently this has been dwarfed by the Criminal Courts of Justice, a circular building rising ten storeys over basement. The CCJ as it is known, (or "the Zoo" as it has been nicknamed) was built on a site that once served as the Garda car pound, at the junction of Parkgate Street and Infirmary Road. Over half of the 400,000 criminal cases dealt with annually by the Irish courts are heard in Dublin. For years, the existing judicial facilities in and around the Four Courts – including the Bridewell and the Special Criminal Court in Green Street – struggled to cope with this level of court traffic.

Criminal Courts of Justice (C.C.J.) Parkgate Street.

Further up Infirmary Road, James Gandon designed the Royal Military Infirmary, which was built in 1786 and gave its name to Infirmary Road. Having accommodated the Department of Defence for a long time, the building now houses the Chief Prosecution Solicitor's Office. The Infirmary was replaced in 1913 by the nearby King George V Hospital, later known as Saint Bricin's Hospital.

I recall hearing a story about the chaplain at St. Bricin's, the Army hospital on Infirmary Road, who was a cranky priest. He had been called in to hear the confession of a patient scheduled for removal of his adenoids. When informed, 'the priest won't be too long,' the patient pointed out that he was Protestant. As the priest would have been annoyed, especially having been called out at night, the nurse woke a Catholic patient and got him to agree to the priest hearing his confession, although he was not for surgery at all.

For years, the Phoenix Park had a wide open entrance until a decision was reached to re-instate the entrance pillars. The largest walled park in Europe, it is traversed by the three mile long Chesterfield Avenue. The Park houses many fine buildings including Áras an Uachtaráin, the American Legation, the Ordnance Survey, Garda Headquarters, St. Mary's Hospital, the Cheshire Home and not forgetting, the Dublin Zoo, the Polo Ground, the bandstand and the coffee shop at the Hollow as well as Park Ranger's houses and gate lodges. Its amenities include the People's Gardens, lakes and sports grounds for football, cricket, camogie, hurling and polo, as well as facilitating horse riding. Cattle once roamed the Park freely until the era of foot and mouth disease. It is still home to deer and a variety of wildlife, flora, fauna and trees.

The Wellington Monument stands high, a memorial to the Duke of Wellington - the 'Iron Duke' - who although he was born in Dublin, resented the fact: *"Just because you are born in a stable does not mean you are a horse."*

Originally planned for Merrion Square, near the Duke's birthplace, the obelisk was built here because of opposition from the residents of Merrion Square. Designed by Sir Robert Smirke, the foundation stone was laid in 1817, two years after Wellington's defeat of Napoleon at the Battle of Waterloo but it was not completed until 18 June 1861 due to lack of funds. Four bronze plaques were cast from cannons used at Waterloo with three of these panels depicting major events in the life of Wellington's military and political career: the Indian Wars, by Joseph Kirk; Waterloo by Thomas Farrell; and Civil and Religious

Liberty, by John Hogan. The Duke of Wellington was the Prime Minister who delivered Daniel O'Connell's demands for Catholic Emancipation in 1829, despite opposition from among his fellow Conservatives.

When Pope John Paul II visited Ireland in 1979, one million people came to celebrate Mass with him at a spot known as 'the fifteen acres.' He was transported for the occasion on a customised golf car, known as a 'popemobile.' The 'Pope's Cross,' made in Drogheda, stands on an elevated site to mark the spot. I heard tell that the cross erected in Drogheda for the Pope's visit was made in Lyons's yard beside our home at Raheen, but I am not sure if this is true.

When the bus swings left over the Liffey at Islandbridge, you catch sight of the weir at Salmon Pool. A renowned fishing spot to intercept the salmon before they go up river to breed, many winners of the coveted title, 'first salmon of the year,' have had their luck here. Clancy Barracks, on the left, closed in the 1990's and sold for redevelopment. On the right, the Memorial Park fringes the banks of the Liffey as far as Chapelizod. Much of the Park was built on landfill – I remember well passing this area when it was the city dump, with JCB's ploughing through rubbish while gulls wheeled overhead. Designed by Edwin Lutyens, the park commemorates those killed in World War I *"to the memory of the 49,400 Irish soldiers who gave their lives in the Great War, 1914–1918."* A building adjacent to the rose garden holds the veterans' records.

On the left at the top of the hill is 'Bully's Acre,' a former public cemetery in the grounds of the Royal Hospital, Kilmainham, however, it actually extends to over three acres. The name is believed to derive from the graveyard's former

Military Cemetery built 1905 for occupants of Royal Hospital Kilmainham. Photo courtesy niah.ie.

use as a place for boxing matches, or perhaps from "baily" (bailiff), a nickname for the officials of the priory at Kilmainham. For over a thousand years, there has been a graveyard here. It is believed to hold the graves of some killed at the Battle of Clontarf, including a son and grandson of Brian Boru. Over time it became more famous as a pauper's cemetery, the land being common ground, with no charges for burials. However, many respectable Catholic citizens were also buried here as there was no official Catholic graveyard in the city after the Reformation. On feast-days the cemetery was used for socialising which sometimes got out of hand, resulting in rowdyism and fighting. The largest of these was the "pattern" on 24th of June, the feast of St. John, when thousands trooped through the cemetery to St. John's Well, located across the road from the cemetery. For years, unsuccessful attempts were made by both the Catholic clergy and the Government, to have these gatherings suppressed. They finally stopped in the 1830s, in the wake of a cholera epidemic.

The Royal Hospital Kilmainham was originally built for soldiers and it is said to have been the model for the Chelsea Hospital. The arched entrance to the Royal Hospital was actually moved from Usher's Island and re-built at this site for Queen Victoria's visit in 1880. It is now in use as the Irish Museum of Modern Art and known as 'IMMA.'

Right turn past Kilmainham Court house and the sombre grey jail, which housed political prisoners. The signatories of the Proclamation were executed by firing squad there in 1916 – Thomas Clarke, Joseph Plunkett, Pádraig Pearse, Seán MacDermott, Eamonn Ceannt, James Connolly and Thomas McDonagh. Eamon de Valera was also sentenced to death but escaped execution because he had been born in America.

On the opposite side of the road was Rowntree's chocolate factory. My bachelor uncles, Harold and Edward Small, lived at Shamrock Cottage in the shadow of Rowntree's factory. The gable end of the cottage could be seen through large wrought iron entrance gates directly opposite Kilmainham Jail. When the factory needed to expand, they persuaded my Uncle Eddie, who was by then on his own, to sell them the site. He moved across the road to a redbrick Victorian house with bay windows adjacent to Kilmainham Jail where he lived for the rest of his life.

The fine houses across from Kilmainham Jail were once home to engineers who worked in the railway works at Inchicore and worshipped at the Methodist, Presbyterian and Protestant churches on this road. St. Jude's was dismantled and the stone was used in the construction of a building on the Guinness estate in Co. Kildare which houses the Steam Museum, its steam engines having come from Inchicore Works. All that remains is the church spire, which still stands as a ruin on the spot. It went up for sale a few years ago but was not purchased. Another church along the same road was converted into a residence.

On to Inchicore and the Naas Road area, the latter being the main artery road between Dublin and Cork and Dublin and Limerick. Inchicore expanded around the Inchicore Works which employed a huge workforce. A maintenance hub for the rail network, buses were also built at the Works. The history of Inchicore and the Works has been well-documented in other local history books.

Father Devine, an oblate father, was well-respected for starting youth clubs, sports clubs, a drama group and a choir in the area between the forties and the seventies, which included some members of the popular singing group, 'The Bachelors.'

When travelling along the Naas Road, the lovely place names strike a chord:- Bluebell, Robinhood, Fox & Geese, Knockmitten, Red Cow, Ballymount, Bushellaloaf, The Ranch, Newlands, Buck & Hounds, Cheeverstown, Kingswood.

The Quaker Lamb family owned the famous Lamb's jam factory at Bluebell. The family had houses on both sides of the Naas Road and their fruitfields were in Donabate, North Dublin. Lamb's chimney was demolished around 1981.

Singing group, 'The Bachelors.'

Other families who lived here and went to school in Clondalkin were the Byrnes, the Mulhares, the Mahonys, the O'Neills, the Healys and the Gallaghers. Immediately after the jam factory on the left-hand side was Lansdown Valley. People used to take a short-cut through the Valley to Drimnagh.

The families living next on the left at Robinhood were the Ryans, the Currivans, the Faulkners, the Behans, the Lazenbys and the Byrons. The Byrne family lived in Snowdrop Cottage between Fox & Geese and Robinhood.

Next came Fox & Geese. Thom's Almanac for 1858 shows 'Michael Flood, Fox and Geese,' while Thom's Almanac for 1882 records, 'Messrs. Flood, Brick and Lime Manufacturers, Fox and Geese.'

Clockwise from top: former home of the Lamb jam-making family at Bluebell; Lamb's ad, kindly shared by Gerard Byrne; Lamb's Factory Bluebell 1933.

Left: Junction Old Bluebell and Naas Road 1952. Credit Thomas Thornton, also Dave Duggan for sharing this photo and photo below.

Below: Long Mile Road, 1950s.

Bottom: Naas Road, early 1960s. Gaynors' house on the right and McCanns shop on the left, with the Slipper Ballroom beside it and the bus stop up to the village.

There was a ballroom located at Fox and Geese called 'The Slipper,' where Peggy Dell and her band played for many years. She was a wonderful pianist who once worked in the music department of Woolworth's Department store. The McCann family had a shop at Fox & Geese that sold bits and bobs such as metal circular patches for repairing pots. A turn-off to the right led to Knockmitten and Killeen Paper Mills.

FOX AND GEESE

Ayrcourt— Burns, M., Ballroom
Macken House—Gaynor, P.
The Stores—McCann, J., grocer
Fox & Geese—Sheehan. D. £10
—Griffin, W.
Kennedy, P. J., poultry store
County Council Houses.
Extract The Directory of Ireland, 1958.

Now we have reached the fringes of Clondalkin, we will leave it for now before Red Cow.

Fox by Monica Sproul (nee Small)

4.
OUR HOME ON THE OLD NANGOR ROAD
AND OUR PARENTS

What was unusual about my parents as a couple was the fact that they belonged to different religions – she was born and raised Catholic and he was born and raised Protestant. Back then, the religion into which a person was born influenced the course of their lives. It impacted on their choice of friends, romantic attachments and marriage partner. Schools were segregated into Catholic and non-Catholic and the religious divide often extended to the areas in which people chose to live.

Following the *Ne Temere* decree, a papal edict of 1907 that placed restrictions on marriage, particularly mixed marriage, non-Catholics had to sign a decree that any children of the marriage would be brought up as Catholics. Many non-Catholics felt that the decree threatened the very existence of the Church of Ireland community, especially as it was swiftly followed by Independence in Ireland and a civil war.

My father being Protestant and my mother being Catholic meant they needed special dispensation from Rome to marry. When it was slow in coming, my father threatened to marry in a Registry Office and he posted the marriage banns. Permission swiftly arrived. Ironically, my father was not a fervent churchgoer. He felt that by the age of fourteen, he had grasped enough of Christ's teachings to follow the right path in life. In the usual way, he had to sign the decree that any children of the marriage would be brought up as Catholics. Even then, their marriage ceremony was conducted at a side altar rather than at the main altar at Corpus Christi Church in Glasnevin.

Before my parents could set up home at Raheen Cottage, my father had to set about making it habitable. He converted the building into a cottage with three separate rooms – a kitchen, a bedroom and a sitting-room, and in 1924, they moved in. The sitting room had a round mahogany table, two carvers and four dining chairs and a china cabinet which held ornaments and Dad's cameras. My eldest sister, Peg, remembered Dad's top hat in a brown paper bag in the wardrobe, which was only worn for weddings and funerals. The kitchen had a black range and a scrubbed deal table, which was covered with American cloth. Shelves in one corner held dinner and tea sets and underneath the shelves was a block for chopping firewood. This was not a good idea as Dad lifted the axe one day and brought down two of the shelves. The broken crockery filled the bath.

A wall divided Raheen Cottage from neighbouring Raheen House. In my older sisters' time, they remembered the Caple family living there, followed by the Jeffrey and Craig families, who were related. Later residents of Raheen House were the Carroll, Cusack, Mullally and Nolan families. Both properties were owned by the O'Brien's, who also owned land up as far as the Oil Mills and more land over by the Green Isle Hotel.

 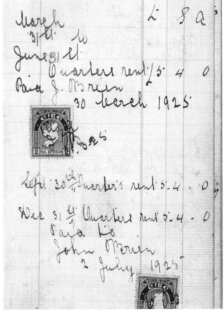

(L) Mary Small with first born child, Peg, 1925, in christening robe. (R) Rent Book. Record of rental payments for Raheen Cottage made in 1925 to John O'Brien, authenticated by affixing postage stamps.

Once children started arriving, Dad had to dispose of his interest in the amusement business because he was not getting home until the early hours. In the still of night, my mother used to hear him coming through the village on his motor bike and side car. The money from these events paid the rent for the year which was £21.16, as well as for a ton of coal for the winter, grocery bills and other bills.

My father set up a painting and decorating business, as well as undertaking general maintenance and building work, mainly working for local families. The hours were long and as he was at the disposal of a small number of people for work and could not travel too farther afield, payment could be sporadic, which put a strain on the family. Many nights he stayed late to finish a job and cycled home in all weathers and was up and gone again the following morning. He was a fiercely independent man with great strength of character who always insisted on working for himself and did so until the age of eighty with only a rare day off. Although the retirement age at the time was seventy, he had scruples about collecting a non-contributory pension and it took much persuasion on my part for him to get him to sign the claim forms I had completed in his name. His life would have been easier if he had taken a job in the paper mill.

You might note the postage stamp affixed where the bill is marked 'paid.' The requirement to affix stamps on receipts was brought in by the 1891 Stamp Act to raise revenue for the Government. Failure to affix the relevant stamp meant the receipt was not valid in a court of law. Although this requirement was brought in during the time of British occupation, stamps on receipts were not abolished in Ireland until 1964.

Most neighbours in the early 1930s had neither a water or electricity supply. Most of my friends

G. Small Billhead marked paid and with postage stamp affixed. Courtesy Patrick Ging and Clondalkin Historical Archives.

did their home exercise and played games either by gas light, candle light or paraffin oil lamp. Well water was fetched in buckets from the nearest pump and used for consumption and cooking. People positioned barrels at the end of drainpipes to collect rainwater for washing clothes and cleaning chores. Once the barrels went dry in summertime, it meant more trips to the well for water. When the water level in the barrels got low, the murky residue had to be rinsed out.

In my time, we had both an electricity supply and an indoor water supply. A well had been sunk at Raheen house that supplied water to both Raheen House and Raheen Cottage and we had a pump inside our gate. My father piped a water supply to inside and built on a bathroom with a flush toilet, a bath and a washbasin under the window. Having installed the water tank above the bathroom door, the bit of surrounding space became a favourite place for our cats to rest. Allied to this convenience, we were pure lucky to be among the handful of families, only on our side of the Nangor Road, and only up as far as Raheen, to be on the power line for Clondalkin Paper Mills. A turbine in the Mill generated electricity.

However, my sister, Peg, remembered the time when Raheen had no electricity and only the pump at our gate. She told us about the oil man who used to call on Wednesday night with oil for the lamps and later, for the Primus stove and bedroom heaters. Turf was delivered on Friday nights in carts painted orange with four strong sticks positioned upright in the corners of the cart to contain the load of turf. Once deliveries were finished, the turf men used to call into Healy's pub. On leaving Healy's they lay back on their carts and let the donkeys take them home from the pub.

The end of the barn in our yard was originally used as a coalhouse, bike storage and an outhouse housing a 'dry' toilet, until my father converted it all into a two-storey workshop to house his extensive range of tools. The upper storey of the workshop had a series of windows to the front that offered a magnificent view of the countryside. From here and from the windows at the back of the cottage, the view took in the Round Tower and the spires of two churches and stretched across pastureland to the Dublin mountains. Added to the view were sounds audible throughout the day - horses, cows, dogs, cats and birds as well as man-made sounds, grinding machinery, tractors and combine harvesters at work. The Mill hooter could be heard for miles around and even the hooter at CIE's Inchicore Works could be heard in Clondalkin and as far away as

Castleknock, on the other side of the Liffey. Church bells also rang out from the Church of the Immaculate Conception and St. John's Church, to add to the order of the day. My father usually kept his workshop locked as it housed his large collection of tools.

One afternoon when I came to visit him with my own family, he announced he had a new combination lock on the door of the shed. This was too tempting a challenge for one of my sons, who arrived in a few minutes later, lock in hand, 'Grandad, I know the combination of the lock.' All he could do was laugh. On another occasion, my son pointed upwards and asked him, 'Grandad, can I use that trowel you have hidden up there? When the roof of the workshop blew off in a storm, all the tools had to be moved downstairs. The upper floor was never re-built.

A retired priest, Father Traynor, used to borrow tools from my father to use for the upkeep of his own car. As a young man, Father Traynor had also been a motor bike enthusiast and I heard tell he was the first man in Ireland to own a motor bike. When Father Traynor died in the 'Old Men's Home' in Kilmainham, he was over 100 years of age. Incidentally, that granite-cut building on the South Circular Road known as the 'Old Men's Home' was more properly called St. Patrick's House. The Little Sisters of the Poor ran it as a nursing home until it was bought by Bovale developments and converted into residential housing in 1995, renamed 'Hybreasal.'

One day I got a telephone call from my father's neighbour, concerned about my father having clambered up on the roof. She was alarmed at the sight of such an elderly man (he was in his eighties then) carrying out repairs. I explained there was nothing I could do to forbid him, because he'd just pooh-pooh my worries and wait until I was gone to get up there again.

Like all fishermen, my father could not resist looking over a bridge to survey the fishing prospects and check if any trout were in. He frequently walked alongside the river, watching for signs of fish. He could be ambivalent about his safety and in his enthusiasm, he often leaned over too far so that every year was characterised by at least one dunking in the Camac.

The worst incident occurred when somebody spotted my father's identifiable leather hat - black leather with a fly-type feather in the band - floating down the Camac, but no sign of George. The alarm was raised. My brother, Jim, organised a search party and nipped back to the house, in case he was there. No George. The search became more frenetic and lasted some time before my father sauntered in with the evening newspaper and cigarettes. It transpired that he'd come home, got out of his wet things and realising his cigarettes were wet, he had headed down to the village for more.

Restless and hard-working, my father liked to be busy and he carried out all his own repairs. He was a motor bike enthusiast and he cycled well into his eighties. He was also a cat-lover, a photographer, and an amateur radio enthusiast. In his youth, he used to make crystal radio sets. His brothers had similar interests. He had a life-long interest in the Holy Land despite not being a church-goer. It is a regret of mine that we didn't club together to send him there.

Nothing was ever wasted. Long before the terms recycling and eco-friendly were coined, my father used to put tea leaves back into the earth and ashes onto the driveway. One of my father's inventions was to fashion a strange implement which he called a 'tamp.' Used tins like cat food or baked bean tins or Fray Bentos steak and kidney pie tins were thrown into a corner of the yard and when a pile built up, he used the heavy tamp to flatten them. This was a task my own children loved.

Dr. Sherry, who worked as a chemist in the Mill, was accustomed to fishing at dusk to catch the trout as they rose. He came up to my husband one day and said, "that father-in-law of yours nearly killed me last night!" He went on to relate how my father had cast out so far from the opposite side of the Mill Pond that his fishing hook latched onto Dr. Sherry's clothing and he found himself getting dragged in, until he managed to free himself.

My father was extremely well read, had a head full of knowledge and he enjoyed conversation and hearty discussions about current affairs and politics. After one heated political discussion, where my father had been pontificating on the ills of the world, my son waited until our car had driven off before making his voice heard, "I don't think Grandad likes a-n-y-thing," he declared. A keen fisherman all his life, he won his last fishing competition the year he died. He never drank alcohol but smoked 40 a day and lived to the age of 89.

George Small at his favourite pastime, fishing in Howth

One final word about my father. He once planted an apple pip which grew successfully, so I wrote a poem about it after he died.

Just a Pip

George was his name
Of little fame
      But his patience did abound
He planted a pip
And awaited the tip
      To show above the ground

With greenfingers driven
Care was given
      Until it began to grow
Then he planted it on
And before long
      The leaves began to show

With Spring anew
Blossoms a few
      It was a rewarding sight
Propped by the wall
So it would not fall
      And let it grow to its full height

Well it grew in time
And looked just fine
      A sturdy trunk it had too
The branches spread out
Above and about
      As I'm sure the roots also grew

Then one fine spring
The sun did bring
      Massive blossom all over the tree
To the ground they fell
And I have to tell

It looked like a carpet to me
The next George knew
From that pip he grew
 Tiny fruits were visible to the eye
They turned from green to red
He scratched his head
 And praised the sun in the sky

George is gone this year
And it does appear
 A little treasure he left behind
In the yard at Raheen
Where he was so keen
 An apple tree you will find.

Gertrude Reynolds 1982

My mother, Mary Small (nee Walsh), had green eyes and long black hair and always a great sense of dignity. When she let her hair down at night, us girls took it in turns to brush it and plait it for her. She was always busy knitting and sewing. Sometimes, she sang old Irish songs or danced around the kitchen. She was never heard to complain although there were many problems in those difficult years of the 1930s. She was generous and kind to those in want who called to the door. There was great pleasure in the home when a new baby arrived but also sadness, with the deaths of my twin sisters in 1938, Mary and Bernadette, who only lived a few days and Patsy, in 1944. The twins are buried at Kilbride graveyard at Baldonnel Camp. Patsy died in the Hospice at Harold's Cross so she was buried in Mount Jerome Cemetery, where Oscar Wilde's parents and sister are also buried. When another little one arrived, it restored the balance. My mother was very caring and she made our lives happy and secure. It has taken me years to write this poem in her memory.

The Dress

Sewing was what she liked to do
Garments she made more than a few

The one I remember most of all
Was a dress of guipure lace as I recall.

An underskirt to the full-length dress
Was made of silk of the best
With drawstring bag of matching lace
It held rosary beads in a case.

The headdress, a circlet of pearls
To hold the veil for each of her girls
The gifted hands belonged to Mary
My mother who was so loving and caring.

Gertrude Reynolds 2019

My parents had six children in all that survived infancy. All the children had arrived in the space of 13 years. My mother died of a heart attack at the age of 55 in 1953. My father died in 1982.

Still Life by Harold Small

5.
RED COW AND UP THE BELGARD ROAD

Back to the Naas Road at Red Cow. The Red Cow Inn has been on the same site since 1690. The origin of the name 'Red Cow' is unknown but the hostelry appears to have given its name to the area. The pub and surrounding land together with some houses were once owned by the Farren family, who lived in the area until recent years. The hill there was known as 'Farren's Hill.' Thom's Almanac for 1858 and 1882 show 'Joseph Farren, farmer, Robin Hood,' while Porter's Guide and Directory for County Dublin 1912, has two entries: 'George Farren, Family Grocer, Tea, Wine and Spirit Merchant, Red Cow,' and 'Joseph Farren, farmer, Robin Hood.' The Thom's Almanac for 1858 also shows, 'Mrs. Margaret Flannagan, Red Cow,' while the 1882 record shows, 'Mrs. Pierce, Red Cow.' Porter's Guide and Directory for County Dublin, 1912, records, 'Joseph P. Somers, Builder and Contractor, Robin Hood.' The Red Cow Hotel, which was purchased by the Moran Hotel chain in 1988, is now located on the site of the pub.

A toll gate once operated opposite the Red Cow Inn, near to where Mr. Byrne's forge stood. In 1663, the First Turnpike Act authorised the placing of barriers across the road and the collection of tolls to fund road maintenance. At that time, coach transport had increased with more frequent passenger use and the establishment of a postal service in 1784. The law caused outrage and mayhem. Mail coach carriers like the Fishbourne family of Cheeverstown House were expected to pay large tolls as 'turnpike revenue.' When the life of the turnpike ended with the advent of rail which offered speed and comfort, toll houses quickly became private dwellings. The Red Cow toll house was owned for many years by Mrs. Mary Delaney until the Naas dual carriageway was built in the 1960s.

From top: Farren's pub, later the Red Cow Inn (photo kindly shared by Gerard Byrne, Old Clondalkin & Surrounding Districts); bill head for Mr. Byrne's Red Cow Forge; advertisement for the sale of the Red Cow Inn (Farren's) 1937; Red Cow Service Station; and Mrs. Delaney's single storey home on the left and Mr. Byrne's forge in the background (photo kindly shared by Gerard Byrne).

Other families living at Red Cow area were the Birchalls, who had a sand and gravel business, the Harris family, who owned a quarry, and the Cullen farming family of Airfield House.

Next on the left was Ballymount, then a collection of cottages where families including the Murrays, the Gormans, the Kanes, the Moores and the Lawlors lived. The remains of an old castle stand about half way along the avenue up to Ballymount House and the ruins of an old fort are in an adjoining field.

Cullen's Farmhouse, Naas Road, Ballymount once stood near where the Red Cow roundabout is now (origin of photo unknown); Ballymount Castle; and Ballymount Castle 1950s (kindly shared by Gerard Byrne, Old Clondalkin & Surrounding Districts).

It was said that several underground passages led from here to the ruined castle on the Monastery Road and to Belgard Castle. This area is now much-developed.

BALLYMOUNT

Marsh, Ethel. Ballymount House
Ennis. —., Isola
Masterson. W.—Garranstown
Dunne Charles—Kilmanagh
Delgattv, A. Iff.—Gort na Blath
Fiddler, J.—Suncroft
Heathering, —.—Green Gables
24 Co. Council Houses

Extract The Directory of Ireland, 1958

In both the Thom's Almanac of 1882 and Porter's Guide and Directory for County Dublin 1912, Charles Blackham is shown as a resident of Ballymount. Apparently, the Blackhams lived in a big house in this area, which became known as 'Blackham's Cross.'

After Red Cow, the bus used to take a right turn onto the Monastery Road for Clondalkin village. This is hard to imagine, given the spaghetti-style interchange that exists there now.

While the name of the roundabout was taken after the former landmark pub in this vicinity, the nickname, *'Mad Cow' roundabout* was commonly used for this junction, which at one time was characterised by miles of traffic tailbacks, in reference to the slang term given to cattle suffering from the brain disease, BSE or 'Mad cow' disease. Nowadays, the terminus of the Luas Red Line is located at the Red Cow interchange park-and-ride station, approximately fifteen minutes' walk from Clondalkin village. This Luas line provides links between Dublin city centre out to Tallaght and Saggart.

Rather than turning, I will instead continue along the Naas Road and in a later chapter, I will take you back to the Monastery Road turn-off of old and bring you into Clondalkin.

The Hunt and Holman families lived further along the Naas Road. Freddie Holman had a huge interest in model-making, model aircraft, steam engines and model ships. Freddie was greatly interested in breeding budgies. The Quinlan family and Noel Hoare also lived along here and further along were the homes of the Dowling family on the left and the McGann family on the right.

BUSHELLOAF (NAAS ROAD)

Clonacool—Hanlon, J.
Ryemead—Quinlan, W.
St. Leonard's—Holman, F.
Landscape—Tracey, G. A., Tia
Garden Products
O'Reilly, Thos.—Bushaloaf Central Garage

Extract The Directory of Ireland, 1958.

There are two theories in relation to the origin of the name Bushelloaf or Bush-a-Loaf. The first and more acceptable one says it is named after a public house of this name that once stood in the area. The second is a ghoulish story of a priest being captured during penal times and tied to a bush and left to starve with a loaf of bread suspended before him out of reach.

BUSHELLOAF, NAAS ROAD, CLONDALKIN, CO. DUBLIN

(2) COMPACT HOLDING OF 14 ACRES 1 ROOD AND 32 PERCHES S.M.

SITUATE AT BUSHELLOAF, FRONTING THE NAAS ROAD, CLOSE TO CLONDALKIN VILLAGE, CO. DUBLIN

(ADJACENT TO NEWLANDS GOLF CLUB AND ABOUT 5 MILES FROM DUBLIN)

Held in Fee Simple, subject to an Irish Land Purchase Revised Annuity of £11-4-6. Poor Law Valuation, £25-10-0 on land.

THE LAND HAS A FRONTAGE OF APPROX. 800 FEET TO NAAS ROAD. ELECTRICITY WATER, AND GAS LAID ON NAAS ROAD, SEWERAGE APPROX. 300 YARDS AWAY.

The land is bounded in front on the south side by the Naas Road, and contains approximately 800 feet frontage. It is bounded in the rere on the north side by a County Council tarred road. The depth from front to rere is approximately 700 feet. There is a gentle slope to the south and the surface is level. The holding comprises two self-contained fields with separate openings from Naas Road. Both fields are practically square and are very compact.

THE HOLDING IS IDEALLY SITUATED, BEING APPROX. 5 MILES FROM DUBLIN.

Full details and Order to inspect lands from Auctioneer.

Solicitors for Vendor: THOMAS EARLY & SON, 63/64 Upper O'Connell Street, Dublin.

Poster for land for sale at Bushelloaf, Near Newlands Golf Club.

The next stretch of the Naas Road on the right-hand side is called 'The Ranch.' These sixteen houses, St. Brigid's Cottages, were built on eight acres of land at Bushelloaf acquired by the local authority under a Compulsory Purchase Order. The families I remember living here included the Smiths, the Nolans, the Callaghans, the Gilsenans, the McNultys, the Coates family and more.

Newlands Cross is now best known for its golf course. Families springing to mind from my time include the McInerneys, Fitzpatricks, Merrigans and the Dowds, who had a farm. Mr. Hughes, father of May Hughes in the Library photograph, ran the forge at Newlands, located beside Frank Waterhouse's garage. The Birchall family once lived there.

As a schoolgirl, Cecilia Loughlin of Leinster Terrace wrote a piece for The Schools Folklore Collection recounting a story told to her by an elderly retired school teacher and Clondalkin native, Mrs. Finn. The story goes that a group of Quakers, led by Isaac Jacob, built a cottage at Newlands, known as 'Shell Cottage' because of its roof made from shells. They were

Mrs. Freeman, 89, with Eileen Mernagh carrying water at The Ranch, c. 1959.

called the 'White Quakers' because of the white garments they wore. They had a reputation as robbers and were much-feared in the area. When Cecilia Loughlin wrote this piece back in 1938, Shell Cottage still existed in fields belonging to the Dowds. However, any Quaker families I ever came across were law-abiding and certainly not robbers.

The right turn at Newlands Cross led to Clondalkin village and the left turn led up the Belgard Road to Tallaght. Katherine Tynan, prolific writer and poet, lived at Whitehall House in the townland of Mooreenaruggan (translation: 'the little bog of the mooreland') on the Tallaght Road until her marriage. Some considered this 200-year-old farmhouse as one of the cradles of the Irish literary revival in the last century. Many literary parties held there were attended by the Yeats brothers, AE (George Russell), Douglas Hyde (later Ireland's first President) Parnell, Michael Davitt, Isaac Butt, J.M. Synge and many of her friends from the Ladies Land League, such as Anna Parnell, sister of Charles Stewart Parnell. Ireland's former President, Mary Robinson, unveiled a commemorative plaque to Katherine Tynan in the Pocket Park on Main Street, Tallaght. The 90-acre farm was bought in 1994 by the Irish Rugby Football Union for possible redevelopment as a sports ground to replace Landsdowne but it has now been sold on. There are efforts to preserve Whitehall in memory of the literary figures who visited there.

Tynan Memorial, Belgard Road. Courtesy niah.ie. Carved stone in Celtic-revival style built c. 1910 to commemorate Katherine Tynan's father who had a dairy farm over opposite.

Belgard cottage, built c. 1860. Former home of Dr. John Jackson. Courtesy niah.ie

Belgard Castle, Naas Road, built c. 1775. Courtesy niah.ie.

O'Rahilly's house: Mooreen House, Mooreenaduggan townland, Belgard Road. Built c. 1936. Photo courtesy niah.ie.

Belgard Castle is a large eighteenth century house attached to a medieval tower with gothic windows and castellated battlements. The castle is first mentioned at the close of the fifteenth century as the residence of Robert Talbot, a branch of the Talbot family, of Feltrim, near Malahide. In his book, Neighbourhood of

Dublin, Weston St. John Joyce describes the castle's location as 'commanding position on the summit of a wooded eminence.' The estate was forfeited during the time of Charles the First when Colonel John Talbot of Belgard took sides with the Confederate Catholics but later restored when he rendered distinguished service to the monarchy in the war at Flanders. As he was the last of the Talbots of Belgard, his estate passed to the Dillon family on his death in 1697 through his daughter who was married to a Thomas Dillon. The estate subsequently passed in succession into the Trant, Cruise, Kennedy and Lawrence families. Sir Henry Lawrence's widow sold Belgard to the Maude family in 1910. The house now serves as the headquarters of CRH Holdings. The Green family used to live in a cottage at the rear courtyard of Belgard Castle.

Ronan O'Rahilly lived near Newlands on the Tallaght Road. In 1964, he was a founder of the pirate station, Radio Caroline, set up to circumvent the record companies' control of popular music broadcasting in the United Kingdom and the BBC's radio broadcasting monopoly. Unlicensed by any government for most of its early life, it never actually became illegal, although after the Marine Offences Act, 1967 made it illegal for a British subject to associate with it. His grandfather, 'The O'Rahilly,' was killed in the 1916 rebellion. He is commemorated by the naming of a lane in his honour off Moore Street, O'Rahilly Parade. The O'Rahilly wrote this letter to his wife as he lay dying:

Written after I was shot -
Darling <u>Nancy</u>
I was shot leading a rush up <u>Moore Street</u>
took refuge in a doorway.
While I was there I heard the men pointing out where I was &
   I made a bolt for the lane I am in now.
I got more one bullet I think
Tons & tons of love dearie to you & to <u>the boys</u> & to <u>Nell</u> & <u>Anna</u>.
It was a good fight anyhow.
Good bye darling

Please deliver this to Nannie O'Rahilly
40 Herbert Park
Dublin

Belgard Road

Ging, Thomas, St. Aleron's £22
O'Rahilly, A., Mooreen House
1 Vacant
2 Cunningham, L.
Ryder, Ml., Mooreen a Ruggan
McGrath, -., Linkfield House
Maude, H.A.C., Belgard Castle
Law, M.F., Belgard Cottage
Hackett, -., Cluainin
Sheeran, -., Lisnagreeve
McTigue, F. – Whitehall Cott.
Brennan, M. – Belgard Lodge
The Rectory – Alexander, Rev. F., B.A.
O'Byrne, A. – St. Columb's

Extract Directory of Ireland, 1958.

Blackbirds by Monica Sproul (nee Small)

6.
'SMALL'S YARD'

Six children in my family survived infancy. Margaret (Peg) born in 1925 and Geraldine (Gwen) in 1928 and a still-born child in between. The boys, Edward (Son) and James (Jim) were born in 1930 and 1932 respectively. When Edward was born, my father used to hold him and sing Al Jolson's popular hit, 'Sonny Boy' so within the family and around the village, he was always called 'Son' or 'Sonny.' In 1934, I came along, Gertrude (Gert), and next to me was Annie Patricia (Patsy) born in 1935; Patsy died of tuberculosis at the age of seven. My mother's babies were born prematurely, mostly in the Rotunda Hospital, but the younger ones were born at home. The twins, Mary and Bernadette, were born at home at seven months in 1938; both died within a few days of birth. The youngest, Monica (Mono) was born at home in 1939. My father was busy finishing off a job to free himself up in time for the birth, but Mono was born while he was away. The nurse handed the newborn baby over to my eldest sister, Peg, while she attended to my mother.

As the family increased, my father added on and converted rooms and continually improved our living

Mary Small with first born child, Peg, 1925, in christening robe.

conditions. Over the years, our home became a long L-shaped cottage with three bedrooms, a sitting-room, kitchen and a bathroom. He installed a roll-top bath with lion's claw feet which had belonged to Johnno.

Our address the world over was: Raheen Cottage, Nangor Road, Clondalkin, Co. Dublin, Ireland. By the 1970s, although Post & Telegraphs (P&T) deliveries had progressed from bicycle to mini-van, the postman had no problem finding our family at this address, despite the numerous houses on the Old Nangor Road, all the way up to Nangor Castle.

Jim, Mono, Gert & Patsy Small.

Living within a more rural type environment meant that we children were very much attuned to the cycles of nature as well as the agricultural cycle. Not alone was it evident by the activities in the fields but many neighbours and family friends worked the land. The 'neighbourhood' encompassed distances reaching up towards Rathcoole, Saggart, Newcastle and the Tallaght Road on one side, to Neilstown, Ronanstown and Cloverhill on another side and to Red Cow, Fox and Geese and stretching towards Bluebell on the city side. We got around by walking or cycling or on the bus for trips to town; very few people had cars.

Signs on it, many of the roads had either a single line of grass up the middle with two ruts on either side or given the frequency of a larger vehicle, two lines of grass up the middle.

A large shed building backed on to the Old Nangor Road, forming a boundary with the yard. At the time of writing, the roadside wall of this structure is all that's left. The top storey was used as an oat loft and the lower portion was divided into areas with separate entrances that opened onto the yard, which housed horses and acted as a storage area for animal feed and farm machinery.

With some of the outhouses deserted during my childhood, it gave us kids free run of a marvellous indoor and outdoor playground.

The farmyard was alive with the sounds of animals. Horses were stabled in the building directly opposite the cottage which backed onto the Nangor Road. The horses were used during haymaking, ploughing and drawing the hay to the barn by bogey. 'Redser' was in the first stable and 'Salamanca' in the second stable. These two stables were on one side of the twin storage areas for binder, scales, horse 'bits,' feed and harnesses. On the other side was the third stable housing 'Snowy,' a Clydesdale horse and 'Blacky' was in the fourth stable. As well as horses, a bull was kept penned here on occasion. Beyond the stables there was a cowshed. Before my time, my father had two ferrets. He used to go ferreting for rabbits and shooting with his friend, Bill Deering.

We were a cat family, not a dog family, although we did have a dog for a time, 'Rex,' a stray that had wandered into our yard. In winter, the cats vied to sit beside the range and as soon as we got home from school, we whooshed them out of the way and competed ourselves for space nearest the range. The rule was that the cats were put out at night time. One time, miaows led us to hay where newborn kittens had been hidden by our missing cat, now a mother.

Our henhouse was next to the kitchen. It not only housed our hens, but also, our obstreperous cockerel. When Grandma Small died, her hens joined those in the yard along with her crotchety cockerel, who became a deadly enemy of our resident cockerel. The two had to be kept apart at different ends of the yard. My mother had to be called upon to escort us kids across the yard to avoid pecks on the legs from the crotchety cockerel who waited in ambush. We'd have to stand outside the gate, rattling it, calling out to my mother.

Beyond the hen house was our rabbit house. One of its occupants was a white rabbit who did not want to be anywhere but amongst the congregation in our kitchen. When we put the white rabbit into a barrel outside for the night, he used to kick up murder and squeal and squeal until he was brought back inside again. In time, the rabbit house went by the wayside to facilitate the hens when the henhouse became the site for a scullery. Later, the scullery became the new kitchen and the old kitchen became the sitting room. When WWII started, it was difficult to procure the henfood, Clarendo, so the hens had to go. A bathroom and a bedroom were built on the site of the henhouse.

Our menagerie of animals included a tortoise, a canary called 'Dickie' and goldfish in a large square tank in the back window of the living room. One day, when we jumped up and rushed to look out the back window at the hunt crossing the field, poor Dickie dropped dead with the fright. Sometimes when the kitchen windows were open, the curly-headed Herefords with big doleful eyes stuck their heads in the window and breathed sweet grassy smells into the kitchen.

A pet cemetery was an alien concept. Like everybody else, we buried any animals that died in a corner of the field, below my father's workshop. The men folk in the family usually dug a hole and in went the animal, to be covered over with earth.

Swallows were among our favourite birds as they were habitual residents in the outhouses, the rafters being a favourite nesting place. They left their droppings all over the earthen floor. Once we spotted them arriving back in Spring from warmer climes, we knew Summer was on its way. They swooped in and out the barn door, their beaks clutching bits of straw or feathers. Soon after, came the cheeping of young ones. In and out the barn they continued to swoop but now with a feeding purpose, bringing flies and worms to fatten them into fledglings. Then they'd progress to flying with the odd one tumbling down until they got the hang of it. You could time the seasons by their comings and goings. Their Autumn gathering in lines along the telegraph poles ready for the great migration marked the arrival of back-to-school time.

We could easily distinguish the various animal and bird noises. At night as we lay in bed, we could hear owls and recognise bats from the whistle they made as they flew. We took a great interest in nature, particularly in bird watching, as the area abounded with robins, linnets, crows, blackbirds, blue tits and other tits, thrushes, larks, yellowhammers, magpies, sparrows, starlings, corncrakes, snipe, plover, herons, swans, martins, kingfishers, wrens, owls, wagtails and many other species.

Immediately outside our front door, a narrow strip of garden was walled off from the yard and gated at each end. This strip had flowerbeds on each side of a crazy paving footpath and a sink and tap at one end, a great place for kids to slop. This piece of garden was stocked with an array of flowers and shrubs – clematis, trapoleum, roses, fuschia, dahlias, delphiniums, hydrangea, geraniums. A large fern grew at the end of the garden nearest to the bedrooms, its fronds stretching over a path built around it. Near the yard's entrance gate, my father grew forget-me-nots in a granite trough beneath a tap.

Another large barn stretched the length of another perimeter of the yard, although it was possible to access the back of the barn. One end of it served as a hayshed while the other end served as storage for mowers and other farm implements and bogies which lay on their ends with their shafts up in the air. The barn was a spacious building with a high slate roof and an open front exposed to the elements where there once had been doors. Bales of hay were stacked up to the roof at one end, depending on the time of the year. Once the farm machinery had been cleared out, we children used to play hide and seek in the barn, especially when it rained. My father slung a rope over the rafters to make a swing. He bored holes in a piece of wood and made a seat by knotting the rope through the holes. When both doors were open, you could swing right through to the open. In later years, when the yard outhouses were no longer in use, my father grew flowers and shrubs all around.

'Small's yard' was renowned as a great playground for youngsters due to its variety of outbuildings and nooks and crannies, ideal for chasing games, such as 'tag.' Kids in the village were often overheard saying 'are you going up to Small's yard?' With games of 'hide and seek,' the kids congregated in a recessed area between the barn and the outhouses where there was an animal feeding tray - a manger - in one corner. The only escape from that area was to climb up onto the manger in order to get over the high wall, a difficult feat when the manger could only accommodate one person at a time. With much consternation and

Gwen, Gert, Peg, Jim, Mono and dog.

shouts, kids used to pile into the corner and you'd be lucky to avoid getting trodden underfoot.

In addition to the large gated entrance between two pillars, a farm gate between my father's workshop and the cottage led into a field that sloped down to the Camac river. Another factor was my tolerant mother, who never minded the yard being full of boisterous children. She encouraged our play by helping to make outfits and feeding us with treats like ice cream wafers. Every now and then Johnno arrived unexpectedly and let a roar at the hordes of kids in the yard, who used to run for cover. Although very fond of my mother since her Sandymount days, he still upbraided her: 'Molly, get them kids out of here.' Having scattered to the four winds, the children used to stay away for a few days but they'd slip back again once the coast was clear.

We were of an age with many other families in the area such as the Hurrells, from Leinster Terrace – Mick, Kathleen and Betty Hurrell used to come to our yard. They also had siblings, Pat and Hugh. Kathleen, Bernie and Miriam Coates, who lived in the Mill Cottages (now part of the Round Tower Visitor Centre) came to the yard. There was also Peter, John, Nancy, Jim, Breda and Tommy in the Coates family. Vincent, Leo, Olive and Imelda McCurtin came to the yard; they also had siblings, Patty, Breda, Sean, Des, Eileen, Ray and Brian McCurtin. The McGraths from Moore's Lane also played in our yard, as did 'Bumpy' Ging, from Ging's shop and Davy Byrne.

Years later, when all the kids were gone, the barn provided a storage space over the winter for a fishing boat we acquired that was usually kept on the Shannon at Lough Ree. At weekends, we'd pile into the car on a fishing trip to Lough Ree. First, we'd have to locate the boat that we'd left tied up in an inlet. This usually involved baling out the boat and teeing up the outboard engine, before it was ready to take out. Eight of us went out in the boat with not a lifejacket between us. Often times, we'd moor at an island in the middle of the lake, where I'd be dropped off with the children, who were blissfully happy pretend-fishing. The menfolk fished across the lake and arrived back for a picnic or a fry, accompanied by a pot of tea, courtesy of my father's trusty primus stove. The boat was brought up from the lake over the winter for repairs and the outboard engine was locked in a shed.

Jim died in 1991, Son died in 2014 and Peg died in 2016. I miss them all.

Swallows by Mary Reynolds

7.
NAAS ROAD TOWARDS KINGSWOOD

At one time, the main artery to Cork and Limerick was essentially a highway called simply 'the Naas road' before it was developed into the Naas dual carriageway in the 1960s. The road later became part of a motorway known as the M7. Back in the day, the road went past an area known as the Book-o-Hounds at Clondalkin, or more frequently, the Buck-and-Hounds. It is believed that the townland took its name from an old public house that once stood in the area, the Buck and Hounds. Rockfield House, built in 1815, was part of a demesne here, once home in turn to John Gerraghty, Henry Brewster and the Hayward family. In 1961, a Statutory Declaration by Edith Maude Colley of Mill Cottages, Kilmatead, records the transfer of the Rockfield House property to her son George Dudley Pomeroy Colley. It states the title in the property had been in the family for generations, and mentions the tenant Mary Josephine Hayward. The Green Isle Hotel was built by the late P.V. Doyle on the site. At the Buck-and-Hounds, Tullys' house was on the left and the Quinlan family also lived in this area, as well as the Murphy family, who had a dairy.

About a mile beyond Newlands Cross is the townland of Cheeverstown, which takes its name from a Doctor Cheevers, who lived there back in the mid-1700s. Cheeverstown Castle was a fortress of the Pale until it fell into ruin. A new Georgian style property was erected beside it and this new building became known as Cheeverstown Castle. The new building was part of an extensive farm, known as Cheeverstown House. Thom's Almanac of 1858 shows, 'Joseph Fishbourne, Esq. Cheeverstown,' but the Thom's Almanac of 1882 shows, Cheeverstown as 'vacant.' The Barringtons and Dr. Kelly then lived there but

Top: Naas Road Motors at Newlands.

Left: Cheeverstown Castle. Origin of photo unknown.

Bottom: Workmen laying a new asphalt surface on the Naas Road, Clondalkin, 1925. Kindly shared by Gerard Byrne, Old Clondalkin & Surrounding Districts.

throughout my childhood, the well-known Clayton family lived at Cheeverstown between 1908 – 1980. Porter's Guide and Directory for County Dublin 1912, records, 'J. Clayton, Cheeverstown House.'

When William Clayton married, he built a house, 'Glenhazel,' on the Naas Road and lived there until his father's death. He then moved into Cheeverstown House and his widowed mother moved to Glenhazel. Back in 1913, a Mr. Robinson was employed as a chauffeur-cum-gardener and he lived in Cheeverstown's gate lodge. Cheeverstown House was eventually bought by Cement Roadstone (CRH Holdings) who demolished all but the gate lodge and commenced quarrying there. Over the years, Cheeverstown was let to various tenants and was most notably used as a children's convalescent home. Eventually, the home re-located to new premises on the Templeogue Road and carried the name, 'Cheeverstown House.'

Cheeverstown House. Kindly shared by Patrick Ging, Clondalkin Historical Society Archive.

Clayton's house: Glenhazel, Naas Road, built c. 1945. Courtesy niah.ie.

BEDLESSHILL NAAS ROAD, UPPER

Breen W.—Buck and Hounds

MeGough. P.—Gibralter

Cleary, P.—Bedlesshill

Doyle, P.—Wood view

Ha'vward, C.—Rockfield

Murphy, P.—Bedlesshill

O'Toole, Cissie—Bushfield

Dowling. Jas.—Bedlesshill

Maginn, Patk.— Bedlesshill

Ferry, E. - Cheeverstown Castle

Clayton, Mrs.—Cheeverstown Hse.

Colley, G. P. D. "Corkagh"

Clayton, Violet—Glenhazel

Hone, P.—Kilmatead

Extract from The Directory of Ireland, 1958

Kingswood. Baldonnel turn on the Naas Road, 1938, cottage in the background. Kindly shared by Gerard Byrne, Old Clondalkin & Surrounding Districts.

I was friendly with Peg, Maura, Eva and Angela O'Connor, who lived in a bungalow along the Naas Road. Angela was of an age with me. Mick O'Brien his wife and daughter, Sheila, lived nearby in a cottage shown in the picture, which belonged to Kingswood Farm. I remember one day myself and Angela called for Sheila and Mrs. O'Brien brought us in for jelly and ice-cream. During WWII, the Irish Army kept an anti-aircraft unit with billet huts on Kingswood farm. The huts were dismantled after the war and re-built in another location, to house civilian families. For years, Joe Carey ran a truck repair business beside the Garden Nurseries on the Naas Road at Kingswood and lived along here.

The famous singer, Joseph Locke, who had a very fine voice, once lived in Kingswood House and at different times, the Connors and O'Brien families lived there. Porter's Guide and Directory for County Dublin, 1912, holds two records, 'Miss K. Walsh, Kingswood House' and 'Walter Walsh, Kingswood.'

KINGSWOOD

Kingswood House—Locke, Joseph, £17.15s.
Callaghan. T
Brownsbarn—Nowlan, K. B
The Cottage—Kelly, Miss
Kingswood—James, A.

Kingswood House, 1935. Kindly shared by Gerard Byrne, Old Clondalkin & Surrounding Districts.

Fox. J.

Foley, —.

M'ulhare. Marv

Mulhare, P. B.

Ard Solus—Humpries, R.

Mooneen Cottages—Alton

„ Collins, —.

Tia—Kingswood Products

Extract from The Directory of Ireland, 1958

In the Duke of Leinster's press clippings, John Cowell describes from 'Dublin's Famous People,' how in July 1815, Charles Bianconi started up a fleet of vehicles, having originally arrived in Ireland to peddle prints of famous Italian paintings. His principal depot was at the Royal Garter Stables along the Naas Road at Clondalkin, where 60 to 200 horses were stabled. Built of limestone rubble and with round windows like wheels on its western end, the building was more commonly known as the Bianconi Coach House. He also had a smaller stable between the gate lodges of Cheeverstown and Corkagh, called 'The Carlow Field Stables,' which he used a base for coaches to Carlow town. His fleet of coaches, painted yellow and crimson, numbered 100 at one time, including mail coaches and different sized cars, holding anything from 4 to 25

Bianconi mail coach in Galway, c. 1880. Courtesy National Library of Ireland

passengers each, as well as carrying mail. Each station employed from 1 to 8 grooms, about 100 drivers and 1300 horses. Ireland being a religious country, Mr. Bianconi's only Sunday work was mail and canal work. The transport vehicles became known as the 'Bians,' short for Bianconi. Although the threat of the railways was already upon him, the 'Bians' lasted for forty-two years. Charles Bianconi died in 1875, aged 89. The premises was sold on to a farmer and it may have become known as 'Brown's Barn' at that stage.

Another building with hay barns and a forge on the Citywest side of the road near Brown's Barn was demolished with the development of the Naas dual carriageway. More recently, the original Bianconi building was converted for use as a bar and restaurant, aptly called 'Brown's Barn,' with many original features kept intact.

The late Jim Mansfield was a well-known person who lived in this area. The story goes that he made his money after the Falklands War, when he bought and re-sold war-surplus heavy machinery. He bought the beautiful Tassaggart House on the Saggart Road and renovated it and he undertook development of the area now known as 'City West,' which is served by the red line Luas tram.

A step further beyond, Connie Holland of The Bungalow at Blackchurch, provided information to the Schools Folklore Collection about the graveyards at Saggart and Coalmanstown. (www.duchas.ie)

NAAS ROAD

Silverdene—McCarthy, L. £19 15s.
Rvemead—Quinlan, W. £24 15s.
Ethnadell—St. Ledger, P. £15 10s.
Light Machinery Co.
Lisheen — Lennon, Patrick, Tia
County Confectioner £3? 10s.
Hyland, B.—Rosapenna, Newlands

Bedlesshill & Kingswood & Naas:
Extracts from The Directory of Ireland, 1958

Kingfisher by Monica Sproul (nee Small)

8.
THE EXTENDED SMALL FAMILY

We had little to do with the Walsh side of our family, in light of my grand-mother's early death, my mother having been raised by relatives in Tipperary and my grandfather having re-married. I recall a photograph of my grandfather as a widower with three children, before the family broke up, but regret there is

Four generations: Mary Small (nee Walsh), her father, James (Jim) Walsh, her daughter, Gwen O'Byrne (nee Small) and infant grandson, Joe.

now no trace of it. One time when my sister, Gwen, was home from England with her eldest son, Joe, my grandfather paid us a visit and we were lucky enough to photograph four generations together.

Our extended family always included the Small side of the family, who had lived on in Drumcondra after my grandfather's death. Around 1928, my two bachelor uncles, Harold and Eddie Small, bought a house in Kilmainham called 'Shamrock Cottage,' in the shadow of Rowntree's factory at Kilmainham. They moved in, together with my grandmother, Margaret Small. They painted black shamrocks on their grained front door.

Every Saturday my father used to visit them and often took us along. My grandmother was renowned for her delicious pot roast. My father used to arrive home with a loaf of her home-baked bread and a bag of sweets for us children. In turn, they were regular visitors at Raheen. Sometimes, we'd meet them in the Phoenix Park where the men raced their motorbikes, caps back to front and coats flying in the wind.

My grandmother died at Shamrock Cottage in 1936, at the age of eighty two. She is buried with my grandfather in Drumcondra churchyard. Her son, Harold Small, paid her some loving tributes:

Shamrock Cottage, Kilmainham.

Harold & Eddie Small, 1936

A Last Request

T'was dismal – dark November
Cold – sodden was the ground.
A watery sun was shining,
And the leaves lay all a-round.
'Whatever is the matter'-
The little sparrows said.
As anxiously they fluttered,
From bush – to garden – shed.
'The old woman in the cottage –
To us was very kind.
She always scattered crumbs around,
And us she well did mind.
But now – we are forgotten –
We'r cold – and hungry too –
And if she doesn't come to us,
I don't know what we'll do.'

About the cottage – silence
Inside it - all was still.
For lying on the sick-bed
the old woman lay so still.
Kind hands tending to her
As standing by her bed
And trying hard to catch the words,
that she so softly said.
To catch that faintest whisper,
they dared not even tread
'Twas low and faint the murmur
"Are the little sparrows fed?"
Again the crumbs are scattered
Though the hearts within are sad
The last request is granted
She made the sparrows glad.

Harold Peebles Small - 2nd December 1936

Firelight

The kitchen seems so lonely,
in the Fire-lights fitful glare.
The High-lights play at hide and seek,
On a well-worn arm-chair.
And as I gaze and ponder,
I can't help though I try.
A glistening tear steals down my cheek,
as I think of the days gone by.
I recall a well loved figure
With brow all lined with care.
And oh! the sadness of the thought,
I helped to put them there.
T'is mother who is absent.
For she's at peace with God.
Travelled that great Highway.
So many feet have trod.
The guardian of my youth,
A true, a trusted pal,
Of all the friends I ever had.
She was the Best- of-All
Our partnership has ended.
We may no longer share.
But Memories Sweet I'll oft' recall
When I see that well-worn chair.

Harold Peebles Small - 1st December 1936

Harold and Eddie remained bachelors. They worked together as a painting and decorating team all over Dublin. They also undertook maintenance work for various customers, including Mrs. Bradshaw, who owned the Mount Temple estate near Griffith Avenue, where Mount Temple Comprehensive was later built. When Mrs. Bradshaw died, the two of them got fixed up with jobs at Cox's Engineering. The Cox family were in some way related to Mrs. Bradshaw. The Bradshaw family were known for their generosity; Thomas Picton-Bradshaw donated a large number of trees and shrubs for planting in Fairview on Arbour Day in 1909.

The pair cycled everywhere and neither smoked nor drank alcohol. They had a touch of Victorian unworldliness about them; they dressed up in Sunday 'best' to go out - tweed coats and shiny leather lace-up shoes which they wore sparingly for years. One time, Harold used the wrong solution in renewing the soles on his shoes. He only discovered his mistake on his way to church, when leaves began to stick to his shoes. To remove the leaves, he brushed the soles of his shoes against a wall. However, he ended up worse off, with moss as well as leaves stuck to his soles, leaving him no choice but to return home.

They pursued a huge amount of interests in their spare time. Both were keen motorcyclists, proficient amateur photographers and early wireless enthusiasts who built their own radio sets. They were great readers and loved classical music. Harold also wrote poetry and he was particularly talented at oil painting and fretwork. He had a keen sense of duty and benevolence and was habitually helping out families. A true Christian, we only discovered the full extent of his generosity to others after his death.

Auction catalogue for Mount Temple, Clontarf

The garden at Shamrock Cottage was divided into two sections and smelled of apples and roses. Harold created a miniature Japanese garden on his patch. They had about eight hens and a cockerel and a pet tortoise, 'Charlie,' who had a box in the garden into which he hibernated over the winter. Harold wrote a poem about Charlie in Peg's autograph book, accompanied by a drawing, which is sadly now lost. They also had a budgie, Bertie. The pair were great favourites with children and used to dress up and play games.

The two also enjoyed fishing. During one of their fishing trips to Howth,

Harold met a lady, who later turned out to be otherwise engaged. He wrote the following poems in 1932 and 1931 respectively;

Good-Bye!

If my love has cast a shadow,
Or perhaps has caused a sigh,
I wonder can you not forgive,
Oh, sweetheart! Won't you try.

What'er my fault it may have been,
'Twas to your charm I fell,
I could not have seen, and known you,
Then failed to love you well.

Not only do I leave you – Love,
One to my heart so near
I leave behind my Boy-hood days,
And scenes of youth so dear.

Good-bye! Sweet countryside,
Green fields, and golden grains,
I dare no longer linger near,
I may not pass this way again.

But as the new road I am travelling,
In the sunshine - through the rain,
I will pause, and looking backwards,
Will think - and think of you again.

My Treasures

Of all the things I value most,
they are neither gems nor gold.

For the things I most value,
are things that are not sold.

Of all the things I value most,
they are like the dew drops clear.
The product of a woman,
to me for ever dear.

Of all the things I value most,
on all the land or sea.
It is the tears my Nancy, shed.
The tears she shed for me.

Daisy, the family dog, 1916 by Harold Small

9.
ALONG MONASTERY ROAD
INTO CLONDALKIN VILLAGE

Let me take you back to the Naas Road and the former junction that led off to the right down Monastery Road and into Clondalkin village. There was a water pump at that junction up to 1974.

Pump at the corner of Naas Road and Monastery Road, 1925

On the left after the turn-off, the Hanlon family lived in a lone house on a hill. A record in Thom's Almanac of 1882 shows, 'Mrs. Hanlon, farmer and lime burner.' As a schoolgirl back in 1937, Miriam Hanlon wrote a descriptive piece for the Schools Folklore Collection about the nearby lime kiln, almost two hundred years old, that was in the hands of the Hanlon family.

A lime kiln is a building shaped on the side like a spinning top, and holds about fifty tons of coal and fire. In a quarry which is quite near the kiln the lime stones are blasted. A hole is bored in the rock and a long cord which is known as fuse is placed in the hole, the end of the fuse being some distance from the rock. Fire is put to the fuse and so goes to the hole in the rock, which is full of powder and almost immediately the rock flies into the air in pieces. These stones are then taken to the kiln. Layers of stone and layers of breeze are put in on top of the kiln. As the stones burn they turn white and when rightly burned they are taken out from a small opening at the bottom. It is then known as lime. It is intensively used for building and agricultural purposes.

Extract from the Schools Folklore Collection. Courtesy of Duchas - www. duchas.ie

Limestone from this area was used in the construction of the Round Tower, the exterior walls of St. Patrick's Cathedral in Dublin and the steps of St. Paul's Cathedral in London.

Hanlon's Lime, Monastery Road. Note the telephone number, Clondalkin 2. Photo credit Gerard Byrne.

A water tower stands near the entrance to a quarry run by the Southern Ireland Asphalt Company. SIAC, its better known name, was set up by Denis Feighery, one of the first in Ireland to use tarmacadam. The company is still run by the Feighery family and is based in Dolcain House. The firm undertakes extensive road and bridge building in Ireland and abroad, to include the flyover at Stanstead.

A mass path near the water tower extends from Fox & Geese to Monastery Road at a point opposite Knockmeenagh Lane. The name Knockmeenagh, meaning 'hill of minerals,' most likely derived from its renown as an area for quarrying.

The area at the top of Monastery Road known as Knockmitten, meaning 'hill of the beautiful plain,' was all farmland at one time. This location used to be a great vantage point for a clear view all over Dublin until bit by bit the landscape changed as field after field fell before excavators and bulldozers.

Clockwise from top: Patsy Keogh Turf Accountant (credit Gerard Byrne); advertisement for point-to-point races, Clondalkin; enjoying the point-to-point races at Monastery Hill from the back of a Hanlon Lime truck; point-to-Point at Monastery Hill with the water tower in the background.

To the right of the road is a large field known as 'Monksfield,' where point-to-point horse races used to be held. The housing estate now built on the land aptly took the name, 'Monksfield.' Because of the style of the houses, with the roof sloping downwards overhanging the walls, the estate is also known as 'the Dutch village,' 'Woodford' estate is adjacent to Monksfield. When they were built, the houses were flanked by small fields lined with hedgerows as far as the eye could see, either populated by cows grazing peacefully or ploughed into drills or blowing with the waves of wheat sheaves.

Next along were the ruins of Mount Saint Joseph's Monastery. The foundation stone of the monastery was laid by the Rev. Fr. A. Cahill P.P. Clondalkin on the 2nd February 1813. A large tract of land was made over to the Third Order of the Lady of Mount Carmel for the purpose of funding and supporting a religious community and establishing schools. The building was surrounded by beautiful lawns and flower gardens. The Brothers maintained a well-stocked vegetable garden and farmyard and killed their own cattle, which made them self-sufficient for food. They also ran a bakery, a coach works and lime kilns, all of which gave local employment. When cholera took its toll, the monks tended the sick and buried the dead in the adjacent graveyard. The record in Thom's Almanac 1858 shows, 'Clondalkin Monastery, Rev. Mr. Brennan, Chaplain,

The Monastery on Monastery Road, c.1930 with nearby quarry. Kindly shared by Gerard Byrne, Old Clondalkin and Surrounding Districts.

Mount St. Josephs. Clothing ceremony. The Little Sisters of the Poor had a Dispensary and they also nursed the sick in their own homes. Kindly shared by Patrick Ging.

Geo. Lyons, supr.' while the 1882 edition records, 'Clondalkin Monastery, Rev. James Beahan, Chaplain, Rev. D.J. Clancy, superior.'

For a long number of years, the monastery was at the centre of life in Clondalkin but education was the main interest of the community. At one stage they had a boarding school, but it was more latterly used as a school for boys. Some pupils had to travel to school variously by horse, pony and trap or donkey carts. Both of my brothers attended the school before moving on to further education - Son continued his education in town and Jim went to the Tech. I remember the lads from the Monastery school used to tease the Convent girls when they met them going to and from school, saying, *'Hay and oats for the Convent goats; eggs and rashers for the Monastery bashers.'*

With the advent of the National School system, primary and secondary schools were separated. When the Monastery was in decline with dwindling pupil numbers and many of the Brothers old or semi-retired, the foundation was dissolved and the schools were eventually closed in 1938. Then the Department of Defence stationed 500 troops there at one stage. In 1945, the Monastery was sold to The Little Sisters of the Assumption and the contents were sold at auction. The nuns had a role at the centre of the community for years and took on all sorts of tasks. One such task was being called upon at time of death to come out to the family home to lay out the dead and comfort the bereaved. The nuns

Floraville, Monastery Road, 1933, demolished in the 1970's. The original entrance gate and lodge still exist. Photo credit Patrick Ging, information credit Emer Ging.

vacated the Monastery in 1980, having decided to work entirely in the community. For a time, the building was leased by the Health Board and accommodated the Rutland residential clinic for those with addictions as well as St. Loman's day care. In 1986, a fire destroyed most of the buildings. The entire premises was demolished in 1989. An estate called Monastery Heath now stands on the site.

Back to SIAC and the entrance beside it to a sports ground, Cumann Luth and Cumann Chloigthi, Chleas Gael, founded in 1884.

Next was Floraville, a beautiful house surrounded by trees and parkland, where hundreds of daffodils raised their heads in springtime. In Lewis's Topographical Dictionary of Ireland, 1837, the record shows, 'C. Brabazon Esq. of Floraville.' Successive residents included William Francis Smith, Captain Sexton, Captain William Browne and Bruno Klinkenbergh. In my time, a single lady, Miss O'Rourke, lived there; she was in some way related to the Hughes family of Nangor Castle. Father Traynor lived at Miss O'Rourke's house after his retirement. The big house was demolished in the 1960s but the former gate lodge, called 'Floraville,' which is directly opposite the library, still survives. Bridget Errity, who worked in Corkagh before she married, lived in this lodge when she became Mrs. Gregory. Bridget is the person who should be writing this memoir as she had an enormous knowledge of Clondalkin, as did Evy Archbold. Monastery Rise estate stands on the grounds of the original big house.

Back across the road again. A bit after the Monastery, the Conlon family constructed a beautiful house called Lexington. Mr. Conlon was a builder who returned from America. Lexington has now been demolished and a nursing home is being built there.

EASTER DANCE
TO BE HELD IN
Carnegie Library, Clondalkin,
On EASTER SUNDAY NIGHT,
APRIL 23, 1916.

MR. A VERSO NAPPER'S STRING BAND.
DANCING 10 P.M.

Tickets (Double 10s. 6d. Single 6s.) can be obtained from Miss K. Vickers, Blackchurch, Harlehatch; Miss M. Hayden, Celbridge, Co. Kildare; Miss R. Cregan, 24 North terrace, Inchicore. Visitors can travel to Clondalkin by 3 35 p.m. train ex Kingsbridge. Taxi to City after Dance 1s. 6d. extra.

Two photos of Carnegie Library, and notice about upcoming dance on Easter Sunday 1916, historical day. Kindly shared by Gerard Byrne, Old Clondalkin & Surrounding Districts.

Beside Lexington was one of the finest buildings in Clondalkin, the red-brick and granite Carnegie Library. Built with the assistance of the Carnegie Trust, it was designed by T.J. Byrne and opened in 1910. It also served as a meeting venue for the Clondalkin area, a polling station, and each month, the upstairs was converted into a venue for monthly dances. The partitions were folded back and ladies were warned to mind their high heels on the 'train tracks.' In 1970, Dublin County Council refurbished the building. In its infancy, the historical society was run from the library.

Opposite the Library is Tully's Castle, a 16th Century tower house, where the Tully family lived for years. In the fifteenth century, it was the home of Betty O'Tullach, who died tragically after the deaths of two suitors and is said to haunt the ruins. Tully's Castle was possibly one of the outposts of the Pale but its origins are mostly undocumented. However, the *"Journal of the Royal Society of Antiquaries of Ireland 1899,"* gives the following information: The name "Castle of Clondalkin"' is applied to Tully's Castle in a number of late eighteenth and early nineteenth century leases, which deal with a place called "The Sheepus." Since 1761 there has been no great change in its appearance. The Sheepus in these leases is referred to as ... *"nearly adjoining the Castle of Clondalkin."*

Major McNally lived in a detached bungalow beside the castle. From about the 1950s, Nielsen's set up a fuel yard in the garden of Major McNally's house, which is still there, alongside several other businesses. Further on, the Guilfoyle family lived in a detached bungalow and the Nugent and Heaney families lived in a pair of detached cottages, where the garage now stands. Mr. Nugent worked in the Mill.

Back to the Library side of the road. A little beyond the Library was a farm, 'Bettyfort,' which presumably took its name from Betty O'Tullach. A record in Thom's Almanac of 1882 shows, 'C. Graham, Esq., Bettyford [sic].' Before my time, James McQuilty lived in Bettyfort's gate lodge which I believe was on the left, inside the gates. The lodge was gone by the time I used to go there to buy

Clockwise from top: Local History Group in library: standing, Peg Nolan, Evy Archbold, Bridie Gill, Carrie Errity, Mrs. Johnson, Joe Connor; seated, Paddy Doran, Miss Hughes, Bridget Gregory (nee Errity), courtesy Historical Society; Tully's Castle c. 1931; row of shops at Bettysfort, Monastery Road, origin of photo unknown; Nielsen's coal depot, Monastery Rd, 1990, originally Major McNally's garden (photo credit Roy Byrne, accessed from Clondalkin Historical Society Archive).

milk from Bettyfort's owner, Maggie Hart, in the late 1930s/early 1940s. You opened a door in the wall bordering Monastery Road and went across the yard to buy milk at the house. Maggie had a dairy herd and she never seemed to take a day off or dress up. The entrance gate to Bettyfort stood at the present-day entrance to Castle Park. The row of shops at Castle Crescent, known as 'Bettyfort Terrace,' and the estate behind were built on Bettyfort land as well as the former technical school, now called Clondalkin Education Centre.

Bettyfort Terrace
£20 each valuation

1. Moran, Laurence
2. 2. Reilly, Francis
3. O'Riordan, Patrick
4. McGillyicuddy, Rev. C.
   Hughes E.
5. Brown, Christopher
6. Hudson, Donald

Extract Thom's directory, 1960.

Nearer to the village, Canon Ryan lived in St. Kevin's Presbytery, a two storey-over-basement house. He was very old, deaf and cross. The Monastery Shopping Centre now stands on this site.

The Freyne family set up a chemist shop in the next premises; their yard abutted the Presbytery. Until then, there was no chemist in Clondalkin and people had to travel to Bowles Chemist in Inchicore for prescriptions. Later on, Freyne's chemist shop re-located to Orchard Road, where it still stands, with a sign above that reads, 'Established in 1935.' Mrs. Freyne was an O'Meara from Ballyfermot where her people farmed.

Maybe the best remembered shop of all was Jacobs; Maisie and Emmy ran a newsagent and grocery

St. Kevin's House,'the Presbytery on Monastery Road, c.1932. Photo accessed years ago Clondalkin Library, origin unknown.

shop. Sweets displayed in tall glass jars were measured out and placed in cones made out of rolled paper for customers, especially cinemagoers. In a room off the shop was the telephone exchange. As all calls came through the exchange, the Miss Jacobs knew everybody for miles around and those they didn't know, they made it their business to find out. Jacob's was later taken over by Eugene Mc-Namara who started off a hardware shop there and expanded to building supplies and tool hire.

In the centre of the village was the Post Office run by the Whitty family in my time. They got to know everybody through their work, especially handling telegrams. The Post Office was run by Mrs. Whitty together with her three daughters, Josephine (Jo), who did not marry, Mrs. Boland and Mrs. Dympna O'Brien, who worked in the Mill office before she married. The Post Office might have been fusty but it was run very efficiently. Mr. Whitty, a dapper man with a waxed moustache, worked in the Time Office in the Mill. A record in Thom's Almanac of 1858 shows, 'Lawrence Hegarty, Postmaster,' while the record in the 1882 edition shows, 'Mrs. Eliza Hegarty, Postmistress.' Porter's Guide and Directory for County Dublin 1912, records for Clondalkin Post Office, 'Telegrams and Money Orders. Mrs. Hegarty, Postmistress.' On the retirement of the Whitty family, Ledwidge's took on the Post Office and the business moved to Tower Road.

A little further on, Hart's pub, formerly known as the Central Bar, now known as 'The Purty Central,' still stands in its original location, on an island site along Main Street.

Back across the road to The Laurels. The Dowling family initially owned this

Jacob's shop and former premises Freyne's Chemist. Maisie and Emmy Jacob in floral dresses.

long two-storey house which had two separate front doors and its gable end to the Main Street. The Dowling name was over the door nearest to Main Street. A gated entrance at the other gable end led into a farmyard. The Dowlings' farm bordered the New Road and stretched way up towards Newlands. Back in the 1920s, Peter and Rita Ging bought The Laurels. They farmed land at the back of the house and used to graze cattle on it. The Ging family developed the

From top: Old Post Office - Westward House; Mrs. W Whitty, retiring Post-mistress Clondalkin, with her daughters left, Josephine Whitty and right, Mrs. Dympna O'Brien, 1964; demolition of Old Post Office, Clondalkin (credit Paddy Ging, Clondalkin Historical Society Archive); Francey Dowling, aged 15, Postman in Clondalkin c. 1948 (kindly shared by Carmel O'Farrell, NSW, Australia). Bottom left: Clondalkin village c. 1900 with The Laurels on the left. Bottom right shows the name 'Dowling,' then owners, over the door.

Tower Cinema (formerly the bus depot)

Tower Cinema on a former bus depot site beside their premises. The building remains but it is now converted into shop units. More about the cinema later.

The Ging family moved to the Diamond House, at the junction of the Nangor Road, Ninth Lock Road, Orchard Road and Tower Road and 'The Laurels' was purchased by the O'Neill family. Dr. Calvert had his surgery in the part of The Laurels adjacent to the Main Street and the O'Neill family lived in the far end. Eventually, the property was sold on and the house became 'The Laurels' public house in the 1930s, taking its name from the two laurel trees which stood outside the door. The land behind was developed and Laurel Park estate stands there now.

At last, we have made into the heart of Clondalkin.

Pheasant by Monica Sproul (nee Small)

10.
DOMESTIC LIFE AT RAHEEN COTTAGE

The family hubbub at our home at Raheen was set against the backdrop of the sounds of nature and farmyard sounds; cows and horses, chickens, cockerels, geese, as well as the peal of church bells and the Mill hooter. The sounds of swallows from our barn, and the coo of the pigeons from the tall trees near the haggard in an adjacent field rivalled the cawing of crows. As the last rays lit the sky each evening, the birds clamoured and took off from the treetops, dispersing and converging again and again until they settled to roost for the night. The noise of the birds was a constant backdrop to the lowing of cattle, the whinny of horses in our yard and the barks of neighbouring dogs. On the odd occasion, a billy goat was put out to graze and depending on the direction of the wind, you could get his strong whiff for about a mile around, hence my aversion to goat's cheese.

As the entrance to our place opened right onto the busy Nangor Road, the gate was always kept shut but our home was always open to callers. Often, you'd hear the gate rattle when you were in the kitchen and glance at the clock to see if one of the family was arriving home. If nobody was expected home, you'd look out the kitchen window to see who was coming. Although our formal front door with its brass head door knocker opened directly into the living room, everybody knew to use the low door which opened directly into the kitchen. A quick rap, the door opened and they'd duck their heads to step inside.

The kitchen was at the heart of our home. In the centre of the room was a red kitchen table with pull-out drawers to store cutlery. My father used to sit precariously on his red Bentwood chair with a foam cushion that had seen better days, a cigarette hanging from his mouth and usually petting a cat on his lap. The kitchen window framed the view across fields laden with cowslips towards Moyle Park and the mountains beyond. The range was not alone a source of warmth, but it was also used for cooking and heating water.

We did not have enough ground to grow our own vegetables and even our yard was a working farmyard. Food was cooked on top of the range or in the oven and we always had a stockpot on the go, full of vegetables, stock and herbs, for use as a base for stews and soups. Large jars were filled for the winter with pulses, such as lentils, green and yellow split peas, dried peas, butter beans and chick peas to thicken soups and for nourishment.

Vegetables were seasonal and all produce was organic but variety was more limited than today. During war time, the selection was more or less confined to root vegetables such as turnips, beans, carrots, cabbage, celery, brussel sprouts, butter beans and potatoes. There were no frozen peas in those days, only marrowfat peas which came in a cardboard pack and had to be soaked overnight before being cooked.

Meat during the week consisted of beef, pork, chicken, fish and mutton. We were never a family for coddle, liver, tripe, pig's cheek or cow heel. Tropical fruit was uncommon but we were always able to buy oranges, apples, pears and bananas. Like most people, we had no form of refrigeration so we placed milk, margarine and butter into a bucket of cold water in a shaded corner to keep it fresh. Packaged food and provisions such as rice and tea were generally bought loose, in bulk, measured by weight. The dessert selection extended from apple tarts, scones and other home baked treats to strawberries and cream, jelly and ice-cream or a piece of Madeira cake topped with fruit and ice-cream. Cupboard staples also included rice, tapioca and sago.

In observance of the religious restriction on Catholics to refrain from meat-eating on Fridays, we always ate eggs or fish, usually kippers, cod or plaice, although plaice was always expensive. On Sundays it was corned beef or a roast cut, usually roast beef, with vegetables and roast potatoes.

All of our family's fare depended on the produce available in the local shops, vegetables from neighbours, or fish my father caught. There was no such thing as vegetarian food or special diets for coeliacs or the lactose intolerant, nor did family members get a choice. My mother shouted out, 'dinner's ready' and you happily ran into the kitchen table.

Jam-making was a seasonal event – my mother made blackberry and apple jam, blackcurrant jam or her own particular speciality, vegetable marrow and ginger jam. She used Seville oranges to make marmalade. I continued with jam-making after I married and in one year alone, I made ninety pounds of plum jam, from the Victoria plum trees in the garden, fifty of which I kept for my father and Jim, as they loved plum jam. However, I had to dole it out frugally, because my father would eagerly share his stash with any visitor that called. In fact, my father and Jimmy loved anything homemade, so I regularly brought over scones and apple tarts and even then, my father might ask were there any sausage rolls or scotch eggs, his particular favourites.

Sometimes a family member arrived home from town with Hafners' sausages that went straight on to the pan no matter what time of the day or night. Every Saturday saw long queues outside Hafners' three shops in Henry Street, George's Street and North Earl Street. The Hafners were *Typical radio back in the day, kept high on a shelf.* an elderly German couple and the story went that they guarded their sausage recipe and it died with them. However, I see the Hafner brand is still in being but I wonder are the sausages the same.

Evenings were peppered with the sound of the radio, our manually-operated Singer sewing machine or the click of knitting needles, followed by short silences while my mother tacked or hemmed or counted stitches.

I mentioned before that my father had built radios since the time of the crystal sets – he used to put the headphones on us to listen so we could listen to London 2 LO. By the time I came along, we had a wireless, a rare asset back then. He was very particular about it and kept it on a high shelf in the kitchen, away from interfering little hands. Radio reception varied - the longer and higher the aerial, the more stations you could get. We had marvellous reception due to the aerial, which stretched in the high trees from Driscoll's to Cusack's. It really was the only source of entertainment in the evenings. Others used battery radios; the battery was a square glass bell jar with a steel handle on top for ease of carriage. The battery needed re-charging so you'd see people cycling by, steering the bike with one hand while holding the cumbersome battery in the other, no mean feat.

Mostly, we listened to the national station, Radio Éireann, but we also tuned into BBC and a multiplicity of other radio stations, including German and other European channels. The wireless was a great source for news and sport updates, the weather and farming programmes. Some programmes ran for years, like The Archers which was on at 7.00 p.m. or The Kennedy's of Castlerosse or the agony aunt, Dear Frankie. Women's Hour was popular with the ladies and Mrs. Dale's Diary in the afternoon. A broad range of music was played – traditional, classical, tango and popular music. My father liked listening to opera and semi-classical music and I remember Nelson Eddy singing with Jeanette McDonald. While we as kids enjoyed that type of music, we also liked popular music such as Artie Shaw's band or Glen Miller's band or Joe Loss and listened as well as crooners like Frank Sinatra and Bing Crosby. 'Half-hour' shows included one called Curtain Up, where you had to try and guess who the murderer was – it was easy enough to identify the characters, when you tuned in. They also had comedy shows and ghostly stories, 'This is your storyteller – the Man in Black.' On Friday nights, they aired a programme, Friday Night is Music Night, then they had a quiz by question-master, Joe Linnane. Sunday was a night for ceilí bands. Radio plays were another favourite of ours.

During the war, we listened to the overseas Forces programmes and live broadcasts, including those of Lord Haw-Haw, as he was known. "Germany calling, Germany calling," he used to say, by way of introducing his talk. After the war, we followed the Nuremberg Trials.

Apart from regular household tasks, my mother was kept busy with sewing and mending. She was a great seamstress who made all our clothes. Back then, people used to 'turn' coats and suits, which meant the seams were unpicked and the fabric was reversed and sewn up again to give fresh wear. When a coat was worn out, it was often cut down for a child. My mother was particular about her finish; she paid attention to detail, adding coloured buttons and piping to garments, her own style features. People used to remark on her knitting skills and neat sewing up of seams that always met perfectly.

Mattresses were put across the clothes line and beaten twice a year. Sheets were made from large flour bags sewn together, then washed and bleached, very hard-wearing. Another regular act of economy was cutting worn blankets and sheets down the middle and then stitching the side seams together. Although it furthered the life of the blanket, it meant a bumpy ridge underneath the body. One good set of bedding was kept in a drawer in case anyone became ill. The set comprised a pair of twill sheets, a pair of pillowcases, a bolster, a pair of white towels, two blessed candles and a 'Happy Death' crucifix.

I remember wintertime for the cold, the endless hours of collecting firewood and darkness falling at four o'clock, reading, radio, and off to bed under a half ton of clothes, with extra heat provided by heavy overcoats. We had stoneware hot water bottles, supplemented by ordinary glass bottles wrapped in a man's sock that was knotted at the top. As children, we slept in brass beds high off the floor. We used to twist off the bed knobs and stuff things inside the tubular bed ends. Territory was an issue, so we used to mark out 'my side' and 'your side' of the bed by counting along the brass bars and drawing an imaginary line. The skylight overhead gave us children a window to the weather, rain trickling down, snowflakes, leaves gathering or a full moon.

The Skylight

Dreams are dreamt when asleep
Now come along and take a peep
For my dreams in my childhood bed
I dreamt as I just stared ahead

The skylight was but two by two
A small space from which to view
To watch the clouds go rolling by
In that huge space, the sky

When the skylight was left ajar
The waterfall could be heard afar
And when the leaves were falling
On the skylight patterns drawing

Rain trickled down the glass

And so the idle hour would pass
To hear the hoot of the owl at night
Or the sound of the cuckoo at daylight

But the stormy night by far
The one which seemed most like war
When massive streaks of lightening fled
Replaced by thunder in its stead

In my bed I would shudder
My dreams replaced by the bedcover

Gertrude Reynolds

My mother made an ankle length lace dress with an elasticated waist for Peg's Communion, with a veil, a headdress and a matching lace pull-string handbag. The same dress was kept by and used for each of the girls in turn for Communion and Confirmation. The dress had been made in such a way that it could be worn long for each Communion and by the time each girl grew, the dress was short enough to be worn for Confirmation as well.

When my cousins, Gertie and Rita Small, started working, they passed their hand-me-down clothes to our family. Garters were a commonplace feature back then to hold up stockings. We rarely got new clothes but one time I was shopping in Bolgers with my mother and sister, Mono, who was being kitted out for confirmation, when I spotted a gorgeous dress with a Peter Pan collar and piping. My mother counted her money and she had enough for the dress, which cost about £2, a rare treat.

Like everybody else, the laundry was dried on a long washing line in the yard, with an eye kept on the sky, lest in rained. On wet days, our laundry was hung on a washing line in the barn. My mother also dried off clothes in the warm kitchen, with a line strung across the room or small items on a type of towel rail that protruded above the range, with three moveable bars.

My father was kept busy with repairs. He mended all the family's shoes, replacing heels and soles. Readymade soles and heels in different sizes were easily purchased in the likes of Woolworth's. He also undertook all the home maintenance as it arose, on top of doing his regular painting and decorating work. The days were long and we all had jobs to do but generally in winter, we went to bed early.

On Saturday nights, all the shoes were polished for Mass the next day and it was also bath night for the children. It was a joint operation with my mother bathing us children in the big zinc bath in front of the fire and passing us over to my father who dried us off and put on our clean night clothes. We never said the Rosary but I knew families who said the full Rosary together which took ages and other families kept it to a decade or two, with different people in the circle leading each decade. We'd sit around the fire for a warm-up and a treat before going to bed, usually a sweet or two or Kerry Cream biscuits or half an orange or apple, or in times of plenty, a whole fruit each.

My father had a penchant for antiques and made use of anything given to him by customers when he was carrying out renovations. An ornate Victorian fireplace had green tiles in the hearth and a fan shaped black canopy above. My father used to get the fire going with a bellows. A mahogany over-mantel surrounded the fireplace and had built-in bookcases on each side. A china cabinet in the corner had cutlery drawers at the bottom. Another built-in press with latticed glass doors held trinkets that children found fascinating – a salt and pepper set in the shape of tomatoes, a green leaf-shaped dish and glass sundae dishes, associated with servings of Neapolitan ice-cream. We all added to his ornament collection over the years, particularly my eldest sister, Peg. One item she brought was a miniature statue of Hamlet with a skull in his hands which sat in the centre of the over-mantel for years.

The original entrance door to the house had an unusual brass doorknocker - the head and shoulders of a man with a tall hat. The kitchen was kept warm with a range on the go and beside it, my father had fitted a Belfast sink below a window with a storage press underneath. Our kitchen dresser had plates displayed on its open shelves and my father fitted in a marble slab for pastry making. The cutlery drawer along one side of the kitchen table was a great attraction for children.

It was the type of household where neighbours and friends dropped in for a chat and a cup of tea. The front door was locked only when everyone was out and even then, the key was inserted into a bracket in the guttering above the door, a place known to all.

Gert, Jim, Eddie and Monica Small with sister Gwen O'Byrne and her son, Joe.

Being seated at either the kitchen table, or around the circular pedestal table in the living room, brought forth lively conversation about current affairs and politics and many family games were played. Avid readers and radio-listeners, the family also enjoyed lively banter. The conversations spanned every topic from films, religion, wildlife, the environment, the weather, ghost stories, politics, literature, history or just local gossip or reminiscences of times past.

Words

Conversations around a table
Is it fact or is it fable?

Trying to communicate
Is it a healthy debate?

Chatter of the girls and boys
Making up the background noise

Teachers never at a loss
To get their message across

Will the young take the advice?
Or the old have to ask thrice

But where do all the words go?
For there is a constant flow

Do they go to the sky?
To build word towers very high

To entertain the folk up there
Interrupting them at prayer

Or was it downward they went?
Prompting those folk to repent

Did they linger in the trees?
With the rustle of the leaves

If they fell in stream or river
Their tones would be drowned forever

Talk of having the last word
But really that would be absurd

Gertrude Reynolds

Ladies who Lunch by Monica Sproul (nee Small)

11.
A CIRCULAR TOUR AROUND CLONDALKIN VILLAGE FROM THE ROUND TOWER TRAVELLING CLOCKWISE ALONG ORCHARD ROAD, MAIN ST AND BACK ALONG TOWER ROAD

Vintage aerial photograph of Clondalkin in 1959. Courtesy South Dublin County Council.

A pump and a horse trough stood in the middle of the road beside the Round Tower, at the junction of the Nangor Road, Orchard Road, Tower Road and Ninth Lock Road.

Next to St. John's Church was a large house called 'Towerville,' built in the 1850s by the Caldbeck family of Moyle Park, who donated this property to the parish for use as a vicarage, 'should the need arise.' However, it was never put to that use. Instead, it was let to various tenants, until it was finally assigned to the representative church body. Occupants over the years included Dr. Burnside, the Dispensary doctor, and later, his wife's people, Mrs. Du Moulin Dockeray and her daughter. Thom's Directory of 1882 records, 'G.S. Burnside, L.S.C.S.I. at Towerville,' and Porter's Guide and Directory for County Dublin 1912, records, 'Mrs. Burnside, Towerville.' After their deaths, Jimmy Bates and his wife Fanny (nee Sheppard) lived there followed by Mr. and Mrs. George Hopley, who had a pharmacy in Queen Street. The property was auctioned off in 1961 and bought by Mr. and Mrs. Eric Graham.

The old Royal Irish Constabulary (RIC) barracks was beside Towerville, across from the pump. Porter's Guide and Directory for County Dublin 1912

Above: (left) pump in the centre of Tower Road, old R.I.C. barracks on left (origin of photo unknown); (right) Towerville, Tower Road. Reynolds Collection.

Left: RIC Barracks, Clondalkin following fire.

records, 'Michael Casey, Sergeant, and four constables.' The barracks was burned down in 1922. Evy Archbold's father was a caretaker in the Time Office at Clondalkin Paper Mills when this happened.

In time, a house called 'Saint Laurence' was built on the site and the Hoffman family lived there before they moved to Orchard House. The Hoffman family had a field across the river from Sallypark and a shed that was home to a cow. The Swantons and then the O'Brien family later lived in Saint Laurence.

When I was growing up, the Hogan family lived in the next house going around the corner into Orchard Road. The Flanagans later moved into the house. I knew Patricia Flanagan. The new Guards barracks came after Hogans. The barracks was then extended and more latterly, the barracks has been further extended and modernised.

Some of the Guards used to drop in to visit Vera O'Neill across the road from the station when she was on a frame with T.B. The O'Neill family kept an 'open' house so that Vera always had plenty of visitors.

Healy's owned all the land stretching up Orchard Road from the Guards barracks to the Main Street, which was always known as 'Healy's Field.' For most of the year, the field was idle, apart from the times it accommodated the circus and the carnival and for two weeks each year, a marquee for dances. Those are times to be remembered with great joy where all the youth in the area gathered to have fun and dance to their hearts content. Eventually, Healy's field was sold and a row of houses was built here.

On the opposite side of Orchard Road, a bridge over the River Camac led to a cul-de-sac row of three cottages. The Murphy family, who have lived in

'Saint Laurence,' Tower Road, Clondalkin and former home of the Hogan family, Orchard Road (Garda Station now stands there). Kindly shared by Patrick Ging.

Clondalkin for six generations, were in the first cottage, which was thatched.

Later on, Con Murphy built a bungalow in the garden and his sister, Kathleen, replaced the thatched cottage with a modern bungalow. The next two cottages were rented by the Smith and Hassett families from John O'Neill who lived in a house behind the cottages, accessed via an entrance just beyond the rectory on the Ninth Lock Road. Eventually, John O'Neill converted these two cottages into one house and he went to live there with his family.

Beyond a field was Orchard House, hidden behind a cluster of trees. Built around 1845, the road derives its name from this property which had an orchard and a huge garden that stretched all the way up as far as Watery Lane. During the season they sold the fruit from the Orchard and I remember well the taste of their sugary pears. A record in Thom's Almanac of 1858 shows, 'Captain Poe,

Clockwise from top: new Garda Station under construction at Orchard Road (photo credit Patrick Ging); Murphy's cottage, 1952 (origin of photo unknown); thatching, Vera O'Neill, 1936; Orchard House, Orchard Road, now Áras Crónáin (origin of photo unknown); homes of Con Murphy and Kathleen Murphy, beyond bridge over the Camac, Reynolds Collection.

Orchard House,' while the 1882 edition records, 'Thomas Hamilton Esq., Orchard House.' Porter's Guide and Directory for County Dublin, 1912, records, 'The Misses Ponsonby, Orchard House.' In my time, the Hoffmans lived at Orchard House and later, the Cusack family, who had once lived beside us in Raheen House. Mr. Cusack was the General Manager of Clondalkin Paper Mills, where he was devoted to his job. In May 1989, Muintir Chrónáin purchased Orchard House and renamed it Áras Cronáin. It operates as a cultural and heritage centre.

Back around 1937, an old Clondalkin resident, Vincent Bracken, related a story for the Schools Folklore Collection, told to him by James P. O'Reilly, about a yew tree in the garden of Orchard House, said to date back to the Battle of Clontarf in 1014. The layout of Orchard Road is a remnant of the outline of the original monastic enclosure -the level of the gardens is above the level of the road reflecting the fosse or protective bank and ditch which originally surrounded the monastery site.

The Kearney family lived in a small lodge at Orchard House – the children were Frank, Jack, Nora and Therese. Therese later became a nun and taught art at St. Wolstan's Holy Faith Convent in Celbridge.

Beyond Orchard House was the entrance to Watery Lane, a narrow laneway with hedgerows both sides, which led down to the Grand Canal. While

Hunt on Orchard Road, 1947. Mr. N. O'Dwyer, Master, Ms. Jean Horsborough, whipper-in. Watchorn's bungalow and shed in background.

it still bears the same name, the road has been widened and it is much more populated. The Murphy family lived at Riverside Farm on the left side of Watery Lane, where they kept pigs and hens. Riverdale Estate stands there now. Further down the lane, the O'Hara and Nixon families lived along a stretch called 'Yellow Meadows.' When they were schoolgirls in the 1930s, Monica Murphy and Sheila Nixon submitted handwritten stories and related about cures for the benefit of the Schools Folklore Collection. Monica Murphy of Riverside Farm mentions the many herbs growing on their farmland which included deadly-nightshade, greasy-blade, marsh-mallows, nettles, docks, foxgloves, prashach, dandelion, chicken-weed, thistle, heart's ease. She then goes on to relate details of how some are noxious and some have curative powers.

The best remembered residents of Watery Lane were the inseparable bachelor brothers, Paul and Joe Shepherd, who lived in a caravan alongside the canal and worked for the County Council. While they were out at work, their caravan was guarded by two fierce mongrel dogs who scared all passersby. It was said that when one of the brothers was admitted to hospital, the other waited at his bedside until his brother was discharged home.

Back to Orchard Road. Bordering the other side of Watery Lane and towards Main Street, the Cowan family lived on a large piece of land. Mr. Cowan had at

(Top left) Cowan's Hardware with flat-roofed home to left, Orchard Rd; (top right) Hawthorn Cottage, Cowan's old family home which burned down in the 1930s while derelict, kindly shared by Sharon O'Sullivan; (left) Greta Freeman with Joe Rigney, leader of the Satellites at the Mayfair Ballroom, Clondalkin, 1957, kindly shared by Gerard Byrne, Old Clondalkin & Surrounding Districts.

one time been the sexton at the Protestant church. The Cowans kept hens and they had lovely flowers in their front garden. In 1947, one of the sons built a flat-roofed bungalow with a shop attached beside the family home, which sold drapery and hardware. Another son had a menswear shop. After my dancing days were over, the Cowans built a ballroom called 'The Mayfair,' which ran for about twenty years, from 1955 to 1975. The Cowan brothers used to be dickied up very smartly for the dances and they got in good bands. As well as weekly dances, St. John's Parish used it once a month for fundraisers.

Beyond Cowans, Healy's long grocery shop stretched around to the post office run by the Whitty's. A barber shop and a solicitor's office now stand on the site of Healy's shop. Jack's sweetshop was along there too.

Directly across the road from Healy's grocery shop was Caffreys' house, home to by the two elderly Caffrey sisters. It now houses Massey's Funeral Home. Next was the Black Lion House, also owned by the Healy's.

Tommy Healy and Mr. Whyte, M.D. of Clondalkin Paper Mills, launched a motor bus service under the name, 'The Clondalkin Omnibus Motor Company.'

Clockwise from top: Healy's 'Corner House' shop c. 1956; Caffreys, building-ing dating to c. 1860, later Masseys Funeral Home, photo courtesy niah. ie; Healy's, The Black Lion House, built c. 1838; Healy's squash (courtesy Patrick Ging, Clondalkin Historical Archive Society).

They used an open-topped bus, called a 'Charabang,' its name deriving from the French word char à bancs, meaning 'carriage with wooden benches.' The Misses Jacobs sold the bus tickets and Pat, the driver, used a little wooden box to help people on board. The Charabang took its passengers as far as Inchicore where they caught the tram into town. A few years later, the bus depot was built on a site beside The Laurels which was later converted into the Tower cinema.

On the other side of the pub was a yard and a handball alley, latter which bordered the short laneway that led on to Main Street. A handball alley was a regular feature adjacent to public houses, hence the name given to a pub in Lucan, the 'Ball Alley.'

Children in a pony trap in front of Healy's Public House (Black Lion) c. 1944. L-R:- Unknown, Nora Cleary, Nuala Brady, Tom Cleary, Unknown, Paul Betjeman. Photo courtesy of Ms Nora Hart, nee Cleary. The trap was owned and driven by Ms Penelope Betjeman who probably took the picture. The details are taken from a local newspaper article that is now held in the Clondalkin History Society archive.

New bus for Clondalkin Motor Omnibus Co. 1920s. Centre L - R, George Guilfoyle, T.F. Healy, P. McEvoy, B. Dowd, M. Hart and F. W. Dawney. Kindly shared by Andru O'Maonaigh.

For years, Jim Holmes had a cobbler's in the laneway. He used to cycle over from Blackditch Road in Ballyfermot, rain or shine. He also made bags and briefcases.

Much later on, Jack Tinkler, formerly of Moore's Lane, had a vegetable shop in the laneway, later run by Ben and Kathleen Tinkler. Carmel's wool shop was another establishment in the laneway. Some called the laneway between the Village Inn and Paddy Powers, 'Pope's Lane,' but it had no name in my day. I now note that Pope's Lane is indeed an historical name from way back in time. Hart's, the Central Bar, bordered the other side of the laneway. This pub is situated on an island premises in the middle of the road. The name changed later to Moran's and it is now called The Purty Central.

Having come up the laneway into Clondalkin's Main Street, the Shearer and Rumgay families lived on the right. Bobby Rumgay was our local postman. I recently bumped into his brother, Billy Rumgay, who told me that Bobby had died.

(Left) Jim Holmes, cobbler in Pope's Lane, Clondalkin

(Below left) Tower Market, kindly shared by Patrick Ging; (below right) Pope's Lane, courtesy Roy Byrne taken from Clondalkin Archive.

Other postmen were Mr. Darcy and Mr. Fox. Beside the Rumgays, Kearney's chemist shop was in part of a house, a window and door. Much later on, a famed boutique was set up next door by Breda Delaney, 'Breda's Fashions,' to which people travelled from far and wide. Ladbrokes betting shops stands there now. Across the road was Molly Reilly's vegetable shop.

Hart's Stores was next; we always called it, 'The Stores.' Essentially, it was an old style pub-cum-grocers. The building in which it stood has been re-developed and now houses a pub known as The Steering Wheel.

Beside the Stores was Leahy's butcher shop. Ciss Leahy was wonderful pianist and she played at all the concerts in the Library. There was a house between Leahy's and the next premises, Rice's grocery shop.

Some of the Rice family operated 'tent' cinemas in Clondalkin, Blanchardstown and Lucan and they started up the Grove cinema at Lucan Bridge. The grocery shop was re-named Fahy's grocery shop when Miss Rice married a Mr. Fahy, who had returned home from America. When you shopped there, Mr.

Clockwise from top: Hart's 'Central' bar, built c. 1850, later Moran's, now the 'Purty Central,' showing the alleyway to Main Street, photo courtesy niah.ie; the Stores pub, c. late 1950s, origin of photo unknown; Fahy's shop, Main Street, Clondalkin; pre 1920s photo taken in what is now the car park of The Steering Wheel pub, Round Tower in background, photo from the Millview Collection of Josephine Byrne nee Delaney.

Fahy would always say as you were finishing your order, "and something else?" My friend, Olive McCurtin, worked in Fahy's before she married Tom Feighery from the Old Nangor Road. Sherlock & Co. Solicitors now stands on the site of these few shops.

Ledwidge's corner shop was run by Mrs. Ledwidge, assisted by her son, Joe, and daughter, Margaret. The Ledwidges had farmed on the Boot Road until Mr. Ledwidge got a stroke. Mrs. Ledwidge opened the shop and continued to run the farm until about 1943, when the shop was well established. Years before the term 'late night opening' was coined, Ledwidge's shop used to open late. Initially, the shop was tiny and sold only bread and sweets as well as milk from the farm, but over the years they bought up adjacent premises and expanded the shop. By the time the Ledwidge family sold out, it was a large supermarket.

At one time, Mrs. Ledwidge had a complete dinner service on sale in the shop. To her annoyance, the delph started to disappear piece-by-piece, until finally, the only item left was a large meat dish, which she was watching like a hawk. One day, she had to take a trip into the back of the shop and found that the meat plate had disappeared too, by the time she got back.

I shall bring you back to the laneway and move to occupants on the left side of the Main Street. Murphy's butcher shop stood on Main Street and they lived in the adjoining house which stretched around the corner into the New Road. Paddy Delaney, brother of Breda Delaney, later set up a shoe shop in that premises, which now houses Coby Jewellers. Right beside Murphy's was Molly Reilly's vegetable shop. Molly was a Tinkler before she married.

Clondalkin village c. 1957 at Ledwidge's Corner. Photo is from the Clondalkin History Society collection shared by Patrick Ging.

Next door to the vegetable shop was Gogarty's, which had once been a shop too, with the name over it. They also had a shop premises on Main Street, Celbridge with a similar shop sign above. An old lady who wore a black shawl lived in Gogarty's in my time. The story goes that at the turn of the century when women wore long dresses, Terry Gogarty used to bring a chair to the side of the road on Sunday mornings and wave his walking stick at any passing lady who was heading to Mass wearing a skirt that showed any ankle. I can't say if he ever married. Porter's Guide and Directory for County Dublin 1912, records, 'Laurence Gogarty, Bootmaker.'

The Minihan brothers, who were related to the Gogartys, lived in the next two houses, a two storey house and then single storey house. In between their houses was a laneway entrance to a yard behind, where there was once a cemetery. Jack Minihan was a bachelor. One of the Minihan's drove a lorry which he parked in the yard. The Kelly family lived in the adjoining single storey house. One of the Kelly lads played the violin, earning him the nickname, 'Strauss' Kelly. William and Nora Gaffney once had a grocery shop called 'the Marian shop,' which they sold back in the late 1950s when the family left for Birmingham.

The O'Brien and McDonald families lived in the next houses. The Dramatic Society held their meetings in rooms over the McDonald's home. My sister, Gwen, met her husband, Brendan, there. This premises was later bought by the bank. The Tower Credit Union now stands there. The Welsh family had a lovely house on the corner of Convent Road with a nice big garden.

Above left: Premises that once housed Gogarty's on Main Street, built c. 1820, courtesy niah.ie. Above right: Main Street Clondalkin, the Dramatic Society met in the upstairs of the building back in the 1940s, photo credit Roy Byrne, accessed Clondalkin Historical Society Archive.

When I was growing up, the long stretch across the road from Ledwidges on Tower Road was a stone wall. The shops and houses that stand there now were all built in the 1950s. The Tuthill family set up their first shop in Clondalkin and lived above it, before expanding to open other Tuthill retail outlets.

Back to Ledwidge's and along Tower Road. Various residents lived in the house beside the shop, including the Sharkeys, Woods and Costellos and beside that house was the McCoy family. Fran McCoy drove Canon Ryan around. An old lady – her name escapes me – lived alongside the McCoys, where she reared hens. I remember her coming up to the Convent to pick up leftover bread in

Top: Tower Road, St. John's schoolhouse on the left and row of shops alongside Tuthills on the right. Kindly shared by Patrick Ging. Bottom: Procession passing Ledwidge's c. 1960s. Kindly shared by Gerard Byrne, Old Clondalkin & Surrounding Districts.

the yard after lunch as feed for the hens. Cruise's butcher shop eventually set
up in that property. The Ledwidge family bought up those three houses as they
became vacant, to facilitate extensions to their shop premises.

The Miss Galvins lived in the last house in that block. Eileen and Kathleen
Galvin were both teachers. Evy Archbold, whom I knew well from working in
Clondalkin Paper Mill, was a niece of the Galvins and lived with her two aunts,
who ran a private school. Evy Archbold's mother, who was a Galvin before
marriage, taught at Palmerstown National School and later, at Newcastle. Kathleen Galvin also taught children privately in their homes. Eileen Galvin ran a
small private children's school in a schoolroom at the back of the house and
she also taught shorthand and typing there. Please don't blame her if you think
my typing skills are not good because she was my teacher. Evy had a wealth of
knowledge about Clondalkin and it is to my regret that I did not record her
great stories before her death.

Next to the Miss Galvins was the dispensary where Nurse Cunnity lived – she
was both a general nurse and a maternity nurse. The Dispensary building still
stands there. A record in Thom's Almanac of 1858 shows, 'McCrea, M.R.C.S.I.,
Medical Officer,' while the 1882 edition shows, 'George. S. Burnside, L.R.C.S.I.
L.A, Medical Officer.' Porter's Guide and Directory for County Dublin 1912,
records for Clondalkin Dispensary, 'Dr. J. McMahon, Medical Officer.'

*Tower Road, 1940. Army light motorised unit in practice. Dispensary in the
background. Photo credit: Terry Crosbie of 'Dublin of Ould' group.*

Beside the dispensary was Lar Connor's yard. Lar had a few cows and sold milk from his small yard. Christy Mulryan lived with Lar Connor and later married, Nancy, a Clare woman. An old man, Johnny Killeen, also lived there. He kept goats and always seemed to be wheeling a wheelbarrow. Tower Shopping Centre now stands on this site.

After Lar Connors, Miss Wall lived in the cottage right beside the Church of Ireland school where she taught.

In 1879, the Church almshouses were built beside the schoolhouse on Tower Road. They comprise four houses, with eleven rooms in all, and a large room to serve as a classroom. By 1955, pupil numbers had risen to 42 and a new teacher, Miss Jones, was engaged to assist the principal, Miss Sheppard. They both taught in the one classroom. As renting only a room rather than a complete house went out of vogue, occupants began leaving the almshouses. In my time, four families lived in Church Terrace - the Kealey, Mulvagh, Pryce and Bailey families.

CHURCH TERRACE

1. Addle, F.
2. Hemmingway, D.
3. Pryce, G.
4. Bailey, H.
Dispensary

Extract Directory of Ireland, 1958.

From top: Rose Cottage, Tower Road. Lar Connors house. Chris Mulryan lived here and held the key to the Round Tower; Schoolteacher's house, Tower Road. Ms. Wall lived there in my day; Schoolhouse, Tower Road, built c. 1870, courtesy niah.ie.

Next was St. John's Church, Church of Ireland. This dates back to about 1787 and was built on the site of a previous church. One day in the early 1950s, Freda Ryan, Anne Bradley and myself found the church door open and in we went. Freda played 'The Bells of the Angelus' on the church organ and then we scarpered.

For some generations, the Galvin family lived in a small house at the base of the Round Tower. In my time, an old lady lived in that cottage and held the key to the tower. Robert (Bob) Galvin, who had been an RIC man, lived in the 1940s/1950s and after he died, his widow moved with the family to the gate house at Moyle Park College. Many of the Galvin grandchildren later lived along Tower Road including Maura, Noreen, Margaret and Paddy.

Now we have come full circle.

St. John's Church. Late 19th century photo kindly shared by Gerard Byrne.

Cast iron water pump Tower Road, courtesy niah.ie.

Coal Tits by Monica Sproul (nee Small)

12.
CLONDALKIN NATIONAL SCHOOL

In the 1930s, playschool, pre-school, Montessori and crèches did not exist. Children started national school at the age of four and finished at the age of fourteen or fifteen. The first written examination was the Primary Certificate, taken in sixth class. The pupils were Catholic children from all walks of life, from the better off to children of farm labourers. There was no class distinction among children at that time.

As if it was yesterday, I remember setting off for school that first day in 1938, walking down the Nangor Road with my older sisters past Ging's shop. It was more than a half- mile walk each way. Many pupils were children of farmers and farm labourers, obliged to walk considerable distances to school.

Presentation Convent. Origin of photo unknown.

There was no school uniform but boys wore short trousers while they were at the convent. I never saw children coming to school barefoot. We sat in pairs on wooden benches with integrated inkwells that were part of one unit with a seat that flipped up.

Boys and girls were educated together at the Presentation Convent until the boys were aged seven and then the sexes were segregated with the boys' education continued at the Monastery school on the Monastery Road. The convent was run on hierarchal terms, staffed entirely by nuns, except for Miss Hanley who taught piano and Miss Galvin, who taught shorthand, typing and book-keeping. Mother Bridget used to remind us that her family were 'The Hanlon's of Monastery Hill.' The nuns had knowledge of the pupils' family backgrounds and often treated them according to their status in the community.

At national school, the aim was to teach the children the three R's, reading, writing and arithmetic; there was no comparison to today's school curriculum. School subjects included arithmetic, Irish, English, geography, history and catechism. Learning Irish was compulsory and it was taught every day. In fact, most subjects except English were taught through Irish and pupils were taught enough Latin to understand the Mass. It was usual to learn by heart and we became proficient at chanting maths tables in a sing-song voice, adding, subtraction, multiplication and long division.

The nuns obviously had vocations but they were not necessarily dedicated to teaching.

The teaching nuns I remember are:– Mother Lawrence, who was in her nineties when she died, Sister Oliver, who also lived to a good age, Sister Kevin, Sister Bernadette, Sister Ita, Mother Teresa and Sister Bernard. The Reverend Mother did not teach but she was in charge of the Convent. Sister Bernadette used to stand staring

Sister Imelda, Presentation Convent, Clondalkin. Photo credit Paul Nixon.

out the window while we repeated tables over and over again and each time we ended our chanted piece, she used to say 'arís' (Irish for 'again'). Using a map of Ireland, the teacher used to point to an area and pick on somebody, asking about typical crops or places where well-known people were born. Others would hiss the answer to help you out. To this day, I can remember the principal exports (c. 1948) being cattle, sheep, horses, pigs, butter, eggs and poultry. Anybody who didn't know their lessons got a slap on the hand. While the nuns had language and painting skills that would have enhanced our education, none of this knowledge was imparted, although they did teach us handcrafts, which we used throughout our lives.

In some parishes, Catholic children attended Protestant schools and vice versa, but this was not the case in Clondalkin. The Presentation Convent was the primary school for Catholic children and St. John's was a separate school for Protestant children, so that children were educated in accordance with the religious divide. Although the schools were relatively close to each other, there was no contact at all between them, a set-up which prevailed throughout Ireland. With no opportunity to get to know one another, the culture of not mixing religions created an 'us and them' divide from a young age which engendered a level of mistrust. However, in my mother's primary school in Tipperary, Catholic and Protestant children were educated together. The Catholic children came to school at nine o'clock in the morning for half an hour of religion before the arrival of non-Catholic children. In line with the custom in schools back then, a lot of religion was taught, however, it is my own belief that those who attended Sunday school ended up with a better concept of the message of faith, as they grew up knowing the Bible.

The Convent's seven classrooms each accommodated about forty pupils. Like most schools at the time, utilities were virtually non-existent. Unusually, the Convent had electricity but there was no central heating, so the place was heated by means of oil heaters and open fires which burned mainly turf, surrounded by huge fireguards. Before school started in the morning, women came and lit the fires and put a big fireguard around them. However, on cold mornings, most left their coats and gloves on until the place warmed up. The teacher rotated rows of students so everybody got a chance to heat themselves around the open fire at the top of the class. On wet mornings, we hung dripping coats on coat hooks that lined the wall.

The school day started with a roll-call where the pupils had to answer in Irish 'anseo,' meaning 'here' or as my son answered phonetically when he started school, 'I'm shook.' Pupils quickly understood commands in the Irish language, 'suigh síos' to sit down, or 'líne díreach' which meant forming a straight line, usually with two pupils side-by-side, holding hands. The teachers were strict on time-keeping and having homework done.

Lunchtime was always spent out of doors; the churchyard doubled up as the school playground and if it rained, children made for a big shed. In winter, children brought flasks of cocoa or hot milk to warm them up, or otherwise drank cold milk with a sandwich. Many children came from poor families. Those who came to school without a lunch went to the dairy window for slices of bread and margarine. In summer, a big trough was filled with cold water and an enamel mug was attached to the handle by a piece of string so the children could scoop out water for a drink.

Typical school desk with slate and chalk.

A shed against a garden wall housed a row of about six toilet cubicles, with no cisterns, that had an unusual feature of intermittent flushing every half hour or so, rather than on demand. Of course, there was nowhere for hand-washing.

Pupils had to come to terms with answering questions and reading aloud, notwithstanding shyness or a stutter. Any engagement or even non-engagement could potentially result in chastisement. A quick lash got a pupil to speed up or to think properly. Fear predominated in the classroom so it was not surprising that school was daunting for kids who had to absorb the strict rules to avoid being slapped on the hands, usually with a stick.

When we started back at school each year, the teacher used to give us a list of the course books we needed. Pupils learned to write first with chalk and slate before progressing to a pen with a nib and ink. The ink was stored in the white china inkwell sunken into a brass receptacle on the top right corner of the wooden school bench. We wrote into blue-lined school copybooks and did our best to avoid blots, but always had blotting paper to hand, just in case. Each pupil was expected to write with their right hand even if writing with their left hand came naturally to them. Left-handedness was considered abhorrent, a weakness to be corrected. A term in the Irish language, 'cíteog,' denotes a left-handed person.

We said prayers in the morning, the Angelus when the bell rang at midday and there were more prayers before school ended. A symbiotic relationship existed between the Catholic Church and the national schools. We were often marched into the church for functions. We had to learn the parables. The priest paid unscheduled visits and interrupted the class to quiz any pupil he chose while the teacher nervously looked on. Mother Lawrence used to ask, 'Hands up who was at Devotions?' and if you had not gone, you had to provide an explanation for your absence. I remember one girl saying, 'I had to mind the house.' Mother Lawrence said: 'Why? Would the house run away or what?'

Sometimes when Father Murphy dropped into the classroom, he made faces behind the nun's back, much to her embarrassment. In addition to visits from local priests, a strange priest came on a pre-arranged annual visit to examine the pupils on catechism, to ensure that standards were being upheld. The school was always extra clean in preparation for these visits, bowls of fresh-cut flowers adorning the window sills. The idea was to keep the pressure on teachers and it worked, because some teachers became stressed leading up to this event and they'd warn certain pupils, who had the propensity to let them down, to stay away from school on the day of the annual visit. Coming up to my confirmation, I remember getting quizzed at school and the dread of not knowing the answer if the Bishop asked you a question on the big day. I also remember the Bishop asking what we wanted to be when we grew up. Some said nuns or teachers or nurses but when it came to my sister, Mono, she said a film star, for shock value.

I sat for years beside a girl called Mairead, who became a chemist in Clondalkin Paper Mill. She later became involved in the preservation of books in Venice. Mostly, class time was deadly serious but I remember some messing.

Although we had singing classes, I think it most strange that we were never taught the national anthem at school. We also had exercise classes, as well as knitting and sewing classes and drawing classes. My sister Mono learned to knit socks on four needles but when she had one sock completed in grey and three quarters of another sock done in grey, Mammy ran out of grey wool and Mono had to finish the sock in red wool, which caused consternation. We had no school tours and no art lessons, apart from the drawing classes. The sports available included, camogie, hurling, football, tennis and badminton were played outside school time and there was nothing arranged like matches or an annual sports day. Several times a month, a library van called to the school and a few of the older pupils got to select books which were kept on shelves to be signed out to pupils. No dentist came to the school but once a year, a medical person came and examined all the children and often made a recommendation that tonsils or teeth required removal. Another memory is the application of bread poultices for all sorts of cuts and gashes that had not healed.

School ended for most children at the age of fourteen when they were expected to get a job or sometimes their family sent the girls to shorthand and typewriting classes. A chosen few who could afford it went to the secondary school, often into town to Eccles Street, until the Presentation Convent built a secondary school in Clondalkin. However, I remember a few won scholarships and went off to boarding school at Mountmellick in Co. Laois. From about the age of twelve, pupils earmarked for secondary school were singled out for extra tuition for the last year or two of their schooling. It seemed more logical that those who could not afford secondary schooling could have done with the extra tuition.

Noreen Galvin, who lived in a cottage near Clondalkin's Round Tower, was my sister Peg's best friend. Noreen's two aunts were teachers. One taught shorthand and typing while the other taught children of national school age privately. Noreen was a cousin of Evy and Mary Archbold who originally came from Milltown in Newcastle, where their mother was also a teacher.

My family paid for shorthand and typewriting classes with Miss Galvin for one hour in the evening. I finished at national school in 1949. After school ended, I went to Yorkshire to help my sister, Gwen, who was expecting her second child.

In 1937, the Government set up a scheme for Officers to attend at national schools around the country to compile a folklore record - The Schools Collection - which is held today at the Folklore Department at UCD. Many pupils from the school were interviewed for this record. The records are available on the internet- www.duchas.ie

The expansion of Clondalkin since my schooldays brought with it a number of primary and secondary schools from many different denominations. Among its present-day primary schools are Sacred Heart of Shruleen, St. Ronan's in Clonburris, St. Joseph's Boys National School, Scoil Íde, Scoil Aíne, St. John's National School (Church of Ireland), Scoil Mhuíre, Talbot Senior N.S. and Scoil Nano Nagle. Secondary schools include: Moyle Park College (boys only), Deansrath Community College, Coláiste Bríde (girls only), Collinstown Park Community College and St. Kevins's Community College. Clondalkin has three Irish language schools (Gaelscoileanna) – Coláiste Chillain, Gaelscoil Chluain Dolcáin, and Gaelscoil na Camóige.

Snowdrops by Mary Reynolds

13.
UP THE NEW ROAD

Back to the turn at the Laurels Pub onto New Road. On the left, where Laurel Park housing estate now stands, was once farmland stretching all the way up to the church. Straddling the corner on the right, was Murphy's butcher shop.

Nurse Brophy lived beside Murphy's shop in a small wooden detached house with a tin roof which stood in its own ground. Her brother lived with her. As the local jubilee nurse, she worked with the doctors in the community and travelled to her patients on foot wearing her uniform and carrying her medical bag. She was always very cross. A solicitor's office stands on this site now.

A pair of semi-detached houses further on were occupied by Mr. Kenny, an army officer, and Mr. Staunton, a member of An Garda Síochana.

Castle View, New Road, built c. 1830. Courtesy niah.ie

Next was the Behan family, who lived in Castle View. Dolores Behan, who worked in the Mill office with me, built a house in the garden, called 'Teach Mhuíre.' Another detached house called 'Moyanna' stands beside it.

A detached house, 'San Guida,' surrounded by a large garden was home to the Church family, then the Dodrill family, until the Cusack family moved there from Orchard House. The chemist, Mr. Kearney, built a house next to San Guida. The jockey, Herbie Holmes, lived in a large detached house, St. Columba's, located beside the church gate.

With a legacy left to him by the Caldbeck family, the local priest, Fr. John Moore, built a convent in the Gothic style. On 8th September 1857, Presentation Nuns arrived in Clondalkin and opened a school for girls. The record in Thom's Almanac 1882 shows, 'Convent, Presentation, Superioress.'

The Convent once had a small orchard, garden and farm and the nuns had their own cemetery in the grounds. Some of the classrooms had names such as the Benefit School, Back Tower, Front Tower and Bake House. As well as the teaching nuns I mentioned previously, the Convent also housed Sister Imelda, Sister Terezina and Sister Columba.

In the church yard, heavy iron rings cemented into the walls were used for tethering the horses of Mass-goers.

One Sunday in 1857, the Parish Priest Fr. Moore held a parochial meeting

Church of the Immaculate Conception

in the Chapel House. He proposed the erection of a new church beside the Presentation Convent.

It is recorded that his suggestion was responded to "in a manner unprecedented in the Annals of Chapel building in Ireland." Certainly a large sum of money was pledged with many parishioners subscribing £50 to £100 each. The church was designed by F. W. Caldbeck in the Gothic style and the foundation stone was laid in July 1857 by His Grace the Most Rev. Paul Cullen, Archbishop of Dublin. In a container placed under the stone were coins of Pope Pius IX and of Queen Victoria, along with an inscribed parchment. In 1863, the Church of the Immaculate Conception was opened.

An unusual feature of this church is the beautiful stained glass window over the High Altar. This window was designed by Thomas Early and installed in 1857. Rather than depict a biblical scene, Thomas Early decided to honour the Patron Saints of the Parish and of the Catholic Church. Starting from the left we see St. Laurence O' Toole, Patron of the Dublin Diocese; the Immaculate Conception, patron of the parish; St. Joseph, patron of the universal church and St. Patrick, patron of Ireland.

The record in Thom's Almanac 1858 shows, 'Clondalkin Roman Catholic Chapel, Rev. John Moore, P.P.,' while the 1882 edition records, 'Clondalkin Roman Catholic Chapel, Rev. John Moore, P.P., Rev. John Healy, c.c.' Porter's Guide and Directory for County Dublin 1912, records for Clondalkin Catholic Church, ' Rev. James Baxter, P.P.; Rev. Michael Traynor, C.C.'

In 1891, an ornamental archway was erected at the New Road entrance to commemorate the Golden Jubilee of Fr. John Moore, the Parish Priest responsible for the building of the church.

Left: Church of the Immaculate Conception - Archway into Avenue. Right: Catholic Boy Scouts 78th troop. Blessing and presentation of the troop's first flag in Sept 1941 outside the main door of the parish church. Photo from the collection of Tom Ging.

The Church of the Immaculate Conception and the Presentation Convent Schools are beautiful granite buildings, but huge and intimidating to a child. There is a majestic copper beech tree in the grounds.

Directly across the road from the church gate, an elderly lady, Mrs. (Mary) O'Toole, lived at Oak Lodge. She used to catch the bus and go to Mass in town. Formerly a Dowling before her marriage, Mrs. O'Toole owned a lot of land from the site on which the bus depot once stood, (later Tower cinema), stretching from there up towards Newlands.

A detached house, 'St. Mary's,' is now situated between Oak Lodge and the Curate's house, 'St. Cecilia's.' Apparently, the Convent's Superior, Mother Cecilia, built this fine redbrick house to accommodate the new curate, hence the name.

Next to the curate's house was once the entrance to Round Tower Football Club. The club now plays on grounds near the Camac on Old Nangor Road.

(Left) Oak Lodge, New Road, built c. 1825. Courtesy niah.ie. (Right) St. Cecilia's, the Presbytery on New Road. Reynolds Collection.

McNulty's former home and shop on New Road. Reynolds Collection.

A secondary school, Coláiste Bríde, is now located on the site. Further on, I recall several of the families living in a row of houses, including the Maguire family (Johnny Maguire was a great football player) and the O'Keeffe, Hughes, Melia, Gilsenan, Kennedy, McGrath and Kelly families, Miss Fox, a librarian, also, a girl in my school, Annie Dowling. The McNulty family had a shop on the corner of New Road and Knockmeenagh Lane. Their daughter, Colette McNulty, an only child, was a little younger than me; she was a cousin of the Coates family. Newlands housing estate was not there in my time, but there was a pocket of local authority cottages along Knockmeenagh Lane which housed several families including the Foran family (Paddy Foran was in the Angling Club) and two cousins who lived with their aunt, Carrie Davis and Annie Hartnett.

Knockmeenagh Lane narrows as it nears the cottages at The Ranch beside the Naas Road. The laneway is bordered by thick hedgerows and now appears little used.

Back down to the New Road. Across from the row of houses I mentioned, the Miss Shepherds lived in a lovely house and kept a greenhouse and a well-tilled garden. They let out an apartment in their house to a Polish couple called Frumpkin, who had no children. Mr. Frumpkin worked in Clondalkin Paper Mill. The couple were sedate and gentle and used to walk a lot with their dachshund. When the Shepherds sold up, the Frumpkins went to live in town, near Smithfield. I heard they had a pact that if one died, the other would commit suicide. They died within days of each other.

(Left) Vintage car rally, Kilkenny Beer Festival c. 1970. Mr & Mrs Jim Boland, Ellis Kelly and Joseph Brown with a 1911 Clement-Talbot. Shared by Patrick Ging, Clondalkin History Society Archive; (right) Harry Reynolds in his shop on St. Brigids Road, Clondalkin, before he retired.

The Miss Shepherds sold on to Jim Boland who lived there before moving to Naas. In 1955, he established a garage there, Boland's of Clondalkin, Car Sales. He had a particular interest in vintage cars and built up a huge collection over the years, including a Crossley Tender, a car once used by the Black and Tans. He often participated in Vintage Car Rallies including the London-to-Brighton run.

St. Brigid's Park, between New Road and Convent Road, was not there during my childhood, nor was the row of shops housing Autosports, a firm of solicitors, Pat Collins Butchers and Reynolds newsagents.

Harry Reynolds ran a shop here for over 55 years. (Obviously showing my age here). People say that the shop never changed a day since it opened and took you back to the traditional local shop experience you won't find anywhere in the Dublin of today. Famous for his jam doughnuts and homemade ham rolls, Harry refused to use his cash register, opting instead for a pen and the back of a Cornflakes box for totting up.

Further along New Road, Bernard Dowd's farm once stood near to the Misses Shepherd. The records in Porter's Guide and Directory for County Dublin 1912, shows, 'Bernard Dowd, Newlands.' A big tree on the corner of *Newlands Villa, being sold by Mrs. Tallon, 1922.*

Newlands Cross, 1930. Tom Dowd's farm on the left. Merrigan's cottage on the right-hand corner.

a newly constructed road, 'Caldbeck Way,' marks the spot where the farm once stood. Next is a house called, 'St. Jude's,' and then a house called 'Rosapenna,' where, to my recollection, the Flynn family lived. Mr. Flynn worked in Urney's Chocolate Factory and had two children, a boy and a girl called Alacoque. The following pair of semi-detached bay-window houses were home to Mr. O'Mahony, Company Secretary of the Mill, and Dr. Keane, who later moved to a nearby house with land, later boought by a Mr. Davitt, on which Newlands Garden Centre now stands.

Beyond those houses, a detached bungalow stands in its own grounds and beside it is another detached house, 'Hillcrest.' The Merrigan family had a small cottage on one corner bordering the Naas Road.

On the opposite corner of the New Road was Tom Dowd's farm. Tom and Bernard Dowd were brothers. A Miss Tallon also lived at Dowds as well as a Mr. Sheils, who had two sons. Porter's Guide and Directory for County Dublin, 1912, records, 'Patrick Tallon, Newlands Villa.'

The Dowds also farmed land elsewhere. They farmed fields behind Raheen House and Raheen Cottage, on the other side of the Camac that are now used as playing fields. They also grazed sheep and cows on land directly across the road from our entrance gate, where Coláiste Chilliain now stands. Their yard was a little way up Moore's Lane. They eventually built a sturdy shed in the yard to house their bull.

Since around 1600, a house had always stood in the vicinity of Newlands

Aerial view Newlands House, 1923. Demolished 1982

House. Regrettably, Newlands House was demolished in 1981, ballroom and all. At least its Bossi fireplace was saved and re-located to the clubhouse at Newlands Golf Club. One of its famous occupants was Arthur Wolfe, Lord Kilwarden, Lord Chief Justice of Ireland, from whom Theobald Wolfe Tone got his middle name. During the 1803 rebellion, Lord Kilwarden was pulled from his carriage in Thomas Street and killed. It was later rumoured that the 'Hanging Judge' had been the real target, not Lord Kilwarden. Some of the White Quaker community lived at Newlands House under the direction of their leader, Joshua Jacob, while he was in the Marshalsea prison. The Crotty family and Mullins family also lived there. John Hawkesby Mullins sold the property on to Newlands Golf Club.

Thrushes by Monica Sproul (nee Small)

14.
EXTRA-CURRICULAR ACTIVITIES

The view from our back window at Raheen was one to be treasured. The Camac river ran through about ninety acres of pastureland which stretched as far as the Oil Mills and provided drinking water for a herd of about 90 milch cows. The river's lovely waterfalls added further interest. Over the fields, there was a heavily wooded area including a stand of chestnut trees. All in all, a great area to roam and be free.

Growing up in the heart of a rural community within striking distance of the city had its advantages - children developed a familiarity with all aspects of farming as well as having access to urban activities. The area afforded a measure of freedom as well as a vast range of indoor, outdoor, formal and informal

Clondalkin farmer 1940. Probably Jim Stynes. Kindly shared by Gerard Byrne, Old Clondalkin & Surrounding Districts.

pursuits, although we spent as much time as possible out of doors. We lived within the cycles of farm life, surrounded by cultivated fields, planted with all types of crops including wheat, barley, corn and other cereal crops. Accustomed to watching farmers furrow, sow and reap, we were often called on to assist at harvest time.

Weather and its effects were a constant topic of discussion and children were attuned to climate. As winter gave way to early spring, primroses appeared on the banks of the river and the odd cuckoo pint, or 'Lords and Ladies,' as some call them. It was commonplace, especially for lads, to wander freely through the fields unrestrained by parents who were probably glad to have them out from under their feet. We plodded about alone or with pals, following in the tracks of birds and rabbits, dogs and foxes or trudged through wooded areas richly endowed with carpets of bluebells where young buds sprouted on the tips of shrubs. We climbed trees and dawdled or waded or fished in the Camac river and the Grand Canal, only arriving home in time for meals. We acquired a knowledge of where best to shelter from rain, the best fields for mushroom-picking, the blackberry bushes that yielded the most fruit and the best fishing spots. We gathered conkers and looked out for wildlife, foxes' dens and birds' nests; we could readily identify a species of bird from the eggs. From toddlerhood, we developed an innate sense towards animals. We knew that cows plodded in single file along their well-worn cow paths, never in pairs. Gates were never locked back then, only bolted or tied with rope but we were always conscious to ensure gates were closed firmly shut behind us in order to secure the animals.

Many relatives visited us in Raheen over the years, as well as friends. School friends, friends from the scouts, football clubs, fishing clubs, dramatic class and later on, boyfriends and girlfriends. As 'Small's Yard' was a favourite destination for playing, the school holidays provided us with lots of friends. Although it was known as 'Smalls Yard,' we didn't own it.

Growing up, the girls played skipping, hoop-la, rounders, badminton and games with sticks and balls and rackets. We tried out musical performances, especially after watching a musical at the cinema. An inordinate amount of time was spent playing shop when we used dock leaves for rashers and broken crockery for money. Ging's shop window was dressed at one time with empty packages of Gold Flake cigarettes and when they changed the window, Bumpy

Ging got us all the Gold Flake packages for our shop, which was a great boon. Another favourite game was dressing up. My mother always helped with costumes. We used to dress the cats up in dolls' clothes and pushed them about in prams. They never minded and in fact, they seemed to enjoy it. Sometimes we photographed the cats all dressed up in a miniature chair my father made for Mono.

The boys played hide and seek, marbles, darts, pitch and toss as well as team sports such as football, table tennis, rounders and another game we called 'relievo.' We also played badminton and tennis on a makeshift court with a net strung across the width of our yard. Their favourite game was probably cowboys and Indians, which they played in the fields, especially after seeing a cowboy film. Naturally, everybody wanted to be a cowboy as they were always perceived the winners; we had been conditioned by *Hopalong Cassidy* and other screen characters. Both girls and boys were across the fields collecting feathers for these headdresses. My mother stitched the material for the Indian headdresses in such a way that the feathers were held in place. The yard was a great venue for games of hide and seek, the downside being the loud screams when somebody was 'found.' Another favourite place to play was the nearby haggard, adjacent to Raheen House.

Gertrude and Monica dressing up.

We also had visits from the neighbouring Cusack children who were younger than us. Once David Cusack (he was a lovely child) came into the yard. He told my father his tricycle was broken. My father told him to bring it around to the workshop where he fixed the broken chain. David was delighted, showed his mother the mended bike and she sent my father 60 Players as a thank you.

Some children worked for local farmers when they were older, hoeing mangolds or picking turnips, strawberries or dropped potatoes. My brothers, Jim and Son, used to help Johnno at haymaking.

As soon as we heard the noise of the threshing machines, we'd head to the haggard to investigate. The reeks were thrown to the top of the threshing machine where their binding was cut and they were dropped into the drum. The grain came out at one end of the thresher and into sacks, the straw came out the other end and the chaff was left in the middle. One person was busy removing sacks, replacing them with empty sacks while another person removed the straw and formed it into reeks. Despite dire warnings, we could not resist jumping into the "chaff" coming out of the chute. The loft in our yard was used to store oats which were turned every day to keep them cool.

Children had great freedom back then and during the summer, they travelled in droves to the Sandy Hole, a shallow pool in a shady part of the Camac River, where the water ran clear over the stones. The older kids were charged with minding the toddlers and teaching younger kids to swim. How it coped with the hordes of children I do not know, as it was only a slight widening of the river. We all aspired to reach a stone ledge in the middle and scrambled to get onto the ledge and then we'd repel all boarders. A block of wood was left permanently at the Sandy Hole for teaching purposes. Once kids gained confidence using the block of wood, they were encouraged to progress to the dog paddle and then on to the over-arm stroke.

There were the boys' changing rooms behind some bushes and the girls' changing rooms behind a stone pillar. There was a lot of giggling and peeking, probably because of the swimsuits, a mix of knitted and cotton. Nobody owned a proper swimsuit. The knitted ones had an especially short life because of the hawthorns around the changing rooms.

Ploughing. Kindly shared by Gerard Byrne, Old Clondalkin & Surrounding Districts.

National Ploughing Championship, Newlands, Clondalkin judged by J. Dowling, examining a fresh furrow.

Sometimes the lads went to the Canal to swim where the older boys dived off the Ninth Lock and the less adventurous stayed in what they called 'the back drain,' which was warmer. The older boys didn't really welcome the girls unless they needed 'fielders' when playing games.

The older girls and their friends used to go on picnics to the Oil Mills. Drinks were put into glass bottles and dangled in the river, which made them deliciously cool.

Other favourite visits were to Corkagh, or off on mushroom or blackberry-picking expeditions. The back field was full of cowslips, buttercups, poppies,

Clockwise: Sandyhole, millrace, built c. 1850, courtesy niah.ie; membership cards for Clondalkin Pike Anglers and rules for Clondalkin Anglers; credit: John Kelly.

sloes and nuts to be gathered, as well as daisies to make daisy chains. Sometimes children went scrumping for apples or the more second-rate crab-apples. The smell of apples in the orchard is a smell that always stays with me.

Cuckoos came in April and we loved to listen out for the first call of the cuckoo, or better still, to spot them. At night it was bats and the sound of owls. Common birds we encountered were thrushes, yellow hammers, robins, blue tits, finches, sparrows, crows, grey crows, jackdaws, magpies, snipe, curlews, wagtails. Swans were regular residents on the Camac river and the Mill Pond and sometimes, you might see wild duck or geese landing there. It was a real treat to see the Kingfisher flying above the river.

The strangest sight I ever saw, and I witnessed it on a few occasions, was the herd of cows running as fast as they could towards the river, with their tails straight in the air. Once they reached the river, they relaxed as soon as their legs were covered by water. The reason for their alarm was the presence of the Warble Fly which deposits larvae on the animals' legs. The larvae travel to the back of the animal to feed and eventually, make a hole in the animal hide to emerge, which distresses the animal and reduces the value of the cowhide.

Fishing was another pastime. Across the back field to where the bank drops sharply to the Camac at the bottom or to the pond to net pinkeens and tadpoles. Childhood fishing expeditions progressed to rod fishing for perch, pike and eels in the Royal Canal, although we never ate them as the canal was a bit murky. Sometimes the lads tried their luck catching salmon, trout or pike. We were well accustomed to coming across salmon caught in a pool and ones that were lice-infested, 'spent' salmon, returning downstream having spawned.

John Walsh (teacher) Moyle Park College, Jim Small, Secretary of Clondalkin Angler's Association and Kevin Harrington, Moyle Park student.

Apart from informal games for fun, we engaged in mushroom picking in the season, usually around the end of August. The best mushroom fields in the area were at Priesttown. Early morning forays were the norm, the earlier the better as you'd find neighbours out there too. My mother used to cook the mushrooms in milk or sometimes she fried them on a pan of butter. We also picked blackberries in Autumn which my mother used for jam-making. Blackberries were plentiful on the hedgerows in surrounding fields – you could fill a basin in no time. Your hands might be stained and scratched from the brambles but it was worth it when you smelled the jam bubbling on the stove and tasted your mother's blackberry and apple tart.

In Autumn, we collected chestnuts, hardened them by the fire, skewered a hole and threaded a string through it to make a 'conker.' Opponents went head-to-head and bashed their conkers against one another until one smashed. The owner of the surviving conker won.

Reading was another pastime – our bookshelves held children's classics such as *Robinson Crusoe, Aesop's Fables, Huckleberry Finn* as well as a large collection of adult fact and fiction. Comics we read included the *Bunty* and *Judy* or boys comics such as the *Beano, Dandy, Topper, Beezer, Rover, Knockout, Wizard* and *Hotspur.* There were boy's books too, such as the *Champion, Magnet, Gem, Film*

Pipe Band. Eamonn McDonnell, Pipe Major with James OBrien and (I think) Gerry Mahady. Credit James OBrien.

Fun, *Adventure*, also, *Billy Bunter* stories. As well as books and newspapers, adults enjoyed the *Ireland's Own*, *Reader's Digest* and the *Freeman's Journal*. Our reading was supplemented by books from the well-stocked local library.

Music was a pursuit for those who could afford lessons. The music teacher in Clondalkin was Ciss Leahy but a Miss Hanley also came into the school once or twice a week to teach music. I do not recall a choir in Clondalkin although we did sing hymns during Mass, which was always in Latin.

The village is home to St Joseph' Pipe band, established in 1937, Paddy Cook was the bandleader – he used to march in front of the band holding a baton. They met for band practice in a hut located between McCurtins and Sherrys on the Old Nangor Road. The band has now become more renowned, having won several All-Ireland Championship titles and then a World Championship in 1990.

My brother, Jim, was in the scouts. These days, Scouting Ireland meet in the Scout Hall on Watery Lane most evenings. Boys' & Girls' Brigades, Guides & Brownies meet at St. John's Parish Hall on Tower Road.

Jim Small in scout's uniform, 1949, alongside father George Small.

Handball was more of a lads' pastime that was played down at the handball alley at Healy's Black Lion Pub, or against any wall.

Both of my brothers played football with the town's oldest sports club, the Round Towers GAA Club, located on Convent Road. Following a meeting set up by Michael Cusack at the pump in the middle of the road beside 'The Diamond'. The club was founded in December 1884, taking its name from the adjacent Round Tower. Club members have represented Dublin in inter-county competition since the nineteenth century. As part of an Oral History GAA project undertaken between 2010 and 2012, some club members gave oral interviews, discussing their collective GAA Round Tower history, including Peg Nolan, Tommy Keogh, Paddy Delaney and Pat Ryder. They described how the club was built up by different families that belonged to the small community of Clondalkin which brought people together both on and off the pitch, between playing games, socialising at ceilís and dances, as well as fund-raising events. (Oral History –GAA. https://www.gaa.ie/the-gaa/oral-history/members-roundtower-gaa-club-clondalkin)

My brothers also played soc-cer. Newer football clubs in the Clondalkin area include Moyle Park Past Pupils F.C., Neilstown Rangers, St. Francis Boys F.C., Ashwood F.C., Booth Road Celtic, Castle Park F.C., Moorefield United, Knockmitten United, Collinstown F.C., Liffey Valley Rangers and Clondalkin Celtic.

Poster for Supper Dance, Clondalkin Celtic F.C., 1994. Photo credit: Irene Harpur.

Clondalkin Celtic F.C.:- 1. John Blackburn 2. Norman Mulvey 3. Paddy Hall 4. (Omitted no. 4) 5.Brendan Callaghan 6. Patsy Blackburn 7. X Kavanagh 8.Billy Maguire. 9. (boy) Damian McGrath. 10. (boy) Micky Boggins 11. Charlie Fox 12. Willie Sheils 13. Jim Mc Govern 14. Jimmy Small 15. Tom Boggans 16. 'X' 17. Mick Delaney 18. Sonny Nolan 19. Sean Boggins 20. Johnny Kelly 21. George Smith 22.George Guilfoyle (Iden-tification thanks to Tommy Keogh).

Later on, the lads played tennis and badminton. For years, Jim was part of the badminton club that played in Baldonnel.

Mary Johnston recounted to the Old Clondalkin and Surrounding Districts about the tennis club in the 1940s at the back of Healys, The Black Lion Inn. People involved included Cyril Healy who ran the pub with his wife, Nancy, Mick Murphy, (who married 'Mertie' (Margaret) Ging, Jack Hanlon from the Naas Road, John O'Neill from Orchard Road, Paddy O'Rourke from Neilstown, Tom and Kathleen O'Neill, Nano Farrell (Hanlon, Monastery Road) from St. Brigid's Road, Lillie and Seán Lombard from Laurel Park, May Hughes from Newlands Cross, Peg Proctor, who had a relative on Boot Road, Bernie Healy, sister of Cyril, Paddy and Peg Johnston from St. Brigid's Drive, Carrie Errity from the Old Nangor Road, Con Murphy from Orchard Road, Patrick Ging, Ed Murphy, Robert Errity and Betty Ward.

Blacklion Tennis Club, Clondalkin (kindly shared by Patrick Ging, Clondalkin Historical Society Archive), and lists of lady and gentlemen members of the club (credit James Robertson).

A host of other sports clubs have sprung up in Clondalkin since my time. At the behest of the Reverend Martin Ryan P.P., who decided to raise awareness regarding the extent of local facilities available, a Clondalkin Parishes Directory was compiled. This acts as a Guide to Community Groups, voluntary and statutory organisations in the greater Clondalkin area. A copy of this Directory was sent back to Ireland from my sister, Gwen, in Yorkshire when she learned I was about to write the book. Gwen and her husband, Brendan, were keen historians and avid collectors of such material. Unfortunately, the Directory is not dated. I propose donating the Directory to the Clondalkin Local History Archive.

Some of the newer clubs include boxing, which brought forth boxers such as Bernard Dunne, from Neilstown, former WBA Super Bantamweight World Champion, and Kenny Egan, silver medal winner in the 2008 Olympics, originally from Woodford estate. Basketball is another more recent pursuit, with Dublin Lions Basketball Club based between Coláiste Bride and Moyle Park

Left: Clondalkin Motorcycle Club. Kindly shared by Christine Coby.

Below: Clondalkin Motorcycle Club Banner

College. O'Malley Field, Corkagh is the home to the Irish National Baseball Team. At one time, Clondalkin had no rugby team but now there's Clondalkin Rugby Club.

Other local community organisations include the Toastmasters, the Order of Malta and youth groups such as Clondalkin Youth Theatre, who practice and put on plays on the stage at Aras Chrónáin. Many of their members have gone on to Drama College and further. The Clondalkin Youth Band, a marching band, was founded in 1986 by Vincent Dolan, a nephew of the late, famous Joe Dolan. Clondalkin has an active Tidy Towns Committee as well as a Committee who managed to stop development adjacent to the Round Tower, which is now a great amenity. The Friends of the Camac actively contribute to the rehabilitation of the river. The Civil Defence established a unit in Deansrath during 2010 which specialises in auxiliary fire-fighting, emergency medical services and swiftwater technical rescue. A notable task was its response to flooding of homes next to the Camac River in 2011, when they rescued families from rising waters.

Two local newspapers, the Clondalkin Echo and Clondalkin Gazette, serve the area. The latter is part-owned by the Irish Times and was launched in October 2005, publication by Gazette Group Newspapers. The Clondalkin News is delivered free into households in the area.

Needless to say, most of the groups I mentioned above were not around when I was growing up, however, the village had its own cinema. Tommy Ging's father turned a former garage premises into a cinema, The Tower Cinema. Hordes of children went to the matinee. More about the cinema in a later chapter.

My older sisters could recall the big snowfall of 1933, when drifts blocked the front of our house and Dad climbing out the back window to dig the family out. Everywhere was cut off and the children were hoping it lasted a long time. Myself and my sister Mono recall the 'Big Snow' in May of 1947, the coldest and harshest winter in living memory. In many parts of the country, the snowfall caused large boughs to break off trees. I remember Dad helping to dig out the cows, the slides we made, the snowmen, throwing snowballs and wellies with holes that let in the wet. Another harsh storm in the 1970s caused many trees to fall, a spectacle which my own children enjoyed. The heaviest fall I recall in recent years was a blizzard in January 1982 which painted Ireland white for the best part of three weeks. News bulletins reported on the hundreds of motorists who had to be rescued from their cars of people stranded in various places, including the airports. It was a bonanza for children who went tobogganing on all sort of improvised sleighs and fertilizer bags.

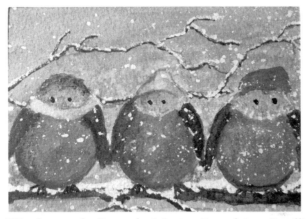

Weathering the Storm by Monica Sproul (nee Small)

15.
UP CONVENT ROAD, THE BOOT ROAD
AND ON TO THE COMMONS AND CORKAGH

Convent Road and Boot Road have completely changed since my childhood. The area is more populated, the road split by the Fonthill Road South, and housing estates now stand where there were once fields.

Starting at the left-hand side of Convent Road, I mentioned before that the Welsh family home was on the corner. Tracing around by Welsh's long garden brought you to Charlie Kelly's small butcher shop, a single storey cottage with a window and a door. When Mrs. Kelly was holding the fort for Charlie, she used the time between customers to knit and she produced some fabulous garments. She'd sit outside on the window ledge knitting away with the ball of wool in her pocket. Tesco supermarket now stands on this site.

An L-shaped building, Moyle Park was built in the 1700's by the Caldbeck family. The first owner, William Caldbeck, also built the adjacent Clondalkin Gunpowder Mills, which was once the sole sup-

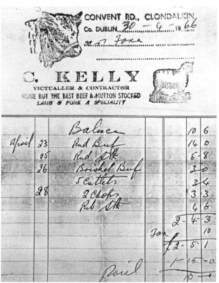

Billhead from Charlie Kelly's butcher's back to 1966. Kindly shared by Patrick Ging, Clondalkin Historical Society Archive.

plier of gunpowder to the English garrisons, until a massive explosion occurred in 1787. The Caldbeck family were prominent members of the Church of Ireland community and influenced parochial and social affairs in Clondalkin. Following the death of William Caldbeck in 1803, Moyle Park remained in Caldbeck hands. In 1810, his daughter-in-law, Mrs. Elizabeth Caldbeck, established a girl's school at Moyle Park Lodge. Although the school closed in 1844, she left a sum in her will for the establishment of a girl's school, as a result of which the Presentation Convent opened in 1857. The Caldbeck family were renowned for their generosity and frequently made donations of money, food and fuel to the poor. Apparently, they arranged for water to be piped to some of the village houses. Both editions of Thom's Almanac, 1858 and 1882, record, 'William Caldbeck, Esq., Moyle Park.' The Caldbeck name is recorded for posterity on a new road, Caldbeck Way.

Old Quinnsworth Supermarket with Penney's on the right, directly across the road is the entrance to Moyle Park. (Formerly Welsh's garden.) Photo credit: Roy Byrne.

Moyle Park, built c. 1780. Courtesy niah.ie.

Moyle Park passed through several hands before it was sold around 1900 to Major Thomas James Ryves, a retired police officer from India. Porter's Guide and Directory for County Dublin 1912, records, 'Mrs. Holmes, Moylepark.'

In my time, Moyle Park was owned by the horse owner and trainer, Jack Nugent, who lived there with his wife and family and his sister Jennie. Two of his horses were called *Nights of Gladness* and *Nights of Delight*. Moyle Park was then bought by the Marist Brothers who opened it as a school in 1957 and retained the house as a residence. Brother Eamonn was well-known and well-liked. It still runs as a secondary school to this day but much of the land has been sold for development.

In my time, the Galvins and the Kieltys lived in the lodges at the entrance to Moyle Park. Mr. Kielty was tall and a member of An Garda Síochana; his wife was a country woman. They had no children, but during WWII, they took in a German refugee. She was a tall, straight girl with natural blonde hair, an object of interest to us because she looked different and because there were no other foreigners in Clondalkin. She went to school in the Presentation Convent and was very intelligent and artistic. She returned to Germany after the war. Years later, the Kieltys accepted an invitation to her wedding.

Back across the road, Finns lived in a two storey double-fronted house and beside them was the entrance to the Convent and the Church. None of the following establishments were there in my time - St. Brigid's estate, Moyle Crescent, St. Anthony's Avenue, St. Joseph's Boys School and Scoil Mhuire. After

Round Tower GAA Club hall, with a sign, 'Established in 1884.'

the entrance to the Convent was Bridie Gill's house. Next was the single storey house where the butcher, Charlie Kelly, lived with his family. Kellys' house was across from the narrow road which led to Corkagh's back entrance, known locally as 'the back road.' (The main entrance to Corkagh was on the Naas Road).

The O'Byrne family lived on the corner junction of the Boot Road and 'the back road.' Mrs. O'Byrne was formerly a Nixon, before she married. Mr. O'Byrne had lorries. A lady named May Foran lived in a cottage beside the O'Byrne's, which is now a business premises.

In my day, there were virtually no houses on the back road, which encompassed a huge piece of commonage land, known simply as, 'The Commons.' This land was eventually taken over by the Council and pockets of local authority houses are now built there. This road is now named St. John's Road and it leads to a housing estate, St. John's Wood. The laneway to Corkagh was always a stopping point for members of the traveller community over the years.

Joe Murphy lived with his mother, until she died, in a wooden house along the back road.

(Above) Old Commons Rd, now St. Johns Rd, view towards Corkagh Demesne. On the left, where the tractor is stopped, was the wooden house where Joe Murphy lived. Credit Paddy Matthews. (Below) Joe Murphy's wooden house and his dog at the gate.

St. John's entrance to Corkagh, known as 'The Back Road' and used by servants and workmen. (Main entrance was on the Naas Road).

The Nolan family also lived in a cottage at The Commons. I remember the sisters, Kitty and Peg, and their brother, whom I always knew only as 'Mutt' Nolan. As he was a tall man, I think his nickname came from the tall newspaper cartoon character of that name. As a schoolgirl in the 1930s, Kitty related a story for The Schools Folklore Collection about a brick field that once existed at The Commons about two acres in size, bounded by a hedge and with an iron entrance gate, as well as the ruins of an old house. Apparently, boys were engaged to gather clay and pick stones from the clay before it was formed into brick-shaped pieces and dried in a kiln. The brick field was levelled and was in use back then as pastureland under the ownership of Joseph Dowling.

The two Smith brothers had adjacent small holdings at The Commons. To earn extra money, they hired themselves out for labour, together with their

(Top) Aerial view of Corkagh farmyard. (Above left) Corkagh House. (Above right) Five terraced cottages in the yard at Corkagh demesne, built c. 1840. Courtesy niah.ie.

horse and cart. Clondalkin Paper Mills used to hire them to cart cinders for dumping up at Mill Lane. One day, they backed the horse and cart too far back towards the pond and in went both horse and cart. As children, curiosity got the better of us and we all tramped up Mill Lane to watch the dead horse being winched out of the water.

On the right of the lane, Kate Carrick lived on a small holding where she kept pigs and hens and a few calves. Kate reared Joan and Celia and Larry Farrell. The Kellys, a large family, lived at the gate lodge at the entrance to Corkagh. I remember Jimmy Kelly well and other family members, Nuala, Kathleen and more. The Clarke family lived on Corkagh Estate, where Mr. Clarke was a steward. I knew the Clarke and Cabena families who lived at Corkagh. Their daughter was Fanny Cabena.

Corkagh Estate was built on the site of a former abbey in two stages. Originally, a small farmhouse was built c. 1650 and a wing was added later in Queen Anne style. Once owned by William Trundell, it was in the ownership of the Finlay family for 225 years, until 1959, when almost all the estate was sold to Sir John Galvin, who demolished the mansion. At its height, Corkagh Demesne employed 25 indoor and 25 outdoor staff.

When Corkagh was sold, the Hone and Colley families, relations of the Finlay family, who had lived at Corkagh, moved into the Dower House at Kilmatead (translates as 'church of Tighe') and the Old Mill House. The writer Elizabeth Bowen often stayed at Corkagh as her mother was a Colley.

Dublin County Council purchased the lands at Corkagh from Sir John

Kilmatead House. Credit: Patrick Healy. Extract SDCC.

Galvin in 1983, designated it as a Regional Park and officially opened it to the public on Sunday 15th June 1986. Since the division of the County, the Parks Department of South Dublin County Council has continued to develop the Park. It has plenty of fine trees and they have improved the water features which now include "put and take" fishing lakes where fish are stocked regularly and must be released when caught. Given its large wetland area and the Camac River running through it, wildlife abounds in the parkland. It also houses an enclosure with animals and a playground.

A particular childhood memory of mine is the hexagonal house in Corkagh, remembered by some as 'The Hex,' which was built for a child but later used as a tea house. It had a thatched roof, a chimney, two windows and a path leading up to the door. Myself and three friends were so intrigued, we had to see inside for ourselves. We opened the door, noted a fireplace and cupboard and then, fearful of being caught for trespassing and being taken to the guards' barracks, we ran off, hell for leather. Now demolished, it is a pity it could not be saved, seeing as it was located close to where the present playground stands.

Jack Dowling and his wife lived at the Oil Mills. Jack worked as a ploughman for Johnno and was very gentlemanly. When the Angelus rang, he broke off from work, took off his hat, blessed himself and prayed. He'd shout at the horses to start them off again. The Dowlings had no children. When we were

The Hexagonal summer house - The Hex - Corkagh Demesne. Courtesy South Dublin Libraries, Tallaght.

playing in the vicinity of their home, we used to knock on the door for a glass of water or to ask the time. We wanted neither; we only wanted to peer in and look at Mrs. Dowling's ornaments, her dresser with its beautiful delph and her chiming wall clock. I always loved the sound of a ticking clock, which brings back childhood memories.

Back to the Boot Road. Earlier, I mentioned Ledwidges' farm. Ledwidges' land bordered the far side of the Boot Road and extended all the way up to the Naas Road. A record in Thom's Almanac of 1858 shows, 'Simon Ledwidge, farmer, Ashfield.' I cannot remember either the entrance to the farm, nor do I remember Ledwidge's house. A pocket of two-storey local authority houses now stand on the farm site. Rockfield Drive is nearer to the Naas Road. A record in Thom's Almanac of 1858 shows, John Gerraghty (sic), Rockfield, while the 1882 edition shows, 'Miss Gould, Rockfield.' Porter's Guide and Directory for County Dublin 1912, records, 'Mr. Hayward, Rockfield.'

Before reaching Ledwidges' farm, a muddy lane, known as Brideswell Lane, led to St. Brigid's Well, a natural spring believed to have been established by St. Brigid in the 5th century. It is said that she put down her staff as she travelled through Clondalkin and up sprang water, which she intended for the baptism of pagans. In return, locals paid homage to her each St. Brigid's Day, the 1st of February. As well as water being drawn from this well for domestic

St. Brigid's Well, off the Boot Road, Clondalkin.

purposes, tradition had it that the well water was good for the eyes. People believed they could be cured by drinking the water from the well or blessing themselves with it. Others believed that in order to activate its curative powers, people had to dip a rag into the water, wipe their face with the rag and then tie the rag or 'clootie' to a nearby tree, usually a whitethorn bush. ('Clootie' is derived from the Scottish for 'cloth').

In 1937, both Kitty Nolan and Peggy Nolan who lived at the Commons related some of the history of

St. Bridget's Well for the Schools Folklore Collection as well as George [O'] Connor, who mentioned various items that were regularly hung from the bush including bits of rags, rosary beads, old coins and pencils – Mrs. Coates had related this aspect to George. The well and surrounding land was 'owned' by William Caldbeck, who rented it to a Mr. Ormsby. It is said that infants that died before they could be baptised could be buried in this area under a lease signed by Mr. Caldbeck. The well is now dry due to diversion of the water flow for road widening in the 1990s. Restoration of St. Brigid's Well took place in 1993. This Holy Well is still highly venerated and kept in good order by the local community.

Time to mention also the talented Mrs. Keogh, who had a large family and knitted beautiful jumpers in complicated fairisle patterns. Mr. Keogh worked as a fitter's helper but he was also what they called a 'lagger.' He was paid an extra sixpence per week, to insulate the steam pipes, with fibreglass or asbestos and he used to wear a bib-type overalls. This contact with asbestos and fibreglass did him no harm - he lived until he was 95, was a pipe-smoker all his life and took four lumps of sugar in his tea and if he had any doubt that the four lumps of sugar had not gone into the cup, he'd put four more spoonfuls in for good measure. He had been reared in the cottages at Mill Yard and his own father had worked in the Mill, until he had an accident. Following the accident, the elder Mr. Keogh still managed to tend to his garden despite his reduced mobility.

Tommy Keogh worked in the Mill as the paymaster. Tommy is a wonderful photographer and community man who won the LAMA All Ireland Commu-

No. 3 Convent View Cottages. Courtesy niah.ie

nity & Council Silver Prize Award as Community Volunteer of the Year for his lifetime of voluntary work for his community. His brother, Kevin Keogh, worked in the Mill's Engineering Stores. Kevin is a keen angler and has an interest in the upkeep of the Camac river.

On further up the Boot Road is the Naas Road, which was entirely different in my day. The 'old' Naas Road still exists and sometimes appears on maps as 'Green Isle Road,' as it leads up to the Green Isle Hotel. To the right of the road,

a new estate was built called Bush-field Lawns. The area to the left, is known as Bedleshill.

With the construction of the new road, a narrow strip of land was left between the 'old' Naas Road and the 'new' Naas Road.. For years, a man who worked for Mrs. O'Brien lived in a house with his wife on this piece of ground owned by Mrs. O'Brien. When the couple left, Mrs. O'Brien sold the land to the owners of the Green Isle Hotel.

This area was also known as the Buck-and-Hounds or sometimes,

Keogh brothers of Boot Road were past pupils in St Michael's CBS, Inchicore between the 1950's & 1960's. Jack, Tommy, Joe and Kevin. Courtesy Dublin City Council.

Coal deliveries by Mr. O'Neill (L) and Jim Stynes (R)

BuckandHounds, one word, without hyphens. The 1901 census shows three households in this area, the Brewster family, the Mulligan farming family and two Dowlings, also, the Philips family, however, as was typical back then, others lived with those families, variously described as, 'boarder,' 'lodger,' or 'nurse child.' The 1911 census also shows three households here, again the Mulligans and Dowlings, the other households being the Stynes and Turner families.

BOOT ROAD
Dwyer, C., The Cottage
Coates. D., St. Bridget's,
Kelly, Mary E., Brideswell
70 Co. Council Cottages, grocer
Extract from The Directory of Ireland, 1958.

Chaffinch by Monica Sproul (nee Small)

16.
OUTINGS

Going on holiday was unheard of when I was growing up. Firstly, few could afford holidays and secondly, holiday entitlements were not yet built into the terms and conditions of jobs. Nobody of our acquaintance went on holidays except those with country roots who took a break back at the old homestead and had country cousins on return visits. Summer was a time for visitors and there was great excitement in advance of their arrival. It usually meant sleeping top to tail in bed to make room for all and giggling until everybody fell asleep.

Once a year, the circus set up in Healy's field. It was a great week for Clondalkin and the tent was packed each night. The circus performances included acts involving lions, elephants, monkeys and ponies. The clowns were well-loved by the audience and although they did a lot of fooling around, they were very talented people who could perform all sorts of acrobatics. A carnival was erected with chair-o-planes, swinging boats, hobby horses, humpback ride and other pieces of equipment designed to jolt human beings, sometimes leaving them dizzy when they alighted. Toft's Amusements

DUFFY'S CIRCUS

WILL VISIT

Edenderry—Tuesday, June 20.
Naas—Wednesday, June 21.
Clondalkin—Thursday, June 22
Bray—Friday, June 23.

GRAND CHALLENGE PROGRAMME
50 CIRCUS HORSES AND PONIES.
A HOST OF STAR ARTISTES.
CLOWNS AND COMEDIANS.

Advertisement for Duffy's Circus, Clondalkin. Kindly shared by Gerard Byrne, Old Clondalkin & Surrounding Districts.

(the Toft family were neighbours of my father) came once a year to Healy's field. A large marquee was erected and for two weeks in the year, huge numbers of young men and women came from far and wide to dance the night away to various bands, and many romances blossomed.

The Tower cinema, which ran from 1939 to 1977, was the main entertainment in the village. Larry Ging ran the cinema, helped by his brother, Tommy. Their sisters also helped selling tickets. The cinema showed films every night and there was also a matinee on Sundays. Prices varied according to the standard of the seats, from 8d in old money up to 1s 4d for the plush seats, which amount to about 5 cents in today's money. Usually, there was a main feature as well as a cartoon and sometimes, the Pathé news. A great variety of films were shown; I recall Laurel and Hardy, the Marx Brothers and later, Flash Gordon and Batman. The matinee, nicknamed 'the fourpenny rush' as it cost 4d. (i.e. four old pennies), was attended only by children, except for one deaf man I knew who brought his children there each Sunday. The drama created great tension in the cinema resulting in deafening noise levels and applause at times when the hero was being pursued or a baddie was caught. How the doorman, Christy Hickey, stuck the noise I will never know. Children often followed serials where episodes often ended with a climax where the star went over a cliff edge or got shot as he rounded a corner. These serials, which we called 'follower-uppers,' reeled children in for a future cinema attendance. The 'follower' to

Left: Gwen, Mono & Gert; Right; Mono (sitting), Gert (standing) in England.

the climax episode often revealed the star clinging to a scrappy bush over the cliff edge or ducking as a shooter took a 'pot shot' at him. I can still recall the screams of the children when the star was 'saved.'

My first time away from home was after national school when I got the boat across to England, to give my older sister in Yorkshire, Gwen, a hand with her children. Once I was working, I crossed the water many times to visit the family and often brought along my younger sister, Mono.

Instead of holidays, day trips and outings were our big treats. Peg and Gwen took us to town, on shopping trips, to the cinema or to a show.

In the school holidays, we got the bus as far as Parkgate Street for a trip to Dublin Zoo in the Phoenix Park. At that time, visitors were permitted to feed the animals, so it was commonplace for hawkers to set up at the Zoo entrance and peddle food for the animals. They displayed their wares on baker boards which sat on top of prams, for ease of wheeling to the Zoo and back home. We bought monkey nuts, which came in a long cone made of newspaper, although we usually had the nuts eaten by the time we reached the monkey house. We bought apples for the elephants – you could experience the rough trunk landing on the palm of your hand. Once we had paid in and passed through the thatched kiosk, the first thing we noted were the beautiful gardens, flowerbeds full of colour, with peacocks and pheasants strutting around, along with ducks and other birds. The first animals we saw there were the huge bison. Cages

Left: Mono & Gert on a visit to the Bronte home at Haworth, England; Right: Gert, Mono and Gwen with Peter O'Byrne.

held monkeys, elephants, lions, tigers, polar bears, seals, exotic birds and even wolves. The reptile house accommodated a variety of snakes and insects. The pets' corner allowed children to get a close look at lambs, calves, ponies, rabbits, pigs and fowl. Feeding time was always a spectacle - the keeper arrived with buckets of fish for the sealions and the penguins performed all sorts of stunts to grab food, sliding on their bellies across smooth rocks. In the afternoon, the chimps' tea party was held on the lawn. The keeper at the snake house took snakes from behind glass and placed them around your neck so you could have your photo taken. You could even ride on the back of an elephant for a small sum. A howdah was placed on the elephant's back and with some difficulty, children were helped on to the howdah and strapped into a seat. Children could also ride on a cart pulled by two miniature ponies.

The Phoenix Park itself was always a great venue for family outings and sporting fixtures.

A large open plain known as the Fifteen Acres accommodated football matches and a polo ground and a cricket ground stand near to the boundary of the Zoo. The Phoenix Park hosted special competitive

Thatched kiosk at Zoo entrance

events such as cycling and running and on occasion there was motor racing, when the day started off with motorcycle racing and went on to motor car racing. The racing cars were built like tanks with extended bonnets and they were driven by world-class drivers. The cars used a clockwise course, zooming down Chesterfield Avenue towards Castleknock, slowing down before Mountjoy corner to negotiate the turn for Ashtown gate. The racing stopped during World War II but it was revived in 1949 and continued for years. In the years leading up to WWII, air displays were held in the Park, to which there was a small admission charge at the Park gates. The pilots were ex-servicemen from World War I who used mostly bi-planes in the pageant. Not alone was there the spectacle of loop-the-loop stunts and parachute jumps, but for 2s 6d, (mere cents these days), you could take a plane ride with two or three people. The pilot usually circled the Phoenix Park before touching down again. For those who preferred music, bands played regularly at bandstand in The Hollow, near to the Zoo entrance.

Some exceptional events drew massive crowds to the Phoenix Park. The Eucharistic Congress was held in 1932, before my time. Years later, people still talked about every house, shop and church being festooned with bunting, flower baskets and flags. People put up flagpoles and hoisted yellow and white papal flags and many an altar was built. Another big event was the visit of Pope John Paul II in 1979. A papal cross stands on the spot in the Fifteen Acres where he celebrated Mass and talked to the people of Ireland. A later Pope also visited this same spot and a few other sites in Ireland in 2018 but the visit did not attract the same crowds.

In summer, we took trips to the seaside, usually to Portmarnock or Killiney. On trips to Killiney, we brought a picnic - flasks and sandwiches - as there were no food venues there. Portmarnock was not well known and was sparsely populated. When our neighbours, the Ollertons

Top: Eucharistic Congress, 1932. The Round Tower decorated with bunting. St. John's Church in foreground. Above: Main Street, Clondalkin during the Eucharistic Congress, 1932.

Left: Advertisement for day trips to Dublin. Kindly shared by Gerard Byrne, Old Clondalkin & Surrounding Districts. Right: Day trip to Laytown. Back L-R, Gert Small, John Hartnett, Vincent McCurtin, X, Martin Whelan. Front L-R, Kathleen Hurrell, Annie Bradley, X, Freda Ryan.

got a car, we went to Malahide, some in the car and some on Dad's motorbike. We made tea on the Primus stove and we ate sandwiches and cake. One trip to Balbriggan was special as we got the train. From about the age of ten or twelve, we joined friends and cycled off on day trips to places such as the Slade Valley, Saggart, Rathcoole, Newcastle, Lucan, Palmerstown, and Tallaght. Our longest outing by bike was to the beach at Donabate. Punctures were a regular feature of life but generally, cyclists mended their own punctures and did their own repairs.

When we got older, we often did cycling trips to Blessington, the Hell Fire Club, the beach or to picturesque places, bringing along a flask and sandwiches. After our picnic, we might treat ourselves to an ice cream cone before the return journey. There were day trips too to places like Belfast.

Boat by Monica Sproul (nee Small)

17.
FROM 'GING'S' CORNER UP THE LEFT HAND SIDE OF THE NANGOR ROAD

Naturally, you know your own end of the village best and so it is with me and the Old Nangor Road. However, the landscape along this road has changed so dramatically that it is unrecognisable in places, especially now it has been cut off by the Fonthill Road South. Even following the road through on the other side of the Fonthill Road, it is hard to credit it was once the main road to Cork, when you encounter it narrowing into a cul-de-sac laneway.

For now, I will confine myself to telling you about the families living on the left hand side of Nangor Road.

Mill Yard. Former family homes of Freeman, Coates, Connor and Matthews.

At Mill Yard were the McInerneys, Freemans, Coates, Connors and Mat-thews families. Maysanne Freeman was a good friend of her neighbour, Mrs. Coates. Mrs Coates and her other next door neighbour, Mrs. Connor, used to go to the pictures together. The interpretative centre was constructed on the footprint of the houses at the Mill Yard. In the upstairs part of the interpretative centre, visitors are taken through the recreated bedroom of the former Coates family home.

The Byrnes lived in Sally Park Cottage at Mill Lane. Davy Byrne was a good friend of my brother, Jim. The Muldowney and Delaney families shared the next house, which was beside the Gavin's house, formerly the old R.I.C.

(Top) L - Delaney former family home. R - once the RIC Barracks. (Above) Old RIC barracks, Old Nangor Road, later home to the Gavin family and later still, the Kinnane's, who operated a small shop from a window to the left.

barracks. This later became home to the Kinnane family who operated a small shop from a window to the left.

Next came the grand Sally Park House which was originally owned by Thomas Seery, who also owned the Paper Mill. Its next occupant was the Mill manager, Mr. Ledwidge. In my time, Marchioness McSweeny lived here with her sister and two brothers whose surname was England. The brothers were barristers but they took such a stance waiting for the bus, they could be mistaken for judges. One of them was a trainspotter who could often be seen standing at

the railway bridge looking onto the track below. The family were said to be related to the German Kaiser and to have received invitations to royal functions in England. The Marchioness used to dress to kill for Mass, swathed in furs and with more than a whiff of perfume left all over the church. A man known locally as 'Bogey' Finn (I never knew his proper name) drove the Marchioness around in a Humber Super Snipe. Their butler, Charlie, was a very small man who dressed impeccably and smoked Woodbines. The word was that he earned two shillings and sixpence a week. The house and grounds were

(Top) Sally Park Mill, discovery of mill stones. (Above left) Sign for C.P.M. Sports & Social Club. (Above right) The 'Gluepot'.

more latterly used by the Paper Mill social club but Sally Park House is now demolished.

Next is a social club that had been run by Clondalkin Paper Mills, and which was subsequently controlled by its paid-up club members. Facilities include a clubhouse and a bar, with competitive alcohol prices, a pool table, darts and a pitch and putt club. In 2016, financial difficulties forced a land sale, to pay bills and maintain finances going forward but the clubhouse and bar – known locally as 'The Gluepot' – were not included in the sale.

Next door to us on one side, my older sister, Peg, remembered the two labourer's cottages within an enclosed yard that were made into a bungalow. The Misses Tutty came to live there from Moyle Park. Following that, the Flynn family lived there but not for long as they were replaced by the Ollerton family, who had three children, Dick, Edward and Jean. The next occupants were the Caseys, then the O'Driscolls and then the Lyons family. The fields behind, where the swimming pool was later built, were owned by the Dowd family.

We were beside this bungalow in Raheen Cottage, tucked away in a yard behind gates. Originally, there were large wooden gates but these were later

Top: Former home of our neighbours, the O'Driscolls and then the Lyons family which also housed a shop and hairdressers at one stage. Credit: Andru O'Maonaigh. Bottom: Raheen Cottage entrance gates.

replaced by smaller iron gates. I am going to skip by our place for the present and bring you back there later for tea.

Raheen House was next. It was built in the 1700's on a hill known as 'The Butts Stang,' a name often used as a place for archery and musketry, the name 'Raheen,' being a name for a little rath. Around 1900, Raheen House and farm were owned by the Tutty family. The Thom's Almanac for 1882 records, 'James Tutty, Esq., Raheen House.' Porter's Guide and Directory for County Dublin 1912, shows, 'W. Fitzgerald, Raheen House.' In 1914, the lands were sold to John O'Brien, a farmer, known as "Johnno."

John O'Brien rented the land to a number of tenants, to include Patrick Nugent, John Caball and W. Jeffries. He also owned Raheen House which was home at various stages to the Craig, Carroll, Cusack, Mullaney families and its final tenants, the Nolan family. Mr. Carroll was a horticulturalist and Head of the Royal Dublin Society for years. He meticulously maintained the large orchard, lawns, flowerbeds, trees and three greenhouses. Mr. Cusack was General Manager of Clondalkin Paper Mills and very dedicated to his job, conscious that the Mill's huge workforce relied on the Mill for a living. Mr. Mullaney was a veterinary surgeon and Head of the Veterinary College in Ballsbridge. Mrs. Mullaney's horse, 'Crackers,' was stabled in our yard. My father often wondered who was more crackers – her or the horse. Mr. John Nolan was formerly an Army man who worked after his retirement as Transport Manager at Clondalkin Paper Mills.

The O'Brien family sold the land for development in 1954. Ultimately, Raheen House was bought by Niall Nolan in the 1980s. In 2006, the entire lot comprising both Raheen House and Raheen Cottage was put put up for sale with planning for development but the sale fell through. At a stage when

Clondalkin Hunt and in the background, left to right: The Haggard, Raheen House and Raheen Cottage.

both properties were derelict, a fire engulfed them. They were finally bought for development and demolished in June 2019 with nice homes set to be built there. I hope the new homeowners will be as happy at Raheen as we were.

While there was no Cherrywood there in my time, I believe this estate has gained prominence since its most famous resident, the actor, Aidan Turner, put it in the spotlight.

Beyond Johnno's land on the Old Nangor Road was a townland called 'Priesttown.' Bridget McNulty, who was in her sixties when I was a child, and her two brothers lived on a small holding, where they kept pigs and hens. One of the brothers worked in Inchicore Works. They used to go across the road to Mrs. Carney's bungalow for water. Next came two pairs of single storey semi-detached council cottages where the Kellys, Behans, Rileys and Briens lived. Mrs. Taylor lived opposite these four houses.

On past 'The Dog's Corner,' you came upon Kilcarberry House. Back in the 1800s, the parish of Kilbride consisted of the townlands of Kilbride and Baldonan, now known as Baldonnel, i.e. Donnell's or Donan's town. The lands of Kilbride extend back to the Anglo-Norman Conquest in the 12th century with

My sister, Monica with 'Crackers,' Mrs. Mullaney's horse stabled in our yard

a castle having been established in Kilbride at one time. The lands eventually came into the hands of the Carberry family, a name that is still reflected in a house in the townland, Kilcarberry House. Henry Philips, the Church Warden at St. John's, once lived there but in my time, the Trench family lived there. Subsequently, Sir John Galvin bought it. Eddie Kavanagh worked for Sir John and lived there with his family. Lewis's Topographical Dictionary of Ireland, 1837, shows Mrs. Anne Connolly as resident there. A record in Thom's Almanac of 1858 records, 'Henry Phillips Esq., Kilcarbery,' while the 1882 edition shows, 'Philips Grierson Esq., Kilcarbery.' 'A. Nolan' is shown for the years 1930/1931 and the Thom's Directory of 1957 records, 'M. Trench, Kilcarbery.'

Beyond Kilcarberry House was all farmland until you reached the Donnellys' farm, where the gate was always kept locked. They lived in a two-storey farm-

house and had apple trees growing in the front garden. A reclusive pair of bachelor farmers, one of them rarely left the farm although the other used to go to the village for messages in a farm cart drawn by a horse. After they died, Michael Carey bought the property; the place was totally overgrown by that stage. Michael set up a garage

(Top) Kilcarberry House, photo courtesy niah.ie. (Above) Former Maxol filling station owned by Mick Carey at Ballybane, Old Nangor Road. Donnelly brothers lived there previously. Kindly shared by John Boland.

there with petrol pumps and did some farming. He used to bring his produce into the market for sale.

Paddy O'Keeffe built a house further on and next is John and Mary Beatty's farm at Ballybane.

Andy Clancy and his wife Stella (nee Browne) lived nearby at 'Derravaragh,' a bungalow built in a large garden, which Aine and Dermot Carberry then bought and lived in. At this stage, we are at Baldonnel Cross. On further towards Milltown, Clery's shop stood on a bend in the road.

Baldonnell House was the principal residence in the small parish of Kilbride. A record in Thom's Almanac of 1858 shows, 'Philips Grierson Esq., Baldonnell.'

(Top) Bringing in the hay – Chris Brown, Ballybane Farm, 1957. (Left) Baldonnell House built c. 1869, photo courtesy niah.ie. (Right) Baldonnel. Kindly shared by Gerard Byrne, Old Clondalkin & Surrounding Districts.

During World War I, the British built a number of airfields in Ireland, including one at Baldonnel, where the Royal Air Force headquarters were based until the Anglo-Irish Treaty in 1921, when the RAF withdraw their air bases from Ireland. Eventually the Irish Air Service became the Army Air Corps. Aer Lingus operated from Baldonnel between 1936 and 1946, until Dublin Airport was opened at Collinstown, another former RAF air base. In 1965, when the remains of Roger Casement were flown home from England to Baldonnel, the air base was re-named Casement Aerodrome. Apart from its official functions, events were frequently held at Baldonnel such as dances, point-to-point meetings and air pageants. My brother, Jim, also played badminton there.

BALDONNEL ROAD
Baldonnel House – Roche, Mrs. M. £130 10s.
St. Bernadette's – Cullen, -
Rock House – Sandal,
St. Joseph's – Corrigan, J., fruit farm
Baldonnel – Treacy, -.
Kilbride House – Vacant
Weston – Dagnall, F.

Extract from The Directory of Ireland 1958

Advertisements for Air Pageant, 1931, and Point-to-Point.

The parish of Kilmactawley boasts some antiquity, going back as it does to the Anglo-Norman conquest in the 12th century. A monastic settlement was established there at the close of the 13th century. Mr. Mangan lived at Castle Baggot, which was in the hands of the Baggot (or Bagot) family for generations. Back in 1937, Sinead Flanagan of Cornerpark, Newcastle, spoke to Mr. Mangan who related some of the history for the Schools Folklore Collection. She wrote how a long avenue leads up the house and continues on past the house to ruins at the back, said to have once been a church or monastery with a graveyard. The ruin is surrounded by a ditch leading to the conclusion that it was once fortified. Before the church went into ruin, Ella Maria Baggot had

the altar and water font removed and placed them into Newcastle Church, in memory of her husband, James John Baggot, who died in 1860.

Grange Castle, a three storey late medieval tower house, was constructed around 1580 and remodelled around 1750.

The name was taken up by the

Top: Castle Baggot, Kilmactawley townland, built c. 1800, courtesy niah.ie. Above: Grange Castle, Clondalkin, 1767. Kindly shared by Gerard Byrne, Old Clondalkin & Surrounding Districts.

nearby Grange Castle Business Park which now houses corporate giants such as Microsoft, Google, Arytza, Wyeth, Takeda and Pfizer. The pharmaceutical giant, Pfizer, the former Wyeth facility, already houses one of the largest bio-technology plants in the world and plans a major expansion of its Grange Castle plant on a site of fifteen acres purchased from South Dublin County Council. The castle also lent its name to the Grange Castle Golf Club.

At the junction with the Newcastle to Lucan road, a pub set up on the corner was called the Happy Brig. The name later changed to Polly Hops pub. It was damaged by fire in 2007 and is now derelict.

Blue Tit by Mary Reynolds

18.
FOOD AND CIGARETTES AND NEWSPAPERS

Neither of my parents drank alcohol but like most people in those days, both smoked. They usually smoked *Players*, *Gold Flake* or *Rothmans* cigarettes. There were no health warnings about damage caused by smoking, nor were there restrictions on where one could smoke. It is hard to imagine now the level of smoke back then in cinemas, on buses and in the workplace. Patients and even visitors smoked in hospitals. The shops sold various brands of cigarettes including *Chesterfield*, *Rothmans* and *Players,* which were considered the very best, in that order. Down the list were *Gold Flake*, followed by *Sweet Afton*, made by

Gings shop - Unknown, Patsy Cleary and Mary Ging. Credit Patrick Ging.

for granted is today market as 'artisan bread,' costing an arm and a leg. Basket loaves, crunchy 'ducks,' 'skulls,' turnovers and Vienna rolls – any of them slathered with butter and jam was enough for tea.

Many shops operated a local newspaper delivery service twice a day within a radius of about three miles. Deliveries were usually by bicycle or sometimes on foot. Sometimes, a schoolboy did a newspaper round after school. The newspapers in vogue were the *Irish Independent, Irish Times, Evening Herald, Evening Mail* and later on, the *Evening Press*. Most people ordered only one daily paper. We did not get papers every day but we always got newspapers at weekends.

Some shops had no electricity supply but despite this, they used a form of cold storage which enabled them to sell even ice-cream which arrived in a special container and lasted for several days. Each week, a van delivered to shops what I shall describe as a tin full of ice, covered in insulation about six inches thick. Essentially, it was an insulated canvas block with ice broken into lumps for food storage, an effective method of refrigeration. However, with the arrival of electricity in the 1930s, shops installed modern fridges. My older sisters remember the ice-cream man who came in summertime on a tricycle with a big box in front. Once he had passed by Leinster Terrace and the bridge over the Camac, he used to blow his bugle. It was a sound that became familiar to all children, prompting them to look for pennies or halfpennies to buy wafers or cornets, latter which are now called whipped cones.

Walnut Whips used to be called a *Whip Cream Whirls* in my time and they came in two varieties. The one with a walnut on top cost tuppence, roughly equivalent to one cent today and the one without a walnut cost one old penny, no equivalent today.

Lar Connor carried milk in churns on a float pulled by a horse. People waited at their doors with jugs and bottles and he dispensed the milk from a tap at the bottom. Goat's milk could be got from Johnny Killeen, who lived on Lar Connors land and reared goats.

Farmers left their milk churns on high wooden platforms built at the roadside for ease of collection, but with the advent of milk trucks, that was no longer necessary and the platforms were taken down. Those working on farms attached to big houses used to bring milk home from the dairy in a billy can. At one time, milk was simply dispensed into the customer's container, until the arrival of glass bottles. Lucan Dairies delivered bottled milk, butter and ice-cream to the shops by van.

Fresh fruit and vegetables were also available at the Clondalkin Country Markets.

Other familiar figures that passed through the neighbourhood included a rag-and-bone man, travellers up from the country and gypsies used to camp on nearby Moore's Lane. They used to call to Raheen Cottage to 'borrow' items - first it was a bag of sugar, then some tea, then bread and so on.

Potato crisps only came on the market after the war, although they were completely different to today's crisps. Firstly, they were a different shape, more like today's chipsticks and secondly, they came with a tiny cellophane sachet of salt inside.

Nora Galvin of Tower House learned from Mrs. Robert Galvin of Tower Cottage about different herbs used of old for culinary and medicinal purposes, information which she shared as part of the Schools Folklore Collection:

Premier Dairies Milk van.

Celery, they made a kind of tea from, to be used with great advantage for kidney trouble. Another herb we hear very little about is Camomile, long ago it had many uses, our fore-fathers used it in many ways. The flowers when dried were drawn like tea and the essence flavoured with milk and sugar, was drunk as a cure for indigestion. The flowers were also made into a poultice for swellings or neuralgia. There is a plant called Hemlock which is poisonous, but which was often used as a poultice for bad sores, and we must not forget the old-fashioned dandelion which has very many uses and the Marigold which was used as a flavouring for soups. There were many very nice wines made long ago, too namely, Cranberry wine, cherry wine, and a lovely wine was made from fraughans - little wild berries that grew in mountainous places.

Peggy Nolan from the Commons described old methods of cooking:

The griddle is only used for the one purpose of baking. It is round like a pan only no sides on it. There is a handle on one side of it. Some people prefer it to the pot oven as it is not so troublesome. One has only to make the cake and put it on the griddle over a slow fire and turn it now and again. It takes one hour to bake one cake and when one has butter-milk it makes delicious bread.

The pot ovens were very common long ago - but they are gone out of date now except in old farm houses. The following people Mrs Byrne St Mark's Lodge, Balgaddy, Mrs Smith, Knockmeenagh, Mrs Melia, Newlands, Mrs Feighery, Nangor Road use the pot oven but I do not know of any others who still use the pot oven. We have a pot oven which we find very useful for baking bread. To heat the pot oven well is the principal difficulty. The lid is put on the top of the pot until it gets very hot. When it is sufficiently heated one puts in her bread and puts the lid on top, which she keeps hot with sprigs or turf. One does not require much heat underneath because it would burn the bread. The bread does not take as long to do as on a griddle. Bread baked in a pot oven is far nicer than other bread because it rises up better and is much lighter. Some people prefer the pot oven bread to any other.

Peggy also described the process of butter churning:

Churning is a very ancient custom, but is not so common at the present time.

There are different kinds of churns such as the wheel churn, the dash churn which is one of the oldest, and the barrel churn. We have a dash churn which we find very useful though very hard to work. When you strain the fresh milk you leave it by to set for cream. When it is ready you put the cream into the churn. After ten minutes you put in one pint of boiling water to bring it to a certain temperature. You keep churning briskly until you see the butter appearing on the churn. You go a little slower when it is nearly finished. You rinse the churn down with some cold water in order to put the butter together. You then put a brick in under the churn and allow it to be rocked to and fro and the butter gathers into a big roll and it is very easily taken off. Butter is put into a wooden butter-dish some cold water to wash the butter-milk out of it is used, for if it is not washed properly the butter will become streaky. You put salt into the butter and rinse again and then you make it into prints which have different designs such as swans, shamrocks and various other things. The design we have is a swan. It is delightful watching people making butter but better still to help as I often do.

Still Life by Monica Sproul (nee Small)

19.
FROM GING'S SHOP UP THE RIGHT
HAND SIDE OF THE NANGOR ROAD

Back to Ging's corner and I will take you along to the families living on the right hand side of the Old Nangor Road.

In my time, the Ging family lived at 'The Diamond' beside Clondalkin Paper Mill – Mr. Ging, Mrs. Ging (a fussy woman) and their family, Laurence ('Larry'), Tommy, Mary, Mertie, Peadar and Paddy ('Bumpy'). The premises comprised a house and single-storey shop with a yard and outhouses behind. At one time, a coaching house stood on the site, then it became the Ace of Diamond pub before operating as a school. One photograph shows the name Furlong over the shop. The Ging family association with Clondalkin stretches back over a hundred years, with history rooted in farming, the corner shop and the cinema.

Gings corner, shown as Furlong's grocer. Early 1900s from long clothes. Credit Patrick Ging.

Mary and Mertie Ging ran the shop which sold groceries, vegetables and lots of other commodities. The far end of the shop was a drapery but they also sold an array of different items there. You could get loose tea and sugar in made-up brown paper bags. Our family shopped there a lot as it was so close. Larry married a refined lady called Lily who came to work in the drapery. I remember her as a natural blonde who wore glasses. Peadar became a priest. Paddy became a draughtsman in the Mill. Tommy worked in the Mill as a fitter and was also

L to R - Alice Matthews, who lived opposite the paper mill, Mary Ging, Unknown, Patsy Cleary and Gerard Grey. Credit Patrick Ging.

Gings shop 1938 playing pontoon. Photo Joe McCreevy, shared by P. Ging, Julie Cotter. L-R, Peter Ging, Mr. Nugent, Joe McCreevy, Jim McDermott, O'Connor & Feeney, boy unknown.

gifted at making model trains. I knew the Ging family well and can say they were very nice people.

As Clondalkin Paper Mills is part of another chapter, I will skip past the 'Time Office' where workers 'clocked' their cards, and the main gate into the yard, where there was a weighing scales for vehicles, and move along to the next residents of the Old Nangor Road.

Right next to the Mill, between the Time Office and Leinster Terrace, Lil

Ging family as members of LDF and Red Cross. Back L to R Larry Ging, Uncle thomas Murphy, Tommy Ging. Front L to R Margaret Ging, Paddy Ging, Mary Ging.

Old Nangor Road showing (L) old RIC barracks (R) Leinster Tce and ahead, Beech Row. Joe Williams photo from 1990s, Clondalkin History Society Archive.

Nolan and her two brothers, Johnny and Tod, lived in a tiny single-storey cottage with a half-door. Lil stood there a lot, looking up and down the road. Sandwiched between the Mill and the cottage was a pig sty where Lil reared a few pigs and at the back of the cottage, she also kept hens. There was a water pump on the road outside Lil Nolan's. Lil hated cars parking in front of her home and she used to throw things on top of the cars.

Christy Hickey, who worked in the Mill, lodged with Lil Nolan for years before he got married. Christy was also a doorman in the cinema which ran in the evenings and for the Sunday matinee. For some reason, he was known as Christy 'Hussey,' although his proper surname was 'Hickey.'

Between the Nolans' cottage and the bridge over the Camac is Leinster Terrace, home to eight families – the Shields, Loughlins, Downeys (Jack Downey was the last of the family to live there), McDermotts (Michael McDermott was the last of the family to live there), Hurrells, Byrnes/Foleys, Muldowneys and the Durnins. As a schoolgirl in the 1930s, Cecilia Loughlin hand wrote several pieces for The School Folklore Collection. Before she married Larry Ging, Lily Ging lodged with the Hurrell family and worked in Ging's shop.

LEINSTER TERRACE

1 Shields. Marv
2 O'Loughlin, J.
3 Downey, H.
4 McDermott. Patrick
5 Hurrell. H.
6 Foley, P.
7 Muldowney, Thomas
8 Durnin, Bridget
Extract Directory of Ireland, 1958.

The bridge afforded a brief glimpse of nature, the river being flanked by greenery, abundant with wildlife and the swans on the Mill Pond, a calm and constant feature.

The Downes, Power and Kelly families lived at Ash Row beside the Mill Pond. Eleanor Kelly (later Goodwin) was the last of the Kelly family to live there.

In the next terrace, Beech Row, Mrs. Devlin, who reared Muriel and Nancy, was in the first house and then there were the Kernans, Cahills, Costellos, Finns and Stynes. Beside Beech Row, the Gorey and McCurtin families lived in a pair of semi-detached two storey houses.

BEECH ROW, Nangor Road

1 Devlin, Mary
2 Devlin, Oliver
3 Murphy, John
4 Cahill, John
5 Finn, Ita
6 Stynes, Bridget
Extract Directory of Ireland, 1958

A tin hut painted green still stands beside the McCurtin's former home. This was the band hut where the local pipe band met for band practice. Passing by you'd hear the learner pipers wailing away on a summer's evening. It was a lovely sight to behold when the band were dressed in their full regalia, all marching to the music, with their leader, Paddy Cooke, carrying their banner. The band played at most local functions.

Practice Hut for Clondalkin Pipe Band. Credit Eddie Mallin.

The Sherry and Erraty families lived in a pair of semi-detached single storey houses with a water pump outside and long gardens behind, which they kept tilled. Both families kept hens and Mrs. Erraty also reared turkeys. Old Mrs. Sherry had a daughter Rosie, who married a man called O'Keeffe. The couple had no children of their own but they raised two boys. Mrs. Sherry grew potatoes and they were the best you ever tasted. Mrs. Sherry and both the Erratys lived to a great age.

An historical society initiative brought forth a piece headed, 'The Erraty Family,' which was published in the journal, 'Sharing Memories,' in summer 1998. It describes how in

Pump on Old Nangor Road between McCurtins and the bandhut. Reynolds Collection 2018.

Old Nangor Rd., view towards CPM, bridge over the Camac and Leinster Terrace. Copy of slide taken by Joe Williams, shared by P. Ging, Clondalkin Historical Society Archive.

1911, the year the Carnegie Library opened, the Erritys went to live over the Library, when Mr. Errity was appointed caretaker-in-residence. Their daughter, Bridget was born there on St. Patrick's night, when a dance was in full swing in the building. In all, eleven children were born in the Library. Tragedy struck when three sons died of influenza in childhood (the '1914 - 1918 'flu').

When he was later employed at Inchicore Works, Mr. Errity used to walk to and from work. He left home at seven in the morning and arrived back as the Angelus bell rang out, when he always lifted his hat. The family eventually moved to the cottage on the Old Nangor Road which was supplied by the Council. I already mentioned Bridget Errity (later Bridget Gregory), who lived at the lodge of Miss O'Rourke's house on the Monastery Road. Another daughter, Kathleen Errity, made a living from sewing from a wooden hut in the garden. Other family members included Carrie, Lil, Vera, Paul, Mannix and Luke.

Next was a field owned by the Dowds which bordered Moore's Lane. Moore's Lane was always a stopping point for the traveller community over the years. It led up to Clonburris House, which was let out. (Strangely, there also appears to have been another house up the Canal called Clonburris House). The McGrath, Brown and Tinkler families lived at Clonburris at different times. George Huddleston, one-time secretary at St. John's Vestry lived in Clonburris cottage. Over the fields from Clonburris House was the ruin of a church ('Old Church') and an old graveyard.

About a mile from the village, along the Nangor Road, fourteen cottages built by the local authority stood in isolation for a long time, backing on to rich farmlands. They were served by a water pump installed by the Council. Some of the families had formerly lived in 'the Huts' on the site of CB Packaging. I can remember some of the families living there – McNallys, Smiths, Hannons, Cooks, Winters,

Clonburris House. McGrath family lived here. Afterwards the Brown family rented it and shared it with the Tinkler family

Delaneys, Gallaghers, McGuinness, Barnes, Smiths, Stanfords, Murphys and McDonalds. When Rosie McDonald married Bertie Higgins, he moved into the McDonald family home. When the Murphy family moved out, the Feighery family, who had formerly lived at the lodge at Deansrath, moved into that house. Those cottages are now surrounded on all sides by new roads and homes.

Next, was an elderly couple, the Goreys, who lived in a tiny cottage in a field with their son, Christy. I knew all the Goreys; Christy, Christy's son Kit, Kit's son Kitser, Kitser's son James and I also met James's three children who live in Kildare. Six generations of the Gorey family, three generations of whom lived on the Old Nangor Road.

Bobby Kelly's house was next. Bobby's great pleasure was tilling his large garden. He kept really straight drills and grew mainly potatoes and cabbage. His sister, Lil Anderson, and Lil's husband, Paddy, lived with him. Paddy Anderson was the only man working in the Mill who could splice a rope, a skill he learned while at sea.

The Andersons, Warrens, Skeffingtons and Geraghtys lived in a row of four council cottages with a water pump outside. Next was a field and then a beautiful bungalow, 'Woodlands,' with manicured gardens, built on Deansrath land. (Mrs. Carney was formerly a 'Hughes').

'Deansrath' was owned in the sixteenth century by the Dean of St. Patrick's Cathedral and was believed to be one of the castles which guarded the Pale. The

Deansrath Castle

Deans sometimes resided there. Occasionally spelt, 'Danesrath,' it was an imposing house on large farm owned by Mrs. Hughes, whom I recall had two boys and two girls. In the Thom's Almanac of 1858, the record shows, 'Peter Hughes, farmer, Danesrath,' while the 1882 edition shows, 'Mrs. Jane Hughes, Danesrath House.' The two Hughes girls married brothers called Carney, both chemists. One of them lived on with Mrs. Hughes and the other I already mentioned lived in 'Woodlands' on the Old Nangor Road. When Mrs. Hughes died, her son, Jackie, returned home from England but he eventually sold up the farm and went back to England. The McGrath family and later the Feighery family lived in the gate lodge at Deansrath. Deansrath is now owned by the State.

As a schoolgirl, Lillie Feighery made several contributions to The Schools Folklore Collection including one about Mrs. Mc Grath's habit of asking her McNulty neighbours to take care of her house when she was going to town on a Saturday. One of them used run up now and again to see if there were anyone near the house. She describes how one such day, Peter McNulty checked the house and although there was nobody there, he saw a little woman combing her silvery hair in an adjacent field, known as 'Mr. Rourke's field.' He ran home and told his mother, who came back with him to the field but there was nothing there at all. She said he must have been dreaming but Peter said he was not, that he distinctly saw the little woman and that he saw that she had a little red comb in her hand.

Deansrath House. Reynolds Collection

Lillie also relates about a place near Deansrath called 'Old Church,' where the ruins of an old castle, church and graveyard were surrounded by a moat. Unusually, there was no public entrance to the graveyard and you had to cross fields to reach it. According to Lillie, some of the tombstones date back to the 17th century and the last person buried there was a Mrs. Gorey in 1925. She also relates how in winter, the moat was full of water, but in summer, a trap-door could be seen but could not be opened. It was said to lead to a tunnel that goes all the way to Maynooth.

The landscape at Deansrath is much changed now, with development having mushroomed around it, but at least St. Cuthbert's Park still retains its hedgerows. The ruins of the fifteenth century St Cuthbert's Church at Kilma-huddrick are still there, near Nangor Castle, but in need of preservation. This church was dedicated to St Cuthbert of Lindisfarne and once belonged to the monks of the Abbey of the Blessed Virgin Mary, dissolved 1539. In 1186, Master Osbertus of Clondalkin gave the lands of Bali-chelmer to the monks along with the chapel and tithes.

St. Cuthbert's Church ruins at Kilma-huddrick

Next was Taylor's bungalow. Mr. Taylor had been a tea planter in India and he suffered at times with the after-effects of malaria. Mrs. Taylor used to show us her gold ring from India, which was in the shape of a snake.

After the Taylor's bungalow, a laneway led up to the home of the McCor-mack family. Mr. McCormack was a fairly raw-boned man who cycled. Mrs McCormack wore a skirt to the ankle, a long jacket and a high-necked blouse. Their only child, a daughter, wore her hair in a 1940s style roll - it was said she was to become a nun – I do not know if this is true.

On past The Dog's Corner was Nangor Castle, a, eighteenth century build-ing in a castellated design. Around 1787, Joseph Budden, a Commissioner for the sale of forfeited estates, bought this property and sold it on to his son-in-law, John Falkiner, who re-built it and added a large Queen Anne style house. When I was growing up, Vincent Hughes owned Nangor Castle and lived there with his wife and family.

A house in the castle yard was home to the Boland family. Mrs. Boland rode a bike with a basket on the handlebars where she kept her handbag. She wore fairly long clothes, a demure lace blouse and a hat. She spoke very softly. Mr. Boland was a big man who smoked a pipe and wore a brown pinstriped suit and a soft hat for Mass. The Boland family cycled to Mass together on Sunday mornings and they used to arrive about ten or fifteen minutes before Mass started. Mr. Boland rode an oversized bike with large springs under the saddle. Their only child, Jim Boland, grew to be tall like his father. He trained as a mechanic with Andy Clancy in his garage at Newlands – Andy lived in a bungalow up the road from Nangor Castle. Later on, the Boland family moved to Laurel Park in Clondalkin village. Jim Boland eventually branched out on his own very successfully and became keenly interested in vintage cars and their restoration. He built up a fine collection of vintage cars.

Later on, Nangor Castle was bought by the Murphy family who farmed there for a number of years. They had three sons; Paddy, Benny and Michael. Both Nangor Castle and Deansrath now belong to the State. The Kelly family lived further along at Ballybane and then, there's Browne's farm.

I heard tell of one young man in this vicinity who fancied a girl who went to a certain Mass in Newcastle but he was too shy to approach her. The story goes that in order to impress her, he used to dress up in riding gear, ride his horse to Mass every Sunday and tie it up outside. However, it is likely that she was never aware he fancied her. Both of them married others.

Foxglove by Monica Sproul (nee Small)

20.
ST. PATRICK'S DAY, EASTER, HALLOW 'EEN, CHRISTMAS, ST. STEPHEN'S DAY AND NEW YEAR

Coming up to St. Patrick's Day, we'd go out into the fields to the best spots for shamrock and gather way more than we'd ever get to use, usually a basin full. As well as shamrock, we wore green rosettes on our coat lapels and green ribbons in our hair, then went to Mass. St. Patrick's Day was a Holy Day of Obligation and we always sang The Hymn to St. Patrick at Mass.

After Mass, we gathered in the village for the spectacle of the St. Patrick's Day parade. Floats were decorated for the parade and participants dressed up in costumes. Lots of bands took part including the Clondalkin Pipe Band, led by Paddy Cook, who had a big head of black curly hair. Children used to march behind the band while Paddy swung his baton. Although there was always a Parade in the city on St. Patrick's Day, we only got to it when our older sisters, Peg or Gwen, took us into town as a treat.

At Easter, we got a mug or a cup, with a chocolate egg on top. There were no birthday celebrations as there are today. We got no presents or cards and did not have birthday parties. Even when there was a cake, there were no candles with everybody around singing 'happy birthday.'

Halloween was another very busy time for children. We'd gouge out

Pipe Band, Clondalkin

the centre of a turnip – not a pumpkin – and make it into the shape of a face. Then we'd light a candle and put it inside. In the daytime, we played games such as 'bobbing apple,' where you bit an apple while it bobbed in a basin of water. Another game was 'snap apple,' where you had to bite an apple dangling on a string - good luck to you if the apple was swinging. We used to eat colcannon, made from a mix of cabbage and mashed potato and afterwards, barm brack, watching out for the ring hidden inside. As darkness approached, dressing up was a big part of the day. Children wore all kinds of clothes and hats to disguise themselves, usually ones that were too big for them. Most importantly, children wore masks or 'false faces,' as we called them, which were held on by an elastic string. The masks varied from images of ghosts, witches and skeletons to animal faces. Some children carried brooms and put on witches' hats. The idea was to cover up completely to disguise your identity.

Groups of us children called to different houses in the neighbourhood. 'Any apples or nuts,' we'd say, once the door opened. We never shouted out, 'trick-or-treat,' which is American. Neighbours used to put apples, nuts or sweets into our collecting baskets. The bigger children often scared the little ones and got a

Hallow 'Een mask ('false face') and typical fireworks.

ticking-off when they got home. The garb was much less elaborate than nowa-days – children improvised, often using the same masks each year.

We never had our own fireworks and I never remember fireworks displays in Clondalkin but the odd time, we'd look out our kitchen window and get a clear view across the fields when any fireworks were let off.

Fireworks were perfectly legal and in plentiful supply; town was the best place to go for the more impressive fireworks. As well as bangers, squibs, rockets, Roman Candles and Catherine wheels, there were nine-hoppers, also called 'gutter bullies' which exploded and jumped indiscriminately nine times, terrorising everybody in their path.

Christmas was a memorable time for us in Raheen; a highlight of winter, the anticipation was enormous. The smell of nutmeg, cinnamon and cloves, while cleaning the dried fruit and the treat of the odd glacé cherry. Taking a turn with the wooden spoon and squabbling to lick the bowl, the taste of the sugary margarine and dried fruit mix. The steamy kitchen and Mam watching the clock.

We made our own mincemeat at Christmas with sultanas, raisins, candied peel, chopped apple, sugar, juice of lemon, cinnamon, nutmeg all mixed together with alcohol to preserve it. Christmas cake used much the same ingredients with the addition of flour, spices, butter, eggs and whiskey.

My mother used to have the cakes and puddings made well before November, wrapped and put away. I remember well the smell of whiskey being poured on the cake again and again. Nearer to Christmas, she'd put on the almond paste and when it was well dried, the Royal icing and then came the Christmas decorations for the top of the cake. Later on came the puddings, mince pies and other goodies.

The real build-up to the festive season started around Our Lady's Feast Day on 8th of December, when people from the country traditionally came to shop in the city. We were among the luckier children brought each year to meet Santa who was invariably ensconced in a decorated grotto or cavern-like corridor in large Department Stores such as Clery's in O'Connell Street, Switzer's in Grafton Street, Tod Byrne's in Mary Street or Pim's in George's Street. All these Department stores are gone now. The city streets were festooned with Christmas lights and jingles played alongside carol singers in full swing. Children wrote to Santa in politer-than-usual terms, listing the presents they hoped to receive. The house was decorated with sprigs of holly and colourful paper-chain decorations hung across from corner to corner of the room. I never remember mistletoe at all. Everybody in the locality was accustomed to going across the fields to collect sticks for the fire but coming up to Christmas, we'd bring home a large tree branch which served as a Christmas tree. Once the tree was home, we hauled out our Christmas decorations and we'd dress the tree with all manner of bobbles and sets of lights. Very few people I knew bought proper Christmas trees. Christmas cards were lined up in the sitting room. We had fires burning all over Christmas, a rare treat.

The excitement reached its peak on Christmas Eve, with the expectation of a visit down the chimney from the great man himself and more importantly, the toys he brought. A glass of whiskey and a piece of cake were left beside the fireplace alongside carrots for Rudolph. Another Christmas treat for some was a trip to a pantomime, usually at the Theatre Royal or the Olympia – my friends, the Coates and McCurtin families used to get tickets every year. Our mother did take some of us to see *Ali Baba and the Forty Thieves* with Jimmy O'Dea and Harry O'Donovan. Getting together with cousins and paying visits over the school holidays made the festive season all the more exciting.

On Christmas morning, my mother was up and out to early Mass and home sharp to start cooking. When the family was smaller, Dad used to kill two cockerels, but later on, we always got a bronze turkey from Mrs. Errity, as we catered for about ten people. Sometimes my father put on the turkey while my mother went to Mass and he always helped with Christmas dinner. The kitchen steamed up with the smell of the turkey as my mother timed the cooking by the pound. I remember the waft of thyme, parsley and lemon, as the turkey was cooking. When the ham was boiled, Mam carefully skinned and scored it and applied a honey-and-sugar glaze. We had all the accompaniments - roast and boiled potatoes, brussel sprouts, carrots, parsnips and celery.

Meanwhile, we were enjoying Santa's gifts, usually dolls and prams for the girls and guns, cowboy outfits and cars for the boys as well as books, games, and annuals. My best presents were dolls and books. The boys in our family got model cars, toy soldiers, trains on tracks and if they were lucky, a new bicycle. Other children were not so lucky – I know of some who got an orange in their Christmas stocking and others who never heard of Santa at all.

Our two bachelor uncles, my father's brothers, Harold and Eddie, always spent Christmas with us. Harold rode his motorbike with Eddie on the back and Grandma in the side car. They brought sweets, usually *Quality Street*, chocolate, nuts, sherry and books such as *Treasure Island, Grimm's Fairytales, Rupert Bear, Bonzo's Annual* and more. We had a big round table that accommodated about six adults as well as a smaller table. We used the window seat for extra seating. All the cutlery was shined and ready, together with best table cloths, napkins and delph. We wore paper hats and pulled Christmas crackers.

After lunch, we played cards as well as board games such as *Ludo* and *Snakes and Ladders*. In the course of the afternoon, we had honey bee bars, sugar barley sweets and liquorice. I remember well the ceremony of cutting the Christmas cake and the taste of cold turkey and stuffing. A sprig of holly decorated the pudding – when the time was right, we poured whiskey on the pudding and set it alight. Nobody in our family drank alcohol but the pudding had stout in it. At teatime, we tucked into Christmas cake and mince pies. The meals and scrumptious food seemed endless.

Afterwards, the tables were cleared and Harold told us ghost stories (he believed in ghosts). If they didn't tell us a specific story we liked, we'd demand to hear it. One well-remembered one is 'The Monkey,' about which they wrote a poem. He also wrote poetry for us, drew for us and generally provided a lot of fun. Uncle Eddie was quieter but loved to play card games such as 'Fish' or 'Snap' or his favourite, 'Old Maid,' when he could be heard laughing heartily at whoever got caught with the Queen. We used to play for sweets. We played for hours, accompanied by lots of noise and disagreements. My father once ticked Eddie off one time for teaching us slang words such as 'okey-dokey' or 'okay, sez you' and so on. When they were gone, we'd gather up our spoils and take our new books to bed for a sneaky read.

On Stephen's Day, the Wren Boys used to call house-to-house, dressed garishly. At one time, the tradition was to carry a wren in a small box singing laments for the unfortunate bird and look to raise money for the funeral. The Wren Boys who called to us were local and they never had a bird with them. Instead, they used to bring a branch of a tree with decorations on it. Our yard gate would creak open and they'd come to the door singing a well-known ditty, usually accompanied by the mouth organ or melodian, expecting to get a few pennies. My mother usually gave them a few pence and off they went. This old Irish custom has almost died out - it is still kept alive in some areas, such as Dingle and Sandymount.

Wren Boys

"The wren, the wren, the king of all birds,
On St. Stephen's Day was caught in the furze;
Up with the kettle and down with the pan,
Pray give us a penny to bury the wran."

Uncle Harold and Eddie joined the family again on St. Stephen's Day arriving on their bikes from Kilmainham. While we always enjoyed their company, it put a stop to us going out on St. Stephen's night as it would have been considered bad manners to leave while they were visiting. They were quite staid and set in their ways. By the times they headed home on their bikes near mid-

Lawlors Hotel, Naas

night, it would have been too late to go out. For that reason, I never got to the most coveted event held on St. Stephen's night, the legendary dinner dance at Lawlor's Hotel in Naas. In 1913, Mrs. Bridget Lawlor had established the hotel in Poplar Square which became renowned in the hospitality business and the hub of Kildare racing. There were many strands to the Lawlor empire – hotel, world-class ballroom and catering business, but my eyes were always fixed on that elusive St. Stephens' night.

On New Year's Eve, Dad used to get us up out of bed to listen out for the peal of the bells from Christ Church Cathedral in Dublin as the clock struck midnight. (He also used to get us up to see the Northern Lights). The ships' hooters in Dublin Port also sounded out to herald in the New Year. I have always loved the sound of bells and the sound of the Angelus ringing out a few times a day. Another sound I love is the ticking of a clock; it is special in old grandfather clocks. The afterglow of Christmas used to take a few days to disperse.

These are incomparable memories I have tried to re-create each Christmas with my own family.

Christmas Geese by Monica Sproul (nee Small)

21.
ALONG THE NINTH LOCK ROAD TOWARDS
LUCAN AND CLOVERHILL

Back to Ging's shop, which stood at the junction of the Old Nangor Road, Orchard Road and Tower Road. I will now take you along the Ninth Lock Road in the direction of Lucan. Right beside Ging's shop, Mrs. Molloy and her children, Nancy and Davey lived in one half of a pair of semi-detached cottages. Next door was Eileen Mahady and her nieces, Mary and Fanny Carroll, who

Gings with Clondalkin Paper Mill in background. Credit Patrick Ging.

came to live there after their parents died. Eileen Mahady married Joe Kelly late in life and they had a son, Jackie Kelly, who still lives along Tower Road.

Originally, the gardens for the Molloy, Mahady and Ging families were directly across the road, but these went by the wayside when the road was widened. A redbrick and granite building which houses the Civic Centre now stands on that corner site, backing on to the Camac river. The Civic Centre provides local access to the services of South Dublin County Council. A sculpture called 'Blip' with its composition relating to the Camac now stands in front of the Civic Centre. The sculpture has four stainless steel elements, one of which is staked in the river bed of the Camac.

Beyond the Camac river was the former rectory, or 'Glebe House,' which was built in the early nineteenth century, on foot of a grant from the Board of Fruits. The Reverend David John Reade was an early occupant but he was reluctant to live there because of the smell of boiling rags from Clondalkin Paper Mill. Although funds were raised to build a new rectory, the money was used instead to extend and repair the Glebe House as the Mill had shut down by the time the funds were in place. In my time, the curate, Reverend Madden, lived there with his family. The Glebe House was eventually sold in 1948 to Clondalkin Paper Mills who used the site to house the Dor Oliver plant.

The former home of the O'Neill family, 'Brookfields,' was beside the rectory. Mrs. O'Neill died young and her husband reared their nine children. He was

CB Packaging Ltd. (Swiftbrook Limited)

strict, but he reared a very nice family. I remember Kathleen, Vera, Mary, Julie and Carmel well and their brothers, John, Tommy, Billy and Mick. I always associate their home with tea and home baking.

An open piece of land beside the O'Neill's was eventually bought by Clondalkin Paper Mills who used to keep a huge truck and trailer there. They used to load up the truck in readiness for a 6 a.m. start to deliver a long-standing weekly order of paper sacks from CB Sacks to a cement factory in Northern Ireland. Beyond this land, a relative of 'The' O'Rahilly kept a piggery.

Two McKeon families lived in houses beyond the piggery. One was a bungalow where the younger McKeon family lived. The McKeon's sold lovely apples and we used to cycle over to buy as many bags of apples as we could carry.

Back to the Mill side of the road. Before the Clondalkin Bag Factory was built, several families lived in wooden huts which once stood on this site. Some families were eventually allocated local authority houses way up the Old Nangor Road, however, it was not an entirely happy event when one of the families was on the move. They could be seen crying and hugging their neighbours goodbye before wheeling away their belongings in a home-made cart or sometimes, a pram.

Hunt passing by the Mill and the 'Huts' c. 1932. Photo accessed years ago Clondalkin Library, origin of photo unknown.

(Top left) House on 9th Lock Rd occupied at one time by Eamon Hynes, Mill Engineer. Kindly shared by Patrick Ging. Clondalkin Historical Archive Society. (Top right) Coursing field, Clondalkin, 1933. (Above) The Committee of the South Dublin Coursing Club. Included in the photo, Captain R.F. Tynan, J. Clyne, B. Hayes.

Micksey Mahon's house, beside the coursing field.

Before CB Sacks was built, the Hynes family lived a large house stood on this site. Mr. Hynes was an engineer in the Mill. CB Sacks, short for Clondalkin/ Bishop Sacks, was built on a long stretch of land at the back of Clondalkin Paper Mills. It was always known simply as 'The Bag Factory.' Several layers of paper made up the paper cement sacks that were stitched together by strong thread. Later on, they changed to stapling them together.

The Dowd family owned the land further on, which was used as a coursing field, known as 'the hare park.' There is no coursing these days. Beyond the coursing field is Micksey Mahon's house and the home of the Barrett family.

Ballymanaggin (9th Lock)
Brookfields – O'Neill, W.
Ellenfield – McKeon, M.
The Bungalow – McKeon, F.
9th Lock House – Palmer, M. publican
9th Lock road, Mahom, M.
9th Lock road House – McCreevy, H.
9th Lock Bridge – Nolan, M. grocer
9th Lock Bridge – Loughlin, P.
14 Co. Council Cottages
Extract from The Directory of Ireland, 1958

The McCreevy lock-keeper family lived in the lodge overlooking the 9th Lock. Nicholas Cahill was also a lock keeper at the 9th lock for a number of years. Lock-keeping tended to run in the same families over generations. Across the road from the McCreevys were the O'Briens. Chris McCreevy and Harry O'Brien made handwritten contributions to The Schools' Folklore Collection.

A cluster of houses around the canal at this point were home to the following families – the Smyths, O'Briens, Murphys, Bolands, 'Jockey' Loughlin and his daughter Marie, James and Mary Power and Kitty and Davey, who lived with them. The foundations and walls of these houses still survive but they are now obscured by trees and shrubs. John Joe Dowling mentioned living in Capps Villa at the 10th lock where his great landlady, Katie McDonald, reportedly gave back some rent if he was absent for a night. Several families lived along the canal – the McDonnells, the Kellys, the Carews and the Sheridans.

10th Lock
Allister, M. Kilmahuddrick
Carey, J. Clonburris Great
McDonald, J., Cappagh

Extract The Directory of Ireland, 1958.

A Cottages at Ballymanaggin, 9th lock, c. 1926. Photo was taken by Emil Otto Hoppe in 1926. Kindly shared by Patrick Ging.

From top: 9th Lock, Clondalkin. Above: Canal boat beyond the 12th Lock, 1959. Kindly shared by Gerard Byrne, Old Clondalkin & Surrounding Districts. Left: Lock keepers cottage, 10th lock, 1940s. Former home of the Stapleton family, was still there in the 1970s. Kindly shared by Gerard Byrne, Old Clondalkin & Surrounding Districts.

The Carey family, who were big dairy farmers, lived at the 10th lock; they originally farmed at Ballyowen House in Lucan. They also owned Gallanstown House at one stage. Mrs. Carey was a Rowntree before she married.

Construction of the Grand Canal started at the site of the 11th Lock in 1756 and by 1779, the canal was officially open for traffic. The first barge that plied the route was owned by Thomas Digby Brooks. Passenger traffic on the canal ceased with the arrival of the railway in 1847 but cargo traffic continued until 1960. Over time, the canal became overgrown and impassable to boats until some clearance in the 1980s afforded access to small pleasure boats.

Back to the 9th Lock. Gibney's pub was across the road and while it still functions as a public house today, it has changed hands and changed name many times. I mostly remember it as 'Palmers,' but for a long time, it was called the Ninth Lock pub. Thom's Almanac for the years 1858 and 1882 records, 'Richard Donnelly, tavern-keeper, 9th Lock.' Porter's Guide and Directory for County Dublin 1912, records, 'Thomas Donnelly, Grocer and Vintner.' Beyond the pub, Station Road branches off to the right, leading over the railway bridge towards Cloverhill, Blackditch, Cherry Orchard, Ballyfermot and Palmerstown. However, I will continue straight ahead towards Lucan and return later to Station Road. First, we pass Nolan's tiny shop on the left and then, the lodge at Cappaghmore.

THE LOUGH & QUAY
The Ninth Lock, Clondalkin
Telephone 573268

Left: Ninth Lock pub, Clondalkin.
Below: Sale of 9th Lock 'country pub'
Clondalkin, 1926.

COUNTRY
THE NINTH LOCK, CLONDALKIN, CO. DUBLIN
(FORMERLY KNOWN AS DONNELLY'S).

LEASE 89 YEARS FROM 1918. YEARLY RENT, £14 4s. 6d.
This attractive Property and Residence comprises—Spirit Bar, with modern
grocery department, large bar parlour, with service window; yard, with gate entrance
stabling and motor house, also paddock (about half an acre), with frontage to the Canal;
residence adjoining has hall entrance, and comprises diningroom, 3 bedrooms, and is
remotely placed from similar business premises, being about 3½ miles from Lucan and 3
Palmerstown. A feature is that a profitable business can be conducted by a resident
small expense. The rent, taxes, and licence duty amount to about 14s. weekly. Or
from AUCTIONEER. Conditions of Sale from
JOHN J. SHIEL, Solicitor, 28 Bachelor
ANDREW J. KEOGH, Auctioneer, 10 LR. ORMOND

Cappaghmore House, situated between the Grand Canal and the railway, was built around 1800 and comprised the main house with yard and outbuildings and the lodge. Its name appears interchangeable between Cappagh and Cappaghmore and it has a history of varied occupation. The first occupants were farmers, the Whitton family. A record in Thom's Almanac of 1858 then shows, 'Patrick Norris, Esq., Cappagh House,' while the 1882 edition records, 'Henry Mathews, Esq., Cappagh House.' Porter's Guide and Directory for County Dublin 1912 records 'N.C. Simpson, Manager of Messers. Kynoch's Paper Mills.' As the property was for use by managers and staff, several residents are recorded, including Thomas McGann and James Dowd, as well as Mrs. Forbes Watson. In 1913, after the death of Alexander Watson, an analytical chemist, the house was sold to Dr. Andrew Ryan, Clondalkin's Dispensary doctor and father of the late Archbishop Dermot Ryan. Later, the Staunton, McGann, Gregory, Mullaney, Mullins and McCausland families lived there. Judge Sealy, sold it on to Frawleys, of Thomas Street Department store fame.

The Gallagher family then bought Cappagh House. Mrs. Gallagher came from the Urney chocolate family who had re-located from Northern Ireland and set up a factory in Tallaght. Apparently, Mrs. Gallagher used to make fudge

Gate Lodge at Cappaghmore, built c.1840. Reynolds Collection.

and toffee for her children and neighbours, then she started to make it for parties and out of that grew Urney's chocolate. Her son, Redmond Gallagher, was keen on motor racing. Johnny Matthews maintained a racing car for him which he raced in the Phoenix Park. The Gallaghers sold Cappaghmore on to Commander and Lady Mack. Lady Mack was the four-times-married sister of the 3rd Duke of Westminster. Apparently, Lady Mack brought her own staff to Cappaghmore, including the stableman and his family who lived in the gate lodge. Tommy Wade, who rode a horse called 'Dundrum' at the R.D.S. Horse Show in Ballsbridge, used to stay with Lady Mack when she lived there. Lady Mack died in 1966.

The next occupants of Cappaghmore House were the Crossley-Cook family, followed by Dermot Ryan (of Ryan Hotels) and then, the Mahon family. Some remember kennels at Cappaghmore, where you could leave your dogs when you went on holidays. The house still stands but most of the surrounding land was sold years ago and re-developed as the Cappaghmore housing estate.

Across the road from Cappaghmore was the Weatherwell tile factory, owned and run by Mr. O'Rahilly, son of 'The O'Rahilly.' The Sheehan family home was before the railway bridge. H.F. Dickson is recorded as the occupant of the next property, Moorefield House. In 1967, Rose Leonard is recorded as living there.

After the bridge, there were four bungalows, however, I only knew two of the families who lived there – Reidys and Higgins. My sister, Gwen, was a friend of Betty Higgins and I also knew Betty's sister, Violet, and brother, Bertie. Bertie Higgins was one of the eldest in the family – first, he became an army man and subsequently, he became a photographer.

NEILSTOWN BUNGALOWS
1 Murphy, T.
2 O'Rourke. P.
3 Higgins. H.
4 Reidy, G.
Cooleven—Logue, J. £29 10s.
Moorfield—Leonard, Bridget
Neilstown House—Smith, Mrs. £183
The Bungalow—Smith, E.
Extract from The Directory of Ireland, 1958.

Neilstown House (demolished)

Continuing towards Lucan, the families I recall living along the way were the Kinsella, Kelly, Grogan and Crosby families. The road eventually leads to Esker, where there are at least three graveyards. Maurice Walsh, author of the renowned story, 'The Quiet Man' is buried at Esker.

Neillstown (sic) House was built in the fifteenth century by Sir William Neill (otherwise 'Neale'), a tanner, who also bestowed gifts on the Church before his death. For a while, the property was home to monks until the O'Rourke family of High King fame lived there. They ran a tannery and bakery. From the 1880s, it was owned by John Smith who resided there along with some of his relatives, the Durie and Haddow families. Thom's Almanac of 1858 records, 'Mr. John Durie, Neilstown House,' while the 1882 edition records, 'Mrs. Durie, Neilstown.' Porter's Guide and Directory for County Dublin, 1912, records, 'Joseph Smith, Neilstown.' Lewis's *Topographical Dictionary of Ireland*, 1837, shows Captain Foss as the occupant of Neilstown Lodge.

NEILSTOWN COTTAGE
1 Kellv A.
2 Roe, P.
3 Kinsella, W.

Extracts from The Directory of Ireland, 1958.

Neilstown Gate Lodge at former entrance to Neilstown House, now Letts Fuel Yard. Reynolds Collection.

Neilstown Lodge on the 9th Lock Road to Lucan. Photo credit Tom Ging.

Mr. Smith was an Englishman and model farmer who had a great plough-man in a Mr. Mahady, who lived with his family in the lodge. When Mr. Ma-hady became an invalid, his son, Jimmy, the eldest of eight children, had to cut short his education at the Monastery School to take over the role so that the family could live on in the lodge. He continued in this role until he married Brigid Kelly from Esker and got a job in Clondalkin Paper Mills. His mother moved into a tiny cottage beside Ging's by the Mill. The local authority issued a Compulsory Purchase Order in 1978 which forced Ted Smith to leave Neill-stown House. The house has since been demolished.

Travelling beyond Neillstown House, the houses became very spread out. Some of the children from that stretch who went to school in Clondalkin included the Sheridan, Fogarty, Sheedy and Ryder children. They Ryders lived in a detached house and any time you passed by, there was a fresh round cake of bread out cooling on the window sill. They had two girls and twin boys and the family cycled everywhere.

'The Bush of Balgaddy' (now gone)

Various families lived opposite the Ryders at St. Ronan's, including J. Mock-ler, then the Doyle, Carroll, Boyle, Stoney and Lawler families. A record in Thom's Almanac of 1858 shows, 'Mr. James Doyle, St. Ronan's,' while the 1882 edition shows, 'Patrick O'Rourke Moran, Esq., St. Ronan's.' Porter's Guide and Directory for County Dublin, 1912, records, 'Mrs. Stoney, St. Ronan.' During my childhood, the Boland family lived there. I remember the Bolands travelling to Mass by pony and trap.

Balgaddy is situated along an old historic route between Royal Tara and the House of Hospitality in Tallaght, in an area once known as 'the Royal Manor of Esker.' In 1901, the population of Balgaddy comprised 85 people. Balgaddy translated from Irish means 'town of thieves,' alluding to a spot where highway-men plied their trade. With the development of modern road networks in this area, only small sections of the original road now remain, such as St. Finian's church ruins.

KISHOGUE HOUSE, CLONDALKIN, CO. DUBLIN
ON 112 ACRES (S.M.) APPROX.
Midway between Lucan and Clondalkin; 7 miles from Dublin

Kishogue House, home of the Mooney family.

Legend has it that one stormy night, a priest called for shelter to a house beside the 'bush' of Balgaddy, at the old junction of Clondalkin Road and Lynch's Lane. The people in the house turned him away because he had performed an unpopular marriage. The priest took shelter in a nearby shed, but before he went, he said that the grass would grow around the door of the house, that the bush would fall and that the name of those who turned him away would never again be in the Bush House. People say that this came to pass. The bush did fall, but was replaced by another, which vanished when development began in this area. According to Deasmhumhan MacCarthaigh in "Gleanings from the District of Lucan," the new bush was an 'unworthy successor.' Today there no sign of either house or bush.

Kishogue House, near to 'the Bush,' was home to the McCutcheon and Mooney families at different times. The Passmore family lived at 'The Bush of Balgaddy.' Records show the occupants of the nearby 'St. Mark's' variously as H. Phillips Esq., Robinson, Hugh Lecky and J. Doyle and the resident of St. Mark's Lodge is recorded as a Mrs. Byrne.

Ballyowen House, c. 1901. Kindly shared by Gerard Byrne, Old Clondalkin & Surrounding Districts.

Balgaddy

St. Ronan's – Boland, Josephine

Goodwin, A., grocer

Cullen, E.

Hickey, C.A.

Byrne, D.

Ryder, C.

Mooney, J.

Callaghan, C.

Nolan, P.

Ballyowen – Byrne, A.

Wynards – Bryne, -.

Sheedy, J.

Kishogue – Mooney, W.   £150

Springfield - Vacant   £178 5s.

Extract from The Directory of Ireland, 1958.

The Bewley family, of Bewley's Oriental Café renown, lived on an estate at Ballyowen. In the 1890s, Ernest Bewley partially re-built Ballyowen House and sold it in 1925 to the Masterson family, who sold it on to the Carey family. Ballyowen House returned to Bewley hands when Victor Bewley bought it. The Bewleys were Quakers, renowned for generosity to their workers, giving them

DOCKRELL LIMITED
AUCTION THURSDAY, 15TH JANUARY, 1925
AT OUR PROPERTY SALEROOMS, SOUTH GT. GEORGE'S ST
(BY INSTRUCTIONS OF ERNEST BEWLEY, ESQ.).
BALLYOWEN & BALGADDY, CLONDALKIN,
CONTAINING 174 STATUTE ACRES
ONE OF THE BEST GRAZING FARMS IN CO. DUBLIN.

Mr. Bewley's famous Pedigree Herd of Jersey Cattle have been grazed on this Farm for many years. It has every requirement and attraction that a farmer can want. The Land is prime, in great heart, and free from disease. There is an abundant water supply on all parts of the farm. The fences and gates are good. The County road runs throughout the Farm, affording easy access to every field. There is a comfortable two-storey House, with new slated roof, and containing 7 rooms, tiled kitchen, hot bath, etc. The Out-offices are all in perfect order, and comprise cow shed for 68 head, fed from the head, with water laid on; call houses, stabling, car sheds, long range of pig houses, engine house, root store, hay barn to hold about 250 tons, lofts, yardman's house, 4 cottages. The farm is exactly 7 miles from O'Connell's Bridge. Held subject to terminable annuities amounting to £176 4/4 per annum. Valuation £210 5/-.
Orders to View can be had from the AUCTIONEERS.

Ballyowen - advertisement for sale of Bewley's farm, 1925.

Ballyowen Castle. Kindly shared by Gerard Byrne, Old Clondalkin & Surrounding Districts.

shares of the business, also, for their benevolence to single mothers in their employment, long before any social welfare benefits were available.

Larkfield was situated between Ballyowen House and Irishtown House, around the Rowlagh area. Larkfield was originally owned by the Lord Chief Justice, Gerald Fitzgibbon. The Mulcahy-Morgan family lived there before the Roche family moved in. They were famous for horse-dealing and provided horses to the army. John Jackman then lived at Larkfield until it eventually became the premises of the Mount Street Farm Club, a charity based at Mount Street, which had been set up for the unemployed of Dublin.

The charity's principle was to get men working to provide for their families, instead of relying on 'the dole' or charity, also, to alleviate food shortages in the city in wartime. As the Club's core functions had been superseded by the Department of Social Welfare services by the 1970s, it changed direction and instead began supporting start-up businesses and training schemes for the unemployed. The Club's property was sold in 2006 and a charitable trust was incorporated.

Although Balgaddy lies on the border of Clondalkin and Lucan, it was part of the Parish of Clondalkin until 1953, when Lucan became a parish in its own right and Balgaddy was absorbed into Lucan parish. Up to then, the people of Balgaddy made the long trudge to the Church and schools in Lucan, but customarily travelled to the Parish Church in Clondalkin for Confirmation.

Mount Street Club Farm House, Larkfield near Rowlagh.

Mount Street Farm Club, Lark-field House. From top: tractor; children's percussion band; piggery (kindly shared by Gerard Byrne, Old Clondalkin & Surrounding Districts). Bottom right: St. Judes, the last pub in Balgaddy.

Left: Houses at Cloverhill Road, built c. 1900. Right: Former Railway Station at Cloverhill Road.

In the early part of the twentieth century, Balgaddy had its own pub beside the roundabout at Earlsfort. The present country house - called 'St. Jude's' - was the local hostelry. Goodwin's shop was the only other commercial business in the area.

Let us return to the 9th Lock and Station Road, which branched off after the canal and led towards Cloverhill. In 1842, the Great Southern and Western Railway Company Limited was formed. In 1846, Clondalkin railway station opened. Initially, the station flourished but eventually it closed to passenger traffic and one hundred years later, in 1947, the station closed to goods traffic as well. The Byrne, Fagan, Blackburn and Fallon families lived along here. Mr Fallon was the station master. The Thom's Almanac for 1882 records, 'John Nonan, stationmaster' and Porter's Guide and Directory for County Dublin 1912, records, 'P. Delahunty, Stationmaster.'

STATION ROAD

Clondalkin Concrete Ltd.
Cullen. Ard-na-Green
Tinkler, J.—Station Bridge
Metal Refiners
6 Co. Council Houses

Extract The Directory of Ireland, 1958

Left: Clondalkin Railway Station late 1940s Ned Gleeson, Signalman, with his children, Kathleen and Joe. Photo credit James O'Dea, courtesy of Breda O'Byrne, nee Kinsella. Right: Stationmaster at work. Kindly shared by Gerard Byrne, Old Clondalkin & Surrounding Districts.

Since the 1990s, commuter trains operated by Iarnród Éireann (Irish Rail) run between Heuston Station in Dublin and Kildare town. North of Bawnogue, a new station, Fonthill, replaced rather than supplemented the previous station. The original Clondalkin station was demolished in 2008 to facilitate a four line track, allowing express trains to pass through without affecting local services on the Kildare line.

Over the railway bridge and on the right was the Daltons' house, Cloverhill, a two-storey bow-fronted late eighteenth century house. In Lewis's Topographical Dictionary of Ireland, 1837, 'D. Kinalson' is recorded as resident at Cloverhill. A record in Thom's Almanac of 1858 shows, 'N.B. McIntire, Esq., Cloverhill.' McIntire's three daughters all married Falkiner men, presumably the Falkiners of Nangor Castle. Porter's Guide and Directory for Coun-

Cloverhill House (demolished), once occupied by D'Alton family (entrance was near to Clondalkin Concrete). Kindly shared by Gerard Byrne, Old Clondalkin & Surrounding Districts.

ty Dublin 1912, records the following residents at Cloverhill, 'Nicholas F. Archdale, Cloverhill,' also, 'William F. Aylward, Cloverhill Cottage.' Subsequently, Cloverhill was home to the D'Alton, Hart and Cleary families, then Bernard Walsh. The Daltons used to travel to Mass by in a trap pulled by a large horse. When harnessed, the shafts of the trap were up in the air to allow the harness to rest on the horse's back which meant that the Daltons had to hang on as otherwise, they would slide to the back of the trap. Cloverhill is now demolished and the land was swallowed up by the construction of the Western Parkway.

Close to their place was the entrance to Clondalkin Concrete, a company with a large workforce.

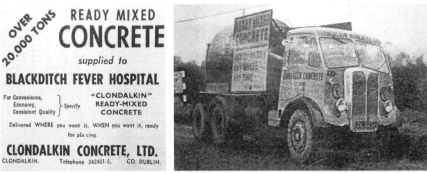

Top left: Clondalkin Concrete 1950. Kindly shared by Gerard Byrne, Old Clondalkin & Surrounding Districts. Top right: Clondalkin Concrete truck. Photo credit Maureen Scott. Above: Group outside Collinstown House.

Collinstown House stood on the opposite side of the road to the present day Wheatfield Prison. The Reverend Hugh Wilson is listed as its earliest owner but many people lived there over subsequent years, either as owners or tenants, including the Cane family, Major Hamilton, polo player and friend of the comedian and film actor, Jimmy Edwards. A record in Thom's Almanac of 1858 shows, 'Arthur Beresford Cane, Esq., Collinstown House,' while the 1882 edition shows, 'Val Brown, Esq., at Collinstown House.' Porter's Guide and Directory for County Dublin 1912, records, 'The Hon. Mrs. McCausland, Collenstown (sic) House.' For a time, Major Kirkwood leased Collinstown House. The poet, John Betjeman, who had already stayed as a guest, subsequently leased the house with his wife, Penelope, when he became press attaché at the British Embassy in Dublin. An elderly lady from the Jameson family, connected to Major Hamilton, was also living there during the Betjemans' time there. The Betjemans became well-known in Clondalkin and John Betjeman served on the Select Vestry of St John's Church for several years.

John Betjeman, an only child, appears to have had a lonely childhood. He took comfort from his teddy bear Archibald (Ormsby-Gore), 'the one person who never let him down.' The story goes that Betjeman used to bring the teddy to bed with him at night. Archibald featured in his children's story, 'Archie and the Strict Baptists,' and in his poem, 'Archibald,' in which the bear is temporarily stuffed in the loft for fear of he would appear "soft" to his father. The poem reflects Betjeman's fondness for his stuffed toy, and helps to explain why Betjeman became, for Britain, 'the nation's teddy bear.' Archibald was famously the inspiration for Sebastian Flyte's teddy, 'Aloysius,' in Evelyn Waugh's *Brideshead Revisited*. Sir John Betjeman was made a Knight of the Realm in 1969 and appointed British Poet Laureate in 1972. He had national treasure status in Britain until his death. Archibald, and Betjeman's toy elephant Jumbo, were in his arms when he died in 1984. He is buried in Cornwall.

In Lewis's *Topographical Dictionary of Ireland*, 1837, Reverend M. O'Callaghan is recorded as the resident of Collinstown Cottage. In my time, an elderly couple lived in the gate lodge.

The walk up to the house, known as Lover's Walk, was said to be haunted. As a schoolboy, John Tully of Collinstown made several contributions to The School Folklore Collection. Collinstown House was unfortunately demolished.

COLLENSTOWN (sic)

Collinstown Pk.—Kirkwood, T. W
Wheat-field—O'Neill, Dr.
Cloverhill—Vacant
Clover Cottage—Walsh. —.
St. Anne's—Tracey, Denis
Extract The Directory of Ireland, 1958.

Wheatfield House was home in its early years to Edward B. Swift, church warden of St. John's, a role also taken by its next resident, Edward Howell. Later residents included the McKenna and Smith families and Cornelius Kehely. Wheatfield House was demolished and the Western Parkway and Wheatfield

Left: Wheatfield House. Right: Fire at Captain Pim's stables, Wheatfield House.

Left: Sir John Betjeman with his toys, teddy, Archibald and elephant, Jumbo. Right: Vera Lawler in front of Irishtown House, c. 1917.

Prison stand there now, as well as Cloverhill Prison. Thom's Almanac of 1858 records, 'Edward P. Swift, Esq., Wheatfield' while the 1882 version records, 'Thomas Long, Esq., Wheatfield.' 'Mrs. West, Gallinstown,' is also recorded in Thom's Almanac for 1882.

COLDCUT

Irishtown—Lawlor, Miss
Harelawn—Connolly. ML
Cherry Orchard—Byrne, -Vera £119 £12

Extract The Directory of Ireland, 1958.

Irishtown House, home of the Lawler family, was situated near Harelawn. Cherry Orchard, as the name suggests, was once a farm before Cherry Orchard Hospital was built on the site.

Wrens by Monica Sproul (nee Small)

22.
THE WAR YEARS

As I was aged five when World War II started, I remember the war years well. Although Ireland was neutral, precautions still had to be taken to combat the difficulties with imports and exports and the danger of attack, so the Government brought in certain measures during this period, which was known as 'The Emergency.'

There was a scurry to listen to news bulletins on the radio and newsreels shown before films in cinemas kept people abreast of the happenings. Everybody was obliged to keep lights off at night and employ 'blackout' curtains to cover the windows, to avoid attracting the attention of stray bomber planes. Any breach was liable to detection by the glimmerman, a 'gas' man and agent of the State, briefed to ensure compliance. His modus operandi was to swoop unexpectedly and touch your cooker to see if it was still hot. Luckily, we did not have gas. At one stage, bombs were dropped on the North Strand and beside the cricket ground in the Phoenix Park.

During the Emergency, The Turf Board, now known as Bord na Mona, was established to organise the cutting of turf on the midland bogs for provision to cities and towns. Thousands of tons of turf were transported to Dublin and stored in high mounds of up to thirty feet along the main road of the Phoenix Park, Chesterfield Avenue, and on the Fifteen Acres. Wire bales and timber bollards, side-by-side and up to roof height, were placed at intervals of about 200 yards along the road, to prevent planes using it as a runway. As this made it hard for cyclists to get by, some got together and dragged the bollards apart, leaving gaps so that cyclists could at least dismount and negotiate around the turf banks. Every now and then, the powers-that-be closed off the gaps again. For the duration of the Emergency, this gaps-no gaps performance continued.

As Ireland was neutral, German and English pilots sometimes strayed off course and once they landed, they were detained at the Curragh Camp in Kildare. Naturally, the Germans and the Allies were held in segregated areas. However, the custody rules were relaxed enough and permitted those incarcerated to attend local dances and as a result, some met and married Irish girls. Many did not want their detention to end, for fear of being repatriated and quickly returned to the front. The film, 'The Brylcreem Boys,' shows some of these men getting into scrapes with their enemies behind bars at the Curragh. Although Ireland maintained its neutral stance, any stray British planes used to mysteriously find their way back to England within a few weeks.

During the war, the Government distributed gas masks to everybody. You had to try them on to ensure they fitted, but they were awfully claustrophobic and left you gasping for breath. Our initials were printed on the square brown boxes that contained our masks. Years later, the gas masks were still in our shed gathering dust.

Turf banks in the Phoenix Park during WWII (before the bales and bollards).

The Government were in constant fear of invasion during World War II, so they kept the Irish army trained up by organising military manoeuvres from time to time. In 1941, one such review took place that lasted about two or three weeks, involving one army group advancing towards Dublin, pitted against another army group in defence. Farmers kicked up holy war because some of the army trucks were crossing their land.

Due to neutrality, Ireland refused England the use of Irish ports during the war, so England remained hostile and disinclined to trade with Ireland. However, there was no issue when Ireland exported milk and meat to England, as they had food shortages and in turn, England sent across coal, but it was the lowest grade of coal, called 'slack.' Slack was difficult to burn and gave out little heat - sometimes it had to be mixed with timber and turf. Inchicore Works built a bricketting plant where the slack was compressed with the addition of a type of concrete 'dusting' into usable fuel briquettes.

All fuel was rationed, petrol, paraffin oil and gas. With the scarcity of fuel, public transport services declined - train services and bus services were delayed or curtailed. Cars belonging to the priest, the doctor, and taxis were considered 'essential' but even then, they had to operate on limited petrol supplies. It meant most people were on foot or on bikes again, and the pony and trap and the horse and cart were back in vogue as modes of transport.

Some more affluent motorists had gas contraptions fitted to the roof of their cars at the start of World War II. This new-fangled invention was used not alone in Ireland, but in England too. A number of vans used to go around, delivering the fuel supply. It looked like a massive balloon fastened to the roof that stretched the full length of the car. The door of the car boot was removed and the boot itself was used as a receptacle for two upright gas cyclinders that supplied the car with fuel - one of them was an open fire fuelled by coke. The car smoked as it went along the road, its huge balloon swaying. In 1940, a new Government Order banned these gas contraptions and rationed fuel supplies even further.

Standard issue gas mask. The Government supplied them for every member of the household.

```
    (iii) in the case of soap powder - at the

          rate of one coupon for twelve ounces

          of soap powder,

(e) where the appropriate number of the

    appropriate coupons in respect of soap supplied

    on any occasion is less than one, it shall be

    treated as one.
```

During the war, it was almost impossible to buy a tube or a tyre for a bicycle, so many tried out ingenious ideas, such as lining the tyre with strips of canvas or stuffing them with hay. Some people with contacts who worked on the docks were able to procure bicycle tyres on the black market - sailors brought them in from abroad. The price was way over the odds, up to a pound per tyre.

As many foods and various goods were scarce during the war, the Government brought in a system of rationing, which meant that some goods were only available by way of coupons supplied by the Government. 'Ration Cards' were introduced for every citizen so that essential commodities such as tea, coffee,

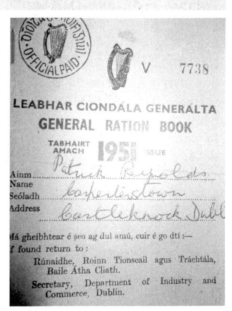

Top: Extract of Government Order, 1942 – rationing of soap. Courtesy of Oireachtas website. Above: My husband's Ration Book 1951 (There was still rationing years after WWII and it was even worse in Britain).

sugar, clothes and other items could be shared out. The 'card' specified the entitlements for each household, highlighting the requisite number of coupons required for their ration of goods such as tea, sugar, butter, rashers, etc.

On a weekly basis, customers went to the shop and were obliged to produce their ration book to shop owners when asking for their rations. At one stage, the tea ration was one ounce per person per week; sugar was eight ounces and butter was six ounces. The rationed items were weighed by the shopkeepers into brown bags, then the top of the bag was folded down and the customer's name was written clearly on the bag. For the duration of the war, some items were not available at all, especially types of fruit that could not be grown in Ireland, such as citrus fruits and bananas. Another prized item was ladies nylons. During the war, the Irish sung a version of Vera Lynn's sweethearts' song 'Bless Them All':

> *Bless 'em all. Bless 'em all.*
> *The long and the short and the tall,*
> *Bless De Valera and Seán McEntee,*
> *They gave us the black flour,*
> *And the half-ounce of tea.*

Clothing and footwear were strictly rationed so if you wanted to look smart, you had to adopt various strategies. Shoes and boots were re-soled and the uppers were patched. Tailors 'turned' suits by unpicking the seams and re-stitching the garment with the unworn side of the material out. Shirts were patched and the collars were 'turned.' Coupons were often 'pooled' to buy items for special occasions. In particular, nylon stockings were prized, so women were vigilant to avoid snagging. Women used nail varnish to stop ladders in nylons and they mended any runs with the finest of needles and thread. As nylons generally had a single seam up the back, some ladies took to using a colour on their bare legs and drawing a vertical line as a 'pretend' seam from the heel up along the calf to mimic the seamed stockings.

Due to the shortage of imports, land in the Phoenix Park was leased to Dublin Corporation for use as allotments. The Government imposed compulsory tillage for farmers as no grain was being imported. Every farmer was obliged to make the best use of any land and sow a certain acreage of wheat, at risk of prosecution for non-compliance. The Compulsory Tillage Order was policed by Government Inspectors. A severe outbreak of Foot and Mouth in March 1941 spread over much of the country - over 550 farms had outbreaks and thousands of animals had to be slaughtered. It took months before the disease was finally eradicated.

As many landed estates lay idle, they had to be sublet in order to comply with the Compulsory Tillage Order. Some farmers rented idle land for tillage, but as manpower was necessary for ploughing the fields and sowing crops, it was sometimes necessary to take on extra help or draft in their children to give a hand. Some tractors were going 24/7 at the busiest times with many staying up all night long to keep things running, with the aid of lamps. People took to cultivating the smallest of patches in order to ensure a supply of food. Even front gardens were dug to grow potatoes, vegetables and fruit trees.

Wages and the prices of all essentials were controlled and any proposed increases had to be Government-sanctioned. As there were few imports, we had to rely on Irish wheat for bread-making, but the bread produced from Irish wheat was dirty white in colour, stodgy and lumpy. You often had to pick the lumps out. It was very unpalatable and hard to get it down without butter and jam to add a bit of taste. It was only then that people realised the extent of our reliance on imported wheat.

Poppies by Monica Sproul (nee Small)

23.
THE CAMAC RIVER AND ITS MILLS.

Our family have been intimately acquainted with the Camac River all our lives. We grew up beside the Camac, fished there, played there and learned how to swim there. I met my husband at Clondalkin Paper Mills, which was situated on the Camac. My late brother, Jim Small, chaired the Clondalkin Angler's Association and often stocked the Camac with trout and rescued swans on the river. When he moved from Clondalkin, Jim went to live in the terrace of redbrick houses alongside Kilmainham Jail, which back onto the Camac. Given his lifelong dedication to the Camac, we scattered part of Jim's ashes in the Camac at Clondalkin. The family therefore had an inextricable emotional link with the river.

The River Camac rises in the Dublin Mountains at Mount Seskin. It is one of the larger rivers in Dublin at 24km in length. Sometimes spelled Cammock, or, historically, Cammoge or Cammoke, in Irish it is An Chamóg or Abhainn na Camóige, meaning 'crooked water.' The river flows through Brittas pond and the Slade valley and flows under the N7 at Kingswood and then proceeds through Kilmatead, where there is a small lake with islands. After this, it flows into Corkagh Park where over centuries it was diverted into numerous ponds to provide water for local mills. Many of the ponds are now in poor condition as water levels have dropped and the ponds have silted up.

At a point we always knew as 'the Sandy Hole,' one sluice controlled water going downstream and another sluice channeled water into tributaries. One tributary went into the big pond beside Moyle Park College and the other tributary went into a second pond. At this second pond, there's a waterfall between two concrete walkways and a second waterfall further along but these waterfalls diminished considerably when the ponds went dry. Beyond this point, the river water was harnessed into use by Clondalkin Paper Mills (formerly Leinster Paper Mills) when it was in operation. The 'Mill Pond,' situated on the old Nangor Road, stored water for future use by Clondalkin Paper Mills. Following demolition of the Mill, this pond was covered over to make way for a car park for the present day Mill Shopping Centre.

After this point, the Camac flows by Watery Lane in Clondalkin and on to Drimnagh and Inchicore, where it is tunnelled under the Grand Canal near Golden Bridge. The river runs behind Kilmainham Jail Museum and under Bow Bridge in Old Kilmainham. Just downstream of the Liffey freshwater limit at Islandbridge weir, the Camac discharges into the River Liffey via a culvert under Heuston Railway Station. Much of its course is now culverted and covered by buildings.

Historically, the Camac river was critical to the development of a monastic settlement at Clondalkin and to the early development of Dublin as a city. During the eighteenth century, small industries such as corn mills, flour mills, oil mills, gunpowder mills and textile mills started to develop along the Camac, as the river provided the requisite power supply for water wheels. It thus became a focal point in the lives of Clondalkin inhabitants as it provided the life blood for many businesses. The Camac receives many tributaries along its course and the water supply could be regulated by means of weirs, sluices, water channels known as millraces and it could be stored for future use by means of mill ponds.

With increasing literacy, the demand for book and writing paper grew and as a result, paper mills sprouted up along the river as water was needed for the pulping process as well as driving the power supply.

I will trace the principal mills along the Camac river down from its upper to lower reaches.

Swift Brook Paper Mill

Swiftbrook was established in the mid eighteenth century. A record in '*The Dublin Book Trade 1550 – 1800*' shows that John McDonnell acquired a flour mill at Saggart and converted it into a paper mill. The mill ran until around 1972 and played an important role in the economic and social life of Saggart, employing more than 400 people at the height of the famine. It also formed a unique industrial aspect of an otherwise agricultural countryside. Swiftbrook was well-recognised as a producer of high quality paper, used in the production of bank notes, stamps, envelopes, official Government documents and note paper brands such as Erin and Ancient Irish Vellum, well-known to generations of Irish people. Swiftbrook also produced the paper on which the 1916 Proclamation was printed. A record in '*The Dublin Book Trade 1550 – 1800*' indicates it was producing '*the best paper in Ireland*' and supplying Government offices.

Top: Saggart Mill. Unloading pulp ready for re-opening in 1929. Kindly shared by Patrick Ging. Above: Swiftbrook Mill chimney and single-storey mill building at Saggart.

Swiftbrook upper mill buildings at Saggart. Photo courtesy National Library Ireland.

Swiftbrook Paper Mill was demolished in 2001. The Swiftbrook mill chimney, rag store and single-storey mill building are protected structures, restored during 2014 with partial funding under the Built Heritage Investment Scheme. They are currently at the centre of a campaign by Saggart residents to retain, preserve and promote the history and heritage of their village in the face of development.

In the early days of paper-making, rags were required for the paper milling process. In its efforts to encourage the paper industry, the Royal Dublin Society in 1746 created a precedent in the history of paper-making by offering premiums for the collections of rags. As a result, £5,000 worth of rags were gathered weekly in the city and county to supply the main paper mills near Dublin. A record exists in 'The Dublin Book Trade 1550 – 1800' that in 1745, Michael McDonnell offered to give ready money for linen rags, 1d-2½d per pound at his house on Merchant's Quay. The use of rags discontinued once pulp could be imported from Scandinavia, but during WWII when no pulp was available, rags and even straw came into use for paper-making.

The McDonnell family had mills at Templeogue and Tallaght and they were also heavily involved with paper mills. The Mill heritage is reflected in the name of a modern housing estate, Millbrook Lawns.

Paper-making machinery was notoriously expensive and had to be constantly improved on, with the result that the Irish paper mills always found it difficult to compete with British paper mills. There were constant calls on the Government to increase duties on imported paper in order to ensure the survival of the Irish paper-making industry. In 1773, Darby McDonnell signed a document in an effort to support the Irish paper-making industry: 'Memorial of the paper-makers for increased duties on imported paper.'

By 1907, only six paper mills were working in Ireland, employing a mere 600 people.

Fairview Oil Mill

Fairview Oil Mill was a small flour mill where grain was ground for local consumption.

The occupier recorded in Griffith's Valuation of the 1850s is shown as a Peter McNally and a Joseph Henry Esquire. The record in Thom's Almanac of 1858 shows, 'William B. Fottrell, Oil Mills, Fairview.' The complex included a house, offices, yard, oil-mill, pond and a small garden. The Oil Mill used a four step process of cleaning, crushing (using mill stones), roasting and pressing flaxseed (and rape seed) to produce linseed oil for use in lamps, medicines and as a base for paint. The waste from the process was made into Linseed Cake, sold as feed for livestock.

Although the mills are marked on the Ordnance Plan of the Parish of

Fairview Oil Mill ('Clondalkin Oil Mills 1861') – Photo courtesy of Clondalkin History Society.

Clondalkin back in 1870, they are marked as 'Old.' Here is an extract from a description:

> A *valuation of the site was recorded in 1845 and it states that there existed a Logwood and an Oil Mill on the site. Both mills operated 10 hours per day and for 9 months of the year but at the time of the valuation the mills were idle undergoing repairs. The Oil and Logwood mills used water wheels of 14.5 and 14 feet diameter respectively. Ponds, culverts and water races were built to harness the Camac River to power the wheels.*
>
> *   It would appear that the former Corn Mill was being used as a Logwood Mill by 1845. Dyes for the cloth industry were made from wood imported from Africa and the Americas. These woods included barwood, brazilwood, sandalwood, ebony, peachwood and shumack. They were collectively known as logwoods. The mill process involved the reduction of the dyewood to 'small chips or raspings that the colouring matter may be more readily extracted by the dyer'. The wood chip/powder was then sold to the woollen, cotton and linen mills for the manufacturers to make up the dyes.*

The Oil Mills. Aerial view of the taken by Desmond Kavanagh while on a flying lesson. Kindly shared by Patrick Ging. The Kavanagh family lived at the Oil Mills.

A newspaper advertisement from 1860 states:

'Linseed Cake and Linseed Meal for Stall Feeding - Reduction in price either at their Mills or Office and Stores, 21, Fishamble Street, Dublin. Orders (per Post) promptly and particularly executed.'

Top: *Oil Mills Bridge.* Above: *Fairview Oil Mill where the Kavanagh family lived and formerly, Jack Dowling and his wife. Photo taken by Joe Williams and shared by Patrick Ging, Clondalkin History Society archive.*

Before the point where the Camac river split at the Sandyhole, farmers customarily dug the ditches in summer and a trickle of water ran down and drained into one of the tributaries. As this has not been cleaned since the 1960s, it has now dried up.

Gunpowder mills in Clondalkin

During the 18th and 19th centuries, gunpowder milling gained national importance. As the odd explosion occurred in gunpowder milling, the mills had to be isolated both from residential areas and each other. For example, in 1733, the production of gunpowder ceased temporarily in Clondalkin as a result of an explosion.

Several powder mills in Clondalkin were spread over an area of about fifteen acres and employed the majority of the local men. The ruins of four such mills are still identifiable in the Kilmatead area of Clondalkin. The gunpowder mills on the Corkagh Estate were operated by several people over the years and provided many locals with employment. Powder mill owners included Nicholas Grueber in the early 1700s, the Arabin family in the 1790s and Richard Chaigneau. Apparently, French Huguenot families had skills in gunpowder

Kilmatead Mill and Pond. Photo credit Patrick Healy, 1988.

processing – mixing the gunpowder, making barrels and manufacture of explosives. Given the many wars in Europe at the time, these were considered valuable skills.

Caldbeck's Powder Mills

William Caldbeck operated a mill close to Moyle Park, built for the British Army in Ireland. A commemorative pedestal near Moyle Park's gate lodge records 'Caldbeck's Powder Mills 1783.' In 1787, a massive explosion at the gunpowder mill in Moyle Park blew the mill into smithereens and caused death and destruction all round. The medieval church in Clondalkin swayed before toppling to become a heap of stones and slates. The magnitude of the explosion was so great that it blew out the windows of hundreds of houses between Clondalkin and Dublin city centre, including windows at Usher's Quay, ten miles away. People were killed or maimed and most of the houses in Clondalkin were wrecked, but the Round Tower miraculously survived unscathed. According to F. Elrington Ball, *'the concussion was felt so severely even in Dublin that it caused the fall of a stack of chimneys on Usher's Quay.'* The much-changed Clondalkin of today displays few scars of one of the most devastating explosions ever experienced in Ireland, but a song sheet printed in the eighteenth century by Bart Corcoran of 23 Arran Quay included a song composed following the event:

1.
Twas on St. George's day, in the year of '87
A day the most dreadful that ever was known;
When all who were in Dublin thought the last Judgment coming
By the great explosion of Calbeck's Powder mills.

2.
That morning I went a walking near unto Clondalkin,
being pleasant weather, and the day most serene;
To my astonishment and wonder, I heard a noise like thunder,
The ground I stood on shook under; dreadful was the scene.

3.
Here were men a dying and others lying crying,
While numbers stood, looking on,
Heads and legs were blown off and mighty stones were blown up,
By the sudden blowing up of Calbeck's Powder mills.

4.

When I beheld these horrors, my soul was filled with terror,
To behold such misery as there I did see;
Children crying for their fathers, others for their mothers,
The whole was great confusion and sad calamity.

5.

Six miles around the country has shar'd this calamity,
Their cabins and gardens and quite torn up,
The fishes from their ponds were thrown upon their lands,
And the poor all about are ruined quite.

6.

I hope those in high station, throughout the Irish Nation,
On the poor will take compassion, and grant them relief;
And to those who are wounded, and with sorrow surrounded;
May the Lord in his mercy ease them of their grief.
To my astonishment and wonder, I heard a noise like thunder,
The ground I stood on shook under; dreadful was the scene.

Fairview Corn Mill

At the other end of Corkagh Park, the remains of a corn mill exist at an area
known as Fairview. This was a small flour mill which would have been used to
grind grain for local consumption. The oil mill which also existed in the Fairview area is recorded in Griffith's Valuation of the 1850s as occupied by a Peter
McNally and a Joseph Henry Esq. The oil mill produced linseed oil which was
extracted from the seed of the flax plant.

GUN-POWDER,
Of the first Quality, made by
WILIAM CALDBECK, Esq;
At his Mills, near Clondalkin,
Now selling by wholesale and retail, on the
lowest terms, for ready money only,
By FRANCIS W. WARREN,
LINEN-DRAPER,
No. 92, Grafton-street, Dublin. (1504

Caldbeck's Gunpowder Mills.

Bridge on Camac river at Raheen.

Leinster Paper Mill / Clondalkin Paper Mill

Another mill located in Clondalkin village was the Leinster Paper Mill, later known as Clondalkin Paper Mill, which was first established in 1819 by Thomas Seery and Son on a site leased to them by William Caldbeck within sight of Clondalkin's round tower. The business expanded and was sold to Thomas Fegan in 1869, but closed in 1875 due to a crippling Government tax on paper. It was re-opened by William Bertram in 1880, trading as the Dublin Paper

Company but it closed again in 1898. It resumed production again as the Leinster Paper Company until it was sold yet again to Kynoch & Co. Limited, a Birmingham munitions manufacturer in 1906, when it was re-named the Irish Paper Company. The board of directors included the future British Prime Minister, Neville Chamberlain. Kynoch had also bought Drimnagh Paper Mills in 1901 and the Arklow-based Wicklow Copper Mining Company.

Having changed hands many times over the years, the Mill was bought in 1913 by the Becker Company who owned paper mills all over the world. Always known locally as 'the Mill,' it was throughout its existence beset by operational problems, characterised by many closures and re-openings. Business boomed during WW1 when British mills switched their focus to production for war

materials but after the war, the Mill went into decline. Despite switching to the production of paper, the Mill closed in 1922. Coincidentally, my father-in-law, who was Secretary of the Fianna Fáil Cumann in Castleknock, was one those who spoke from the back of a truck to promote the re-opening of the mill. It re-opened in 1936, under the name, 'Clondalkin Paper Mill.' This mill, with its extensive buildings, covered a vast area between the Old Nangor Road and the Ninth Lock Road to include CB Sacks abbreviated locally to 'The Bag Factory.'

I admit to being biased when it comes to Clondalkin Paper Mill as this mill was at the core of Clondalkin throughout my childhood and early adulthood. I worked in the Mill office, met my husband there and although I had to leave on marriage, he continued to work

Blessing of Clondalkin Paper Mills by the Very Reverend Canon Ryan, P.P. with Mr. McEntee, Minister for Industry & Commerce.

there for the next 33 years. As much of life in Clondalkin revolved around the Mill and many depended upon it for a livelihood, my account is long and personal. Indeed, Clondalkin Paper Mills (C.P.M.) employed a workforce of hundreds during the time it functioned, to include many neighbours, friends, relatives and colleagues, such that I could venture to write a separate book, there are so many stories to be told. Not alone did the Mill give great employment to the area, but locals also benefitted from offshoot businesses, for example, gaining employment as deliverymen, contractors and suppliers. Local shops and businesses also earned their living from money generated by the Mill. It also gave temporary employment during the 'August shut,' a holiday period which facilitated a massive maintenance overhaul that required extra manpower.

Before the term 'noise pollution' had been coined, the sound of the hooter at Clondalkin Paper Mills governed the day in the village. It rang out clearly for workers at 7.45 a.m. and again at 7.55 a.m. so that any potential latecomers were well-warned. It sounded again at 5.30 p.m. for knocking-off time. In the 1940s, almost all the employees travelled to work on bikes, although some travelled by bus. Very few had cars – Mr. Cusack, the General Manager of C.P.M. for years, had a 10 horsepower Hillman Minx and later on, an American Chevrolet. Mr. O'Mahony, the Company Secretary, drove a Ford 8 and Mr. Swanton, the Engineer, rode a motorbike.

Typing Pool, Clondalkin Paper Mill. L-R, Kathleen O'Neill, Freda Ryan, Gert Small and Anne Bradley.

The prohibitive expense of starting up the machines meant the Mill had to run continuously 24/7, unless there was a breakdown or during 'August shut' time, when all but the maintenance crew took holidays. Given health and safety concerns and the operation of heavy machinery, it was compulsory to have a qualified nurse in the premises, although Miss Ryan worked office hours. She was a contrary woman who huffed and puffed if she had to bandage a finger.

By way of a very rough 'take' on paper-making, raw timber of particular types was mixed with water and china clay (pulp), which happened in the beating loft in Clondalkin Paper Mill, then other chemicals were added, which made it into a papier-mâché type substance. This material was fed into the 'wet' end of the paper-making machine, then dried under pressure. The water was pressed out of it with the application of steam and intense dry heat to turn it into rolls, or what we know better as 'reams' of paper.

Any boiler man there would tell you the oil they burned in the boilers was very thick. But to keep the boilers in good working order, they had to use distilled water. The permutid plant contained distilled water that was so pure,

Clondalkin Paper Mill. Flowing paper pulp in the beating loft. Kindly shared by Gerard Byrne, Old Clondalkin & Surrounding Districts.

people used it for their car batteries. Apart from the noise pollution, there was visible pollution from the Mill, between materials used in the laboratory and in the paper-making process, such as dyes and bleach and in addition, spillages and effluent. Essentially, the paper residue ended up in the Camac as a white effluent, which was the subject of many complaints.

Mill chimney, c. 1990s. Credit Eddie Mallin.

With the building of the Dor Oliver plant beside the Rectory on the Ninth Lock Road, excess water and residue was instead pumped under the road into this plant for the extraction of paper residue. Ultimately, everything ended up in the clariflocculator and trailer loads of a papier-mâché substance used to be dumped at an infill quarry up beside the Round Towers Football Club, much to the disgust of the residents who complained about the smell, which was not surprising, seeing as dumping had been going on there for decades.

Tommy Keogh, who grew up around Camac River and worked in the Mill for more than 25 years until its closure, said you used to be able to tell the quality of the water in Clondalkin by the colour of the paper manufactured that week. My husband remembers a newspaper heading, 'Liffey Turns Red' apparently caused by a recent run on foot of a particular paper order. The culprit was apparently the red cover of 'The Messenger' magazine.

Every now and then, a blip might occur in the paper-making process resulting in the rejection of an order. One such blip occurred when a large order of lined school copybooks were returned as faulty because the paper in parts did not take ink. The rejected pile was destined for incineration, probably for brand maintenance purposes, however, the pile quickly diminished with Mill

Paddy (Bumpy) Ging, Barney Fitzpatrick, Tony Reynolds, Joe Donaghy. Photo taken by Joe Donaghy, a wonderful photographer.

employees siphoning off copybooks. I had schoolgoing children at the time and warned them to secrecy about the origin of their copybooks. Truth be told, the children did end up with patchy essays but I don't think we ever had to buy another copybook.

The Mill managed to continue running throughout WWII, a time when it was hard to come by materials. As much of the regular British labour force who worked their mills had gone to war, Britain was glad to avail of paper supplies from Ireland, as paper was scarce there. For decades prior to its next closure in 1982, business and industrial relations remained good and the Mill managed to ride out successive global crises.

Essentially, C.P.M. was a 'jobbing' mill, where manufacturing was done in 'job lots,' in accordance with small customised orders from businesses who requisitioned a certain grade of paper and specified certain colours. It meant the 'runs' were generally shorter, in line with demands. High quality paper was produced to order, much of which required particular treatment, for example, paper for the production of cheque books, or special paper for wrapping surgical instruments which was ordered by the National Health Service in England. However, the Mill did not compare favourably with the bigger paper mills in

Engineers Dept. T. Reynolds, J. Pluck, T. McGovern, B. Glennon, W. Pentz, J. Lynch, X, B. Fitzpatrick, T. O'Neill. Bottom-B. Brant, S. Carroll, J. Geraghty, B. Cusack, H. Hurrell, J. Campion

Britain, where frequently one type of paper might be produced on a run that lasted an entire week and this aspect always represented a challenge to the Mill's ongoing longevity.

In the 1970s, industrial disputes between the workforce and management dogged Clondalkin Paper Mills. Another negative factor that impinged upon the Mill's success was Ireland's membership of the E.E.C. (now E.U.) from 1973, given the cheaper labour rates in other parts of Europe. The death knell sounded for the Mill with the discovery that manufactured paper could be purchased cheaper from abroad than it could be made in Ireland.

My husband tells the story about his work colleague, Brendan Halford, who was concerned when he got wind of news that the Mill was closing. He called around to the home of another work colleague, Eddie, who lived nearby. Eddie had heard nothing but as they were speaking, they became conscious of a motorbike sputtering along the road. The courier was stopping and starting as he checked house numbers, but they just knew. Eventually he stopped outside Eddie's house and delivered a redundancy notice.

On the announcement of its closure in 1982, workers staged a sit-in to prevent its demise, with many employees, but not all, occupying the premises on a scheduled rota basis. The sit-in lasted a year and culminated in a hunger strike by two workers, many Dáil debates and protest marches in the city centre. Fianna Fáil promoted the re-opening of the Mill and on foot of a commitment by then Taoiseach, Charlie Haughey, the Mill re-opened briefly under new management as part of a deal with Charlie Haughey's Fianna Fáil government, supported by State loans. However, its new life under the resurrected name 'Leinster Paper Mills,'

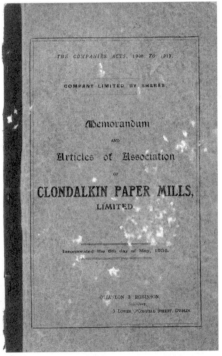

Clondalkin Paper Mill, Memo and Articles of Association

was short-lived. It ran for just over a year and closed for good in 1987. It was the last remaining paper mill in Ireland.

In its last days, a bonfire was piled high and set alight. My husband spotted and rescued a document from the pyre which turned out to be the original Memo and Articles of Association for Clondalkin Paper Mills. (I must point out that it is not his wont to go through rubbish piles but the particular instances I itemised happily bore fruit.)

The entire site was later sold on and 'The Mill Shopping Centre' stands there now, with Dunnes Stores as its anchor tenant. Its name reflects its former milling heritage and acts as a reminder of how the architectural landscape of the area has changed.

I always believed they should have preserved part of the paper mill as a reminder of the employment it gave in the town and surrounding areas, which helped to raise generations of children. The Clondalkin Mill Group also contributed to the education of some employees' children by the award of an annual scholarship fund to cover university fees.

Drimnagh Paper Mill

Drimnagh Paper Mill, based in the Landsdowne Valley, was formerly known as 'The Dock Milling Company' was bought as a 'sister' company by Clondalkin Paper Mill. Although Drimnagh Mill had been in existence since the early 19th century, before the Clondalkin Mill was built, it had not modernised over the years. It still had steam engines driving its two paper machines, years after the Clondalkin Mill had electricity-driven machines. Drimnagh Paper Mill was also characterised by problems posed by competition from abroad; a record exists of Dáil questions being raised back as far as the 1940s where workers at Drimnagh and Clondalkin Paper Mills complained to the Minister for Industry and Commerce about 100 men and women having been laid off by Drimnagh Paper Mill as a result of the effects of unrestricted imports of British paper and a consequent falling off in orders. The Minister was asked to take steps to remedy the position by restricting the importation of paper into Ireland. The high protective tariff on most of the types of paper manufactured by the Drimnagh Paper Mill which had been suspended in 1943 was restored in 1945.

My husband recalls the paper makers going on strike at Drimnagh Paper

Killeen Paper Mills

Mill. When others turned up for work such as electricians, fitters and helpers, they were reluctant to pass the picket at the gate but had no choice as the strike was unofficial. When more workers gathered at the entrance, they wondered again should they join the picket. Mid-discussion, one of the engineers came along, grinning, to let them know that all of their jobs would be gone within the week anyway as the plant was closing. The workers had been given no indication of the impending closure. Indeed, a huge vat was under construction on the premises at the time, which seemed to belie this information. However, Drimnagh Paper Mill duly closed the following Friday and some of the workers were transferred to Clondalkin Paper Mill.

Going way back, Killeen Paper Mills also had problems with competitors. A file of documents exists in the National Archives dating back to a 1828 report from Christopher McDonnell of Merchant's Quay to Ireland's Chief Secretary, Francis Leveson Gower, about an attempted arson attack on his paper mills at Killeen. He claimed his establishment was being targeted because of his intention to install modernising machinery and he offered a reward of €50 for information on the outrage. By 1836, Sir Edward McDonnell was running the mill. Thom's Almanac of 1858 records, 'Sir Edward McDonnel (sic), paper mills, Killeen,' while the 1882 version shows, 'Edward Nolan Esq., Killeen,' as well as 'Messrs. Nolan, paper mills, Killeen.'

Ault Wiborg Newspaper Ink factory

This was a London-based firm which came to Ireland in the early fifties and had its plant in the John F. Kennedy Industrial Estate at Bluebell. It manufactured and distributed paints, inks, lacquers, thinners and dyes.

Goldenbridge Mill

In the 18th century, Goldenbridge Mill (Glydon Bridge) was producing paper and flour. In the late nineteenth century, Inchicore village developed into a significant industrial and residential suburb due primarily to its engineering works

Kilmainham Mill. Courtesy Dublin Inquirer.

Kilmainham Mill

and the west city tramway terminus. While much of the industrial archaeology has disappeared, remnants still exist in the area.

Kilmainham Mill

The Kilmainham Mill, a water-powered mill dating back to the 1500s and originally part of Kilmainham Castle, is one of the last standing structures of water-driven industrial heritage in Dublin city. Occupied continuously since the Middle Ages and largely unaltered since the early 19th century, this mill is designated as a *Recorded Monument* (Ref: DU 18:20 (288) and the site at Rowserstown is entered in the Register of Monuments and Places any development will be subject to the provisions of the National Monuments Act. The 'Save Kilmainham Mill' campaign recently succeeded when Dublin City Council bought the site with the intention of turning it into a heritage site.

Over time, each of the mills along the Camac river ceased operation, either because demand for various products waned or the functions of mills changed as their ownership changed or because demand for a different type of product grew. The years of pollution took its toll on the Camac river. The water went idle and static and the ponds dried up. Culverting to facilitate urban-style development further served to diminish natural habitats and the ecosystem along the Camac, in addition to the natural soakage provided by waterways.

The local authority set up the River Camac Flood Defence Scheme to prevent flooding at Leinster Terrace and the Old Nangor Road area. A local volunteer group '*Friends of the Camac*' was set up in Clondalkin to preserve the river and protect its ecosystem, in an effort to take it back for the community. Bird expert, Eric Dempsey, described how the natural heritage, birds in particular, indicate the state of any environment as they can fly and therefore have the capacity to leave the area, if the environment becomes unsuitable. Although there is evidence of mallards, grey herons, moorhens, grey wagtails and even the odd kingfisher, the Camac should be richer in birdlife. In addition, birdsong is another indicator, in circumstances where some birds can only survive in thick undergrowth, such as the black cap, the robin and the wren, who sings 27 notes per second, also swallows, swifts and sand martins, among many others. Other river dwellers who act as an indicator of an improved environment are butterflies and fish, the latter who rely on insects and larvae to survive.

Dublin City Council are fully supportive of incentives to achieve a better environment, given that they are charged with the implementation of the EU's Water Framework Directive, obliging all water bodies in the EU to achieve "good ecological status." The rehabilitation of the Camac must be achieved by 2027. At the lower reaches of the Camac, Kilmainham residents are campaigning for a long proposed pedestrian and cycle greenway, known as IMMA Avenue, as part of a larger plan for a greenway along the length of the River Camac, a key part in joining up the Grand Canal Greenway to the Liffey.

In his poem, Camac Maiden, the prize-winning poet, Paul Murray, captures the essence of the Camac more eloquently:

Camac Maiden

South East of Saggart, the lady was born
before her descent towards grey city walls
where first she entered the mind-set of man
who pursued her not for her downhill dance
but more those pulsing currents she bore
that could be cajoled to linger a while
seduced by industry to follow its code
down precast spillways paved in fool's gold.

And it came to pass across ripples of time
that mill and still claimed a handmaid to toil
amid smoking stacks and steaming realm
of weavers, dyers and craft-brewing game
who left in their wake but a tainted flow
as out lady floundered sad and forlorn
shedding mud tears from an oil-stained face
for the pristine banks of her bog-meadow place.

But when all seemed lost for this tarnished jewel
slumbering elders awoke to the light
to clean up an act that shamed us for so long
releasing the maiden from unwaged chores

allowing her waters to dance once again
returning life in a babbling cascade
to a city at last taking time to rejoice
never forgetting her Camac's sweet voice.

With kind permission of Paul Murray
Prize-winning and published poet and
former employee of Killeen Paper Mills

Kingfisher by Monica Sproul (nee Small)

24.
GROWN-UP PURSUITS

We used to take pleasure whenever we could to walk the fields and simply enjoy nature.

Our neighbourhood teemed with birds and their distinctive sounds were in the air. Although some are relatively rare in Ireland now, where has the rest of the bird population gone? The more colourful birds are gone missing too - jays, finches and the barn owl that glows under the light of the moon. Wildlife was more abundant too – hedgehogs, badgers, foxes, even mink. Back then, red squirrels were more commonly seen – now, you mainly see grey squirrels.

Sheep shearing in Small's Yard. Gert, Mono, Jim and other children with Jim Doyle in braces.

Several men in the neighbourhood who worked for Johnno used to frequent our yard, where the horses they used were stabled. These included Mr. McInerney, Willie Tully, Jack Dowling and Pat 'Mac' (McDonald). Jack used to harrow with the two big Clydesdales, Blackie and Charlie, while Pat Mac hitched Redser and Salamanca up to a float each day to bring hay or milk to Sandymount, depending on the time of the year. Anyone who has experience of a travelling on a horse and cart knows that the horse plods along when it has a load but once that load has been shed, they start travelling along at a fair lick. The pace quickens on the homeward-bound journey when they start to trot faster and faster and yet faster still, until it turns into a gallop on the final stretch, so much so that when the horse turns in the gate to home, there's a risk of the cart overturning. Any time horses turned into our yard after a day's work, they'd wait impatiently to be unhitched and once they'd shed their harnesses, they'd make for the trough inside the gate, where we'd have to pump in more and more water to keep up with their thirst.

Two men came each year on a Sunday to clip the horses' manes. One operated the clipper while the other wound the handle. The horses never seemed to mind, although it took nearly all day. All ploughing was done with two horses,

Farrier at work

also harrowing, hay cutting and turning. Threshing was a busy time when Percy Lawler came with the traction engine. Hedges were trimmed and weeds removed once a year and hay-making was another busy time. Even if you weren't from a farming family, everybody gave a hand bringing home the hay, stacking it and drawing it home on a bogie, which was a flat cart pulled by a horse. Once August came, the bogies stored in the barn were dusted off and the Shire horses put to work pulling them along the roads to collect the haycocks. The haycocks were wound onto the bogies, brought back to the big haggard nearby and hauled in there to be stored as winter fodder.

It was great fun to hitch a ride on the empty bogies that were heading to the fields to collect haycocks. We knew there'd be no room for passengers on the way back as the bogies were loaded to full capacity. The drivers' roars echoed down the road, 'get off the back of the bogie.' Johnno used to bring buttermilk for the men, which they sometimes shared with us. Once when my brother, Jim, was driving a bogie with my sister, Mono, on board, he asked her to nip into Raheen for something. As she jumped down, her shorts got caught in a hook and pulled her under the horse. The horse stepped over her but the big wheel took a chunk of skin from her knee which needed ten stitches but I think

Small's Yard. Horse hitched ready for work. Boys names unknown.

she got full benefit in the way of treats and visits during her recovery. Speaking of which, it is noteworthy that given the freedoms afforded to us growing up, younger kids in the charge of older kids, being gone all day and what we got up to, nobody broke bones, suffered injuries or drowned.

People were accustomed to travelling distances for evening entertainment, films and dancing. My older sisters remember seeing their first films at Rice's Marquee, which was set up in the village. Peg recalled seeing Charlie Chaplin in an old silent film, 'City Lights' around 1931. Prices back then were four pennies, eight pennies and one shilling, hard-

Gert & Monica Small with David Cusack and Cusack's dog Rex on top of a grain pile in Small's Yard

Tower Cinema with film posters from 1947. Courtesy Patrick Ging.

ly measurable in today's currency. The Ging family took over the old tram shed and turned it into a cinema and called it the Tower Cinema. The cinema shows usually involved a double feature, often a cartoon before the main film. Even when there was no double feature, they often showed what we called 'shorts,' starring Charlie Chaplin, Laurel and Hardy, the Three Stooges, Buster Keaton or the Marx Brothers. The feature films in black and white often starred actors such as Gene Autry, Roy Rogers and his horse Trigger in cowboy films, Rita Hayworth, Elizabeth Taylor and many more. Posters were pasted up in the area to announce forthcoming films and shop owners readily obliged in turn for free cinema tickets. The posters used to be printed in a little shop near the Premier Cinema in Lucan (it was later called the 'Grove' cinema).

The bench seats, called 'woodeners,' were cheapest, about half the price of the seats with backs. A projector was operated from the back onto a screen in front of the audience. Once everybody was seated, the lights went out and the film started. The film was sometimes interrupted by a break, so that the projectionist could change the reel. Cheers went up when the baddie was captured or the hero was saved. As smoking was the norm, a haze of smoke rose up to join the tunnel of light from the projector.

The cinemas in town, like the Capitol, the Ambassador and the Savoy provided a different experience, often starting with a live stage show or a stand-up comedian followed by the Pathé News which in wartime comprised live news reels. Before the feature film got going, they often put on a cartoon show or comedy sketches and showed trailers of films to come.

Once, my friend Annie Bradley and I sneaked into a cinema in Grafton Street, to see a film starring Silvana Mangano, 'Bitter Rice,' which was considered risqué. By the late 1940s, Italian films were all the rage as everyone was sick of war films. We got a fit of the giggles when the projector broke down in the middle of the film. Although the film turned out not to be risqué at all, we were still terrified coming out, blinded by the light, in case we'd bump into someone we knew. Another time, we went to see 'Mandy,' a bit of a tearjerker. We were crying so much, it started us on a fit of laughing. It was embarrassing when the lights came on and we realised a row of sailors nearby had been listening to our sobs.

Dancing was another great social outlet and a means of meeting partners. The Cowan brothers built a dancehall in Clondalkin and they ran dances there for many years until the 1950s. I think they may have left it a little late as dancehalls were going out in the 1950s. There were weekly dances at the Slipper Ballroom at Ballymount and two dances a week at Saggart, on Wednesday and Sunday nights, with music provided by a record player. There was also a proper dancehall in Newcastle, where bands used to play. On occasion, dances were also held at Baldonnel. While we managed to venture into town on occasion, we used to hear tell of fabulous ballrooms in Blackpool such as the renowned Tower ballroom, Empress Ballroom and the Winter Gardens, but I never got to them. My dancing days were long over by the time Clondalkin's only night-club, the Blue Banana (known as the 'Bluer') opened. The bouncers probably wouldn't have let me in anyway, "Are you a regular?" they used to ask, before turning you away.

The South County Dublin Harriers featured in the locality during my child-hood, headed by the Harvey family. For a drag hunt, the huntsman went across the fields in the early morning with a dead rabbit or hare to leave a scent. The hunt met at the back of Healy's pub in Clondalkin village. We often watched as the dogs raced across the fields at the back of our house, barking wildly, fol-lowed by the horses. Eventually, the spread of the city and the suburbs forced the hunt towards Kildare and Wicklow.

South County Dublin Harriers - hunt passing Clondalkin Paper Mill, 1953. Courtesy Gerard Byrne.

Baldonnel. Kindly shared by Gerard Byrne, Old Clondalkin & Surrounding Districts.

Motor Racing. Courtesy Patrick Ging.

Clondalkin Garden Fete, 1929, official opening of bazaar by the Reverend Monsignor Watters. Kindly shared by Gerard Byrne, Old Clondalkin & Surrounding Districts.

Other events occurred at intervals, such as the Clondalkin Garden Fete, air display and motor racing.

Occasionally we took a trip into town, generally on Saturdays, to take in Woolworths and buy some of their ice cream and sweets or we queued down the street for a pound of Hafners sausages.

Still Life by Monica Sproul (nee Small)

25.
RELIGION

Religion played a huge part in the life of Irish people but it was also the source of a divide even down to village life where one was expected to mix with one's own brethren. During the Reformation, Protestant churches were built in the towns and Catholic churches could only be built on the outskirts of the town; many villages today are left with the vestige of this legacy. Members of gentrified Protestant families were accustomed to socialising together at events - hunts, balls, the Royal Dublin Horse Show and many were members of the same clubs, such as the Kildare Street Club. Although this provided a level of cohesion among Protestants, it also cultivated a natural divide that extended beyond church attendance to school attendance and social structure. I have already mentioned the Catholic *Ne Temere* rule which represented another divisive factor. Despite the religious divide, many Protestant families such as Mr. Becker and the Caldbeck family contributed to the building of Catholic schools and churches.

The Parish of Clondalkin and Rathcoole was served by two Protestant churches - St. John's Church in Rathcoole and St. John's Church in Clondalkin, latter which is located directly across from the Round Tower. In his *Topographical Dictionary of Ireland,* 1837, Lewis describes how the Clondalkin living comprises a rectory and a vicarage. Back in the early 1800s, the school room was built by subscription on land given by William Calbeck Esq., who also provided land in 1833 for the erection of a house for the R.C. clergyman and for a dispensary. In my time, Miss Wall lived in the schoolteacher's house alongside the Protestant school. The Reverend Dr. Reid established four almshouses adjoining the church *"for destitute widows, a poor shop, a repository, Dorcas institution and a lying-in hospital."* The bells rang for service at 10.30 a.m. and I recall the some of the parishioners who attended the Protestant Church services in Clondalkin – the Shearers who lived on Main Street, Mr. Maud who lived on the Tallaght Road, Jack FitzPatrick, Cecil Ellis, the Harris farming family who also had quarries, the Claytons of Cheeverstown, Herbie Holmes, the jockey, who lived up the New Road, the Beatties and the Lyons family. Due to dwindling numbers, there has been little expansion in the Church of Ireland and the practice nationally is to merge parishes in an area. The Catholic faith has been in decline too, with many choosing to continue only as à la carte Catholics. The lukewarm reception for Pope Francis in 2018 bears testament to this, especially when compared to the last Papal visit of Pope John Paul II in 1979.

The Reverend Madden lived in the Rectory which was located opposite the 'Bag Factory.' Mrs. Madden, the rector's wife, dressed in a long costume with a fox fur worn loose over the shoulders and she carried a woven shopping basket. I overheard her in Ging's shop one time ordering Vienna roll and mentioning that they were having rabbit pie for lunch.

When I was growing up in the 1930s, the Catholic Parish of Clondalkin

Rev. Richard Charles Madden, Rector of Clondalkin from 1936 to 1948, attending the Armistice Day commemorations in 1943 presumably at Islandbridge. Photo credit: Shared by Roy Byrne.

was spread over a wide area, extending from the Third Lock Bridge at Inchicore up to Ballymount, as far as Tynan's Cross on the Belgard Road, Kingswood, Baldonnel, Milltown, Balgaddy, Cloverhill and Knockmitten. That entire parish was served by a single church – the Church of the Immaculate Conception in Clondalkin, where the bells for Mass rang at 11.00 a.m. In fact, many parishioners came by pony and trap from as far away as Lucan and even Palmerstown, before Palmerstown had its own church. I remember collections in Clondalkin to fund the building of a church in Palmerstown. I also remember the day Archbishop McQuaid came to consecrate the newly-built church, called St. Philomena's, as my brother, Jim, was among the scouts who formed the guard of honour at the church in Palmerstown.

Canon Ryan lived in The Presbytery, a large house on the Monastery Road. Fran McCoy used to drive Canon Ryan around. Prior to that, Father Traynor used to live in the redbrick Presbytery on the new Road, opposite the Church. Retired before my time, he went on to live to the age of a hundred. Father Murphy lived in that Presbytery too. Porter's Guide and Directory for County Dublin 1912, records for The Presbytery, Clondalkin, 'Rev. James Baxter, P.P.'

Catholic churches built in the parish in more recent times include the Church of the Sacred Hearts Priests of the Parish at Sruleen, the Church of the Transfiguration at Bawnogue, the Church of St. Ronan at Deansrath and a Chapel of Ease at Knockmitten, called the Church of the Presentation of Our Lord in the Temple.

Catholics were obliged to go frequently to confession and go to Mass at least once a week. It was usual for Catholics to bless themselves by making a sign of the cross when they were passing a church or a funeral, even when they were passengers on a bus. People rarely missed Mass or even a church ceremony, and nobody left early. Way back in time, the exceptions were women in advanced state of pregnancy, who were expected not to go to church and more or less hide away in their homes. After the birth, Catholic rites required mothers to be 'churched,' before they were considered sufficiently 'clean' to receive the sacraments. The new mother attended a specific 'churching' service to thank God for a safe delivery and go on her knees before a priest to be 'purified.'

Back then, passing judgment on people because of the clothing they wore was not that unusual. A single lady of my acquaintance once got ticked off for wearing a 'swagger' coat, which was the height of fashion at the time. As its

Lady being 'churched.'

Priests in confession box

'loose' effect resembled a maternity coat, it was not acceptable for a single girl to wear this type of coat.

Every Saturday evening saw a line-up for the hearing of Confession, in readiness for being 'free of sin' before Sunday Mass. Generally, the Confession box had three compartments. The priest seated himself behind a curtain in the middle compartment and slid across a wooden door to one side compartment in order to hear the list of sins from the kneeling penitent through a metal grille.

"Bless me Father, for I have sinned. My last confession was three weeks ago."

Mumbling prayers as he made a sign of the cross in the air constituted absolution and then the priest meted out penance.

"Say two Hail Marys, four Our Fathers and a decade of the Rosary, and beg God for forgiveness. In ainm an Athar agus an Mhic agus an Spioraid Naoimh, Amen." (In the name of the Father, the Son and the Holy Spirit. Amen)

Meanwhile, a second penitent was kneeling in the other side compartment waiting their turn.

Although it was a whispered exchange through closed doors, those waiting in the pews could fairly well get the drift of what was being said. Even if they couldn't quite hear, they often gauged from the raised voice of the priest or the reaction of the penitent emerging from the side compartment whether they had much sin on their soul. Another pointer was the length of the penance the penitent had to undertake while kneeling at a pew.

I recall confessions conducted by one old priest, who was very grumpy and hard of hearing. '*Speak up*' he used to say, and you'd have to elevate the pitch of your voice, so he could hear your awful sins. He could very well shout at you in the darkness when you revealed your evil nature. There was a confession box each side of the church but his queue was a lot shorter that the other priest's queue as nobody wanted to be overheard. When he fell short of penitents, he'd leave his central spot in the confession box, come out and beckon waiting confessors to his side, who all ducked their heads. Even when a selected penitent was seen to follow him, they had often sidled back to the 'easy' priest who was light on penance by the time the priest got back to his box.

Back then, the priest used to say Mass with his back to the congregation, except when he moved to the pulpit to deliver a sermon. The sermon might very well involve the priest thumping the pulpit with a rousing sermon for half to three quarters of an hour, breathing hell, fire and damnation and warning us of the evil that would befall us for breaches and sins. Of course, the Mass was always in Latin right up to the 1960s – there was no Mass in English at all.

Years ago, the 'dues' were read out from the altar at Sunday Mass, after Christmas and Easter. Starting with the highest donor, it was usual for priests to read out publicly the names of donors and the amount of each, from the top all the way down. It was a source of shame to some who could ill afford to donate, especially when the priest skipped mention of their house, which indicated no donation at all had been made. Unlike other parishes, not all the donations were read out in Clondalkin but I remember well those who ranked at the top of our list which always included 'Marchioness McSweeny – five pounds.'

Other status markers were the geographical demarcations in the church itself – approximately three-quarters of the church, towards the back, was given over to the poorer members of the congregation who generally contributed to

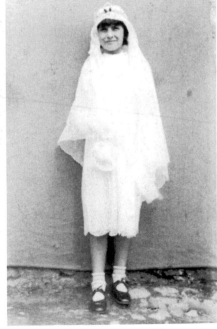

My sisters Peg (left) and Gwen (right) making Confirmation.

'the penny collection' or 'copper collection' – they were expected to enter via the main entrance at the back. 'The silver collection' denoted those who had made a 'silver' donation - they were expected to enter through the side entrance door to the church. It is hard in this day and age to believe that a gated rail stretching right across the side aisles divided worshippers belonging to the 'silver' and 'copper' collections, but it did. There was another gated rail further up the church which divided the priest from the congregation. In preparation for the sacrament of Holy Communion, a white cloth used to be draped over the railing before the altar at the top of the church. A lady who lived beside the Mill Yard was a particularly avid Mass-goer. She used to open both gates and march right up to the altar, much to everyone's amazement.

In keeping with tradition, men assembled for a chat outside the church gates after Mass. You were expected to fast before Mass, in preparation for receiving Holy Communion, so the pangs of hunger stretched as you walked home afterwards in eager anticipation of a fry, accompanied by toast and a big pot of tea.

In addition to Mass on Sunday, other church attendances were required.

My brothers Son (left) and Jim (right) making Confirmation.

Devotions in May or October entailed devotion to the Virgin Mary. Holy Days of Obligation, major feast days in the Catholic Church, had to be observed. Lent brought the Stations of the Cross and Holy Hour, which was on the first Friday of every month. On the first Sunday of every month, parishioners were broken into pious groups called 'guilds' for devotion to spiritual works of mercy, whose attendance was required at a particular service called 'Sodality,' which is now long gone.

On Ash Wednesday, the priest applied ashes to the foreheads of the congregation, to symbolise the dust from which we are made, speaking the words, "*Remember that you are dust, and to dust you shall return.*" It was permissible for ashes to be brought home to a sick person. The Easter ceremonies included Palm Sunday and Good Friday, which was an exceptionally quiet day when no shops or pubs were open, a day of contemplation. Hot cross buns featured on the menu on Good Friday.

The Feast of Corpus Christi in late May brought the place to standstill as everybody took part in the procession. The Rosary was recited, hymns were sung and Benediction took place. When there was Rosary or Benediction, everybody stayed until the last hymn had been sung. We had Benediction with

Corpus Christi Procession in Mount St. Joseph grounds. Credit Breda O'Byrne nee Kinsella. Kindly shared by Patrick Ging.

the Blessing of the Blessed Sacrament accompanied by singing and the release of incense from a thurible.

Apart from being baptised and christened, young Catholics also had to undergo the sacraments of Holy Communion and Confirmation which were quite onerous. At the age of seven you were decked out for First Communion or if you were a younger sibling, you wore clothing handed down from an older sibling which had been kept aside specially for the occasion. Few had cameras, so photographs of these occasions were rare, as were celebratory meals. Our Uncle Harold was the family photographer when we were young. Afterwards, those clothes were kept for best until they were either worn out or passed on to a sibling or cousin.

Gertrude Reynolds (nee Small) making Confirmation, c. 1946, and May procession 1925.

Intending Communicants had to participate in a May procession which involved a slow walk behind three priests under a canopy. The May Procession started at the Catholic Church and continued around the village, often escorted by the Boy Scouts Association, of which my brother, Jimmy, was a member. Another procession, 'Forty hours for the Exposition of the Blessed Sacrament' took the same route. Scouts in full uniform had to attend for the duration of the ceremony. A few scouts were detailed to stand still on the church altar - the detail was changed hourly. The prohibition on chewing the Eucharist and touching the Eucharist eventually went by the wayside.

Children between the ages of about eleven and fourteen from the wider locality were all confirmed in Clondalkin. For months beforehand, you'd be dreading the thought of Archbishop McQuaid going from pew to pew asking religious questions, in case you did not know the answer and brought shame on the teacher, the school and your family. Both Communion and Confirmation brought forward gifts of medals, rosary beads and prayer books and, it was hoped, the gift of some money.

Some became altar boys after Communion and served at Mass until about the age of thirteen. They wore white starched surplices with a red soutane. Altar

Left: Anne Patricia Small (Patsy), died in childhood. Right: My sister Mono making First Communion.

boys had three main duties, serving to the 'right,' serving to the 'left,' and ringing the bell. Some used to dash up to the church early so they could choose the bell. Altar boys had the honour of holding the bishop's mitre or crozier during confirmation ceremonies.

New priests used to get stuck doing the early morning eight o'clock Mass and to count the collection money at the weekend. One curate managed to sidestep that one nicely - when the priest asked how much was there, he pretended he wasn't much good at counting and gave a most unsatisfactory rough guesstimate, which stuck the priest himself with a re-count.

On Sundays, it was a sin to do manual labour and generally, shops only opened for a short time in the morning so people could buy newspapers and provisions. You had to observe the rule of abstinence – no meat on Fridays - many Catholics designated Friday a 'fish' day. 'Quarter Time' was a four-times-a-year Catholic rite where abstinence from eating meat on Friday was extended to Wednesdays too. Fully aware of this, the shopkeepers used to stock extra eggs during quarter time. Over time and with the decline of the hold the Catholic Church had on parishioners, these rules were observed less and less and many are now gone.

The long arm of religion stretched into people lives to the extent that during Lent, all dancing was cancelled. This was made possible because the parish priest usually controlled the parish hall or community hall where dances were generally held. Interestingly, Protestants were accustomed to attending 'Catholic' dances but although 'socials' and dances were held at the Protestant school in Clondalkin, no Catholics attended because they wouldn't get to hear about the event. It was usual practice for the Catholic church to provide the land on which a community hall was built but the parishioners raised the funds to build it. However, ownership of such halls was in the hands of the church because in recent years, some halls were sold off by the parish priest without any recourse to the parishioners.

Allied to religious policing, the moral police in an area would not approve of any gaiety during Lent either. Nobody required notice of this because the practice prevailed throughout Ireland whereby no dances were held during Lent apart from those which ran on a commercial basis in Dublin city centre. Even the Slipper Ballroom at Fox and Geese stayed shut during Lent.

Catholic Boy Scouts. Brothers Benny and Mick Kinsella each end back row. Tommy Keogh 3rd row. Joe Keogh, Mick Palmer, Jimmy Tinkler, middle row. Credit Caitlin Kathleen Kinsella Bent.

Retreats were also regular feature in the parish. Each year, there was a week-long retreat for women and a week-long retreat for men. At one adult weekend retreat which took place in Merrion Square, part of the sacrifice was for participants to maintain silence and not talk for the entire weekend.

Weddings at the church were a commonplace sight. The grooms generally wore suits and brides wore dresses in white or cream, but many brides wore a simple wool suit. Buttonhole carnations with stems wrapped in tinfoil were the order of the day for the wedding party. In advance of the marriage ceremony, the church required formal notification of the intended marriage. Marriage banns were either 'posted' or read out from the altar on three Sundays in order to notify the public and ensure there was no impediment to the marriage, for example, that neither party had been married before. Couples could pay a fee not to have the banns read out and this became a snobbery thing as couples who didn't pay the fee were perceived as poor.

The marriage ceremony took place in early morning, hence the term wedding 'breakfast,' which was usually hosted in hotels such as the Harcourt Hotel or Jury's Hotel at the Four Courts. Mostly, the guest list was confined to immediate or extended family. Outside the church, people threw confetti in dolly mixture colours over the couple, rather than showering with them with rice for good luck, as they did elsewhere.

As the churchyard beside our school doubled as a playground, we often came upon a funeral as 'removals' generally took place around three in the afternoon, the time we got out of school. Out of morbid curiosity, we'd shuffle into the midst of the congregation to watch the goings-on. The coffin was carried within a horse-drawn hearse and funeral horses were always black in colour, festooned with plumage – black feathers for an adult deceased, white feathers and a white coffin for a child.

Once a family member died, a notice with a black border and sometimes, a black ribbon, was placed on the front door. After the doctor and priest had left, the deceased was laid out in a habit called a 'shroud' provided by the undertaker, not in 'best' clothes as they are today. These days, the house is often cleaned top-to-bottom in readiness for visitors and the deceased is covered with a fresh white sheet, however, in my time, it was not customary for the coffin to be left 'open.' Relatives and neighbours helped the bereaved with arrangements and often baked a cake or provided ready-made meals. When the coffin was leaving the house, neighbours closed their curtains out of respect. Catholics in the area were brought to the church and the coffin placed up at the altar rails, much like it happens today. The funeral procession often travelled past the deceased's home, where it paused for a few minutes. As well as conducting ceremonies for the dying and dead, priests also had a role in comforting the relatives and paid house visits.

The bereaved wore a black armband or a black diamond stitched to the left arm of their coat, a visible reminder to people of their bereavement. A widow wore all black clothing for six months and often changed to black-and-white clothing for the next six months.

Wakes were commonplace outside Dublin, when the coffin was placed in the middle of a room, usually the 'best' room. Sympathisers were seated on chairs against the walls. It was usual to have refreshments placed on tables in the room, sandwiches, cake and bottles of ale or porter. I myself have never attended a wake.

Of course I attended Uncle Harold's funeral which was held in a Protestant church. When I mentioned my attendance to the priest in confession, he said: "I'll give you absolution this time." Years later, I arranged Uncle Eddie's funeral which presented a great difficulty as he had very specific instructions about being buried with his parents and when I discovered there was no room in the grave, I had to arrange a cremation in order to carry out his wishes.

Back in 1937, Kitty Nolan of The Commons and Maura Ryan of Drimnagh Road wrote pieces for the Schools Folklore Collection about the seven ancient churchyards in the parish of Clondalkin as well as the graveyards and who could be buried there.

Withering chrysanthemums in russet or gold in the shape of a cross were a common feature in graveyards; they were replaced at Christmas by a holly wreath. All too often, the faded plastic flowers under glass globes on the graves remained there for ages as nobody wanted to be the one to discard them.

Peaceful scene by Monica Sproul (nee Small)

26.
LIFE FOR THE SMALL FAMILY AFTER NATIONAL SCHOOL

Up to the 1950s, most children left school at the age of fourteen and got jobs locally. Around Clondalkin, school-leavers generally got jobs in the Mill or at Urney's chocolate factory in Tallaght, the Aspro tablet factory in Bluebell on the Naas Road, or at Lamb's Jam Factory, all within twenty-five minutes cycling distance. Some went on to apprenticeships to qualify in trades such as mechanic, electrician, tailoring or they trained for secretarial work or in jobs such seamstress. Most were too young to go to England but some did go when they were older, on the promise of better money and job prospects.

When I was about twelve, my parents started gearing me up for office work and put my name down for classes with Miss Galvin, who provided a secretarial course at our

Gertrude Small

school. However, as I mentioned before, my mother had arranged for me to travel by ferry to England when I left school to help out my older sister, Gwen, with her toddler, Joe. At that stage, she had another baby on the way. I spent the next six months with Gwen, her husband Brendan, and his father, minding baby Joe. In the evenings, I attended a secretarial course at a nearby college, where I learned English, Commerce and Arithmetic, as well as shorthand and typing. Just before Christmas, I made my way home to Dublin.

Office staff Clondalkin Paper Mill. Freda Ryan, Annie Bradley, Teddy Lee, Kitty Whelan, Gert Small, Kathleen O'Neill, Betty O'Reilly, Dolores Looney and Evy Archbold.

C.P.M. staff. Back, Dolores Behan. Middle L-R, Nurse Maureen Ryan, Freda Ryan, Teddy Lee, Gert Small, Dolores Looney, Annie Bradley, Paddy Johnson. Front, Kitty Whelan.

In the New Year, I attended at Miss Galvin's Secretarial School; classes were held in her home. I got a job as a legal secretary with a solicitor based in Dawson Street, Mr. Little. (The irony, Miss Small working for Mr. Little). A few months later, Miss Galvin contacted me to let me know there was a job going in the office at Clondalkin Paper Mill. Starting in the Mill was like going into the bosom of one big family, as I knew most people working there and it was about three minutes' walk from home.

Top: Office outing to the Spa Hotel turned rainy. Back L-R, Joan X, Maureen Kelly, Gert Small, Bunty McCreevy, Marie X, Evy Archbold. Front L-R, Jean O'Neill, Dolores Looney, Mary Bradley. Above: Great Southern Railways advertisement for holidays.

Everybody worked a five and a half day week, to include a half day on Saturday from 9.00 a.m. to 12.30 p.m. There were frequent outings with work colleagues, usually local trips or day trips, but sometimes several days away together. By the time I started work, the former one-week holiday entitlement had been extended to two weeks. Only then did going away on holiday become a regular feature of life.

One time, I went on holiday to Galway with my friend, Anne Bradley, and we stayed in a guesthouse in Salthill. We had paid our return train fare but miscalculated the cost of the accommodation as 5 guineas, instead of 5½ guineas, which left us short. We had to lug our suitcases (no suitcases on wheels back then) all the way into the train station at Eyre Square as we had no money for a taxi. The whole journey back to Dublin, we were wondering what we'd do, as neither of us had the few shillings bus fare home. When we reached Dublin,

Gertrude Small and Tony Reynolds with Pip.

we went into a church and prayed. Eventually, we decided we'd go into a police station and ask for assistance to get us as far as Raheen, where my parents could arrange to get Annie home to Rathmore Road in Rathcoole. Outside the church, who did we bump into but Anne's boyfriend, (later husband), Myles Mathews, from the Mill Yard, who was wondering where we were going. We crushed into Myles's sports car, with me scrunched into the 'dicky' seat at the back, very glad of the lift home.

When I met my husband, who had a car, we often took trips along the coast to Arklow, a holiday mecca at the time. We'd spend the day there, sometimes on the beach, have our tea in Hoyne's Hotel on the Main Street and then make our way to the Marquee dance-hall, which had originally been a tented marquee dance but by that stage, it had become a proper dance-hall.

Like many couples back then,

Top: Dublin Airport back in the day. People dressed up for the Airport. After goodbyes, the passengers walked across the tarmac while those seeing them off waved from the outside balcony. Above: Tony & Gertrude Reynolds (nee Small) departing for honeymoon, Dublin Airport.

we married before the 5th of April, to get the benefit of a tax rebate covering that tax year. It was not the ideal time for hunting down glamorous but warm bridal wear and white shoes. Honeymoons were usually a few days long and spent in Ireland - getting the train to Drogheda, Arklow or Belfast was not unusual. Our honeymoon to London by plane was considered exotic. Some of the wedding guests came along to the airport to wave us off. Everybody used to dress up for a trip to the airport back then.

Many couples moved in with their parents after the honeymoon as few new houses were built until the late 1950s and in any event, most couples could not afford to buy their own home. Before we married, we put a deposit down to purchase a house and this caused some anxiety in both families. My Uncle Harold cycled all the way out to Clondalkin, worried about the idea of a mortgage and terrified of debt. Meanwhile, my father-in-law was raising the same concern with my husband. As a result, we sold our car, banked the money and did without a car for the first two years or so of our marriage. In a cruel twist of fate, our old car frequently passed us as we stood at the bus stop. Eventually the money that was sitting in the bank all the time bought us another car, so we could have afforded a car all along.

Gertrude Reynolds (née Small)

SIBLINGS

As the eldest, my sister, Peg, was expected to help in the busy household - minding the younger ones, shopping, laundry and cooking. When the youngest, Monica (Mono) was born prematurely at home in 1939, my father was away, busy finishing off a job to free him up for the arrival of the new baby, who instead arrived early. The newborn baby was handed to Peg by the nurse soon after the birth while the nurse attended to my mother.

Although Peg got the benefit of shorthand and typewriting classes, she favoured becoming a nurse. She worked first in Urney's and then, in Redmond's grocery store in the city centre as a shop assistant and childminder, until she spotted an advertisement in the newspapers:

"Join the ATS at 72 Clifton Street, Belfast."

(The Auxiliary Territorial Service was the women's branch of the British Army during WW2).

Peg enlisted for four years at the barracks in Belfast (Army number: W279926, No. 18 A.T.S., stationed at T.C & R. Depot) and after a month of induction training which involved drill ("square-bashing"), her plan of switching to nursing was scotched when she was told she'd be in the A.T.S until the end of the war. While qualifying as a cook, she got a telegram from home, *"Patsy sinking fast, come home."* Patsy had contracted T.B. As all leave was denied with talk of a German invasion, Peg never got to see Patsy before she died. Patsy is buried in Mount Jerome Cemetery in Harold's Cross, beside the Hospice.

After the war, Peg returned home from a posting in England and worked as a cook. She returned to England in 1950 and settled in Coventry with a Welsh man, Ned Evans, who had a lovely tenor voice. Peg was very upset some years later to receive a devastating telegram, 'Mother died Sunday.' The fact that several days had passed since Sunday added to her grief because she could not understand why the family had not made contact sooner. It was only when she reached home that she realised the words on the telegram were wrong. The telegram should have read: 'Mother died suddenly.'

Peg had a wonderful pair of hands and could turn her hand to embroidery, sewing, threadwork and knitting. She often sent home hand knits as presents to Ireland. She was a gardener with 'green fingers,' whose seeds and plants always thrived. Throughout her life, her garden was always a mass of flowers for months on end. As well as growing all sorts of vegetables such as runner beans and tomatoes, she also cultivated rarer plants such as vines, Birds of Paradise, orchids and banana plants. The pair enjoyed fishing, car boot sales and collecting; Peg collected ornaments and Ned collected records from Bing Crosby to classical music. Their travels included bus trips, continental holidays and visits back home to Ireland.

Gwen came next. After school, she worked in various offices. In her spare time, she undertook advanced Irish language classes and she also belonged to the Dramatic Society who met in rooms opposite Ledwidges. It was here she met a young man, Brendan O'Byrne, from Drogheda, who was based at Baldonnell where he worked as a draughtsman. They settled in Yorkshire and had a family of nine children, two of whom pre-deceased them.

My brother Eddie (known as 'Son' or 'Sonny' Small) attended school at the Presentation Convent in Clondalkin, then the boys' school on Monastery Road before going on to secondary school in Inchicore. When he left school, he worked at Aspro and Clondalkin Paper Mills. He was keen on following horse racing. He studied the

Edward ('Sonny') Small.

Gwen outside Raheen Cottage.

form, put on his bets and followed the races and often travelled down to the Curragh for the day. My mind wanders back to the time Son bought himself a trendy new bri-nylon shirt. There I was ironing it for him, more used to cotton than nylon, and when I started on the collar, it unfortunately shrivelled up, so I had to replace it. Son was a great lover of nature, always keen on birds.

Having taken a rare trip to the beach, Son was on his way home on the bus, when a chap he knew came up and shook hands, sympathising with him on his mother's death – that was how he learned his mother had died unexpectedly. Son emigrated to England in the 1950s, married Phyllis from Newcastle and they settled in London and had a family. Son worked for the Royal Mail until retirement, as being outdoors suited him better. He kept up his love of sport and particularly, horse-racing.

Jim attended the Presentation Convent in Clondalkin and the boys' school on Monastery Road before going on to study at Lucan Technical School. He started as a cabinet-maker's apprentice at Heron's in Leixlip and used to cycle to work there until he contracted tuberculosis. He was lucky that streptomycin was used as a treatment by then and it proved successful. While Jim was hospitalised in Jervis Street, he did a lot of wood carving but sadly none of this work survives. Afterwards, John O'Brien gave permission for the health board

Jim working on a vintage car.

Gwen pays a visit to see the vintage car Jim is working on.

to place a hut outside the back window with a bed inside. Back then, it was considered the best way to treat T.B. Jim never completed his apprenticeship as he had been advised to leave the job because of the dust. He worked with my father at painting and decorating, mainly in the Clondalkin area. During the 1950s, while Jim was on a rare trip to Yorkshire, helping Gwen and the family to paint and fix up their new house, a telegram arrived there on the 7th of August 1953, announcing my mother's sudden death.

A keen sportsman, Jim took part in most local sporting events and excelled at badminton, fishing and swimming. He was secretary of the Clondalkin Angler's Association. He was an outdoor person, keen on nature and he was always on hand to help with re-stocking the waterways and rescuing birds in distress. He was skilled at handcrafts and often helped to refurbish vintage car interiors. If somebody invited him off fishing few days, Jim was gone off like a shot, to the consternation of many women who wanted to see their kitchen finished or their room re-decorated. Jim remained on in Raheen Cottage until he inherited our Uncle Eddie's house alongside Kilmainham Gaol in 1989.

Sadly, Jim died two years after his move to Kilmainham. He is buried in Mount Jerome cemetery with our parents and our sister, Patsy, who died in childhood. Part of his ashes were scattered at his favourite place, along the River Camac in Corkagh Park.

My younger sister, Mono, lost her mother when she was only fourteen. Initially, she worked for a time at a jewellers until she gained entry to nurse training in Yorkshire and followed it up with midwifery training in Bristol. She married twice and has a daughter, Grace and a son, Joe, one grandchild and two great-grandchildren. She lives in Hertfordshire. As well as being an accomplished painter, she is very well-read, has a good command of French and is gifted with her hands, especially at sewing.

Jim and Mono outside the hut provided by the Health Board beside Raheen Cottage when Jim was recovering from T.B.

J. SMALL————————————

CONTRACTOR
RAHEEN, CLONDALKIN, CO. DUBLIN

J. Small Bill Head

Standing L-R, Mono & Peg. Sitting L-R, Gert & Gwen.

Nurse Monica Small

The Small family L - R, Mono, Gert, Jim, Son, Gwen, Peg

Woodland Wildflowers by Mary Reynolds

27.
POLITICS

Growing up I didn't have much interest in politics. Most families supported a specific political party and this information was known to all and sundry, including the politicians who banked on their votes. Generally, politicians' sons took over from their fathers - there were few female politicians and not much has changed in Ireland in that regard. As some schools were used as polling stations, many schoolchildren got the day off school when an election took place, but we didn't as the library was always used as our polling station. My parents tended to vote for particular candidates, rather than a particular political party.

Unlike the 'First Past the Post' method in the U.K., the system of election in Ireland is by proportional representation with single transferable vote. Until 1932, Cumann na nGaedheal ruled as a minority government, but having merged with two smaller groups, the party became known as Fine Gael. I recall three political parties when I was growing up– Fine Gael, Fianna Fáil and Labour. There were some Independents and a new Party called Clann Na Poblachta. From the formation of the first Fianna Fáil government in 1932, the Fianna Fáil party was continuously in office for almost sixteen years, up to 1948.

To drum up votes coming up to an election, politicians and fellow party men undertook election tours, canvassing house-to-house by car and on foot. Some political meetings were attended by hundreds of people. In some areas, they held torch-lit processions, which involve party supporters marching behind a colourful party banner. In some parts of the country, they used to soak sods of turf in oil, place the sods on top of pitchforks, then light the sods, before raising them upright. I never remember any of this happening in Clondalkin.

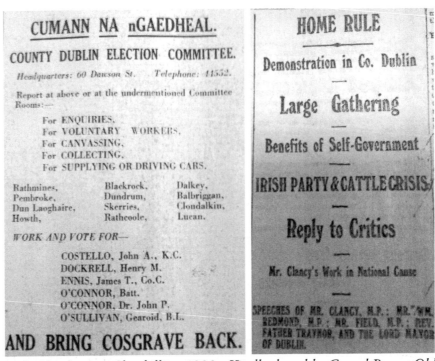

Left: Blueshirts in Clondalkin, 1930s. Kindly shared by Gerard Byrne, Old Clondalkin & Surrounding Districts. Right: Politics and the Priest - Rev. Michael Traynor C.C. Lord Mayor.

Approaching election time, candidates waited outside the Catholic church after Mass on Sundays. They never attended outside the Protestant church. They'd choose a convenient spot to park a flat-backed truck in order to way-lay some Massgoers. After Mass, a speaker stood on the back of the lorry with some sort of microphone in hand to address a gathering of people to entice them to vote for their party. Having pontificated about their achievements, public positions they had held, and their involvement in voluntary organisations, they proceeded to address popular issues. Sometimes, it was only their faithful followers who stayed to hear them out. The cants became familiar as they made promise after promise, looking for your vote. Elections could be won or lost on the strength of a speaker's oratory.

Some staunch supporters used to supply both the flat-backed truck and a microphone to their favoured candidates in the area. Each area had a local Cumann and in turn, the Cumann had a secretary whose duties included tak-

Typical Mobile Advice 'Clinic'

ing the minutes at party meetings, writing reports and meeting politicians. On polling days, the secretary called around to houses ensuring voters had a lift to the polling station and supporters put cars at the party's disposal for this purpose, as lack of transport and even the weather could influence the turnout on voting day. The O'Driscoll family, who lived next door to us on the Nangor Road, sup-

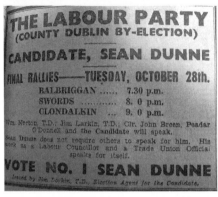

Politics. Election time 1948. Kindly shared by Gerard Byrne, Old Clondalkin & Surrounding Districts.

plied a lorry to support local candidates during elections. They favoured Clann na Poblachta.

The banter was often accompanied by music from a local band. Some bands backed certain candidates and if there was more than one band in an area, it roused excitement if they were backing opposing candidates, with marching and counter-marching going on. Victory was met with scenes of jubilation - the tricolor waving, speeches of gratitude, cheering and shouting. In some places, church bells tolled and tar barrels and bonfires were lit in celebration. With the arrival of television in 1965, candidates paid more attention to party political broadcasts and radio and TV time was allotted by agreement. Some parties ran mobile advice clinics.

The Dublin Mid-West parliamentary constituency was created for the 2002 General Election, composed of parts of the Dublin South-West and Dublin West constituencies. It contains the areas of Clondalkin, Lucan, Rathcoole and Saggart, following the recommendation contained in the constituency review of 2004, it also includes the town of Palmerstown. The Electoral (Amendment) (Dáil Constituencies) Act, 2013 defines the constituency as:

> *"In the county of South Dublin the electoral divisions of: Clondalkin-Cappa-ghmore, Clondalkin-Dunawley, Clondalkin-Moorfield, Clondalkin-Rowlagh, Clondalkin Village, Lucan-Esker, Lucan Heights, Lucan-St. Helens, Newcastle, Palmerstown Village, Palmerston West, Rathcoole, Saggart; and that part of the electoral division of Clondalkin-Monastery situated west of a line drawn along the M50 Western Parkway."*

The constituency elects four deputies, commonly known as TD's (Teachtaí Dála) who represent the constituency in Dáil Éireann the lower house of the Irish Parliament or Oireachtas. Four T.D.s from different political parties were elected to Dáil Éireann in 2016 – one from Sinn Féin, one from People Before Profit, one from Fianna Fáil and one from Fine Gael.

Fox by Monica Sproul (nee Small)

28.
NIGHT LIFE

Mostly, our night time entertainment involved going to dances in the locality such as Saggart or Newcastle or to Baldonnel, or going to the pictures. Some were members of the dramatic society and put on plays. At the present time, Clondalkin has several drama groups - *Clondalkin Dramatical and Musical Society, Sruleen Amateur Drama Club, Bawnogue Players* and *Olpha Players* at Dean-

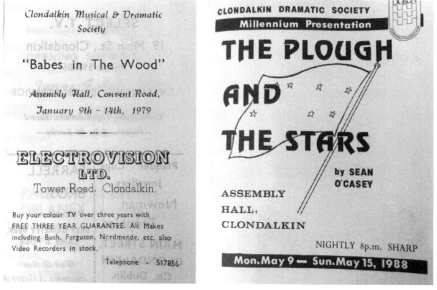

Left: Clondalkin Musical and Dramatic Society, Babes in the Wood, 1979. Right: Clondalkin Dramatic Society, The Plough and the Stars, 1988. Credit to Carmel Jordan who kindly shared.

Clondalkin Dramatic Society, The Righteous Are Bold, 1970. Newspaper clipping taken from scrapbook of Mary Heaney, nee Ging.

srath. Other pursuits were card-playing and listening to the radio. My favourite was dancing.

A large wooden building in Saggart was the premises for the Social Club of Swiftbrook Paper Mills, which was also used as a dancehall. We danced to records there as they never had bands. I learned to dance there, taught by others. Naturally, you learned the easier dances first, like the waltz. When a more difficult dance like a foxtrot or tango came on, you'd head for the ladies in case you were asked, as you didn't want to have to refuse anybody who asked. Social club members could practice their dancing each evening and many became really good dancers and were generous in teaching others.

We'd get to know the regulars, but sometimes not their names, so we'd describe them by some identifying feature. We referred to one chap as '*The Diamond*' as he wore not one, but two, flashy signet rings. We used to see another chap there who was known around Clondalkin Paper Mill as '*The-Man-Who-Killed-a-Cow.*' Apparently based on a truth, the story goes that he ran into a cow on his motorbike; he survived the collision but the cow died. Another rascal who frequented Saggart seemed to get a kick out of raising hopes and then breaking dates. Another fellow's cruel ploy was to dance passionately with a girl all night long until she'd think she had it made, then he'd tell her at the end of the night that he was about to emigrate.

In reference to someone we fancied, we often used their real initials – one pal of mine used to mention '*The Parish Priest*' in reference to a chap she fancied whose initials were 'P.P.' We called another regular, '*The Dear Kid.*' Occasionally, there was announcement at Saggart: '*Only club members will be admitted to the dance in future,*' which made us duck our heads. Although it was a real cause for consternation, we'd nevertheless slip up there for the next dance and never had any trouble getting in.

I will never forget another announcement at Saggart towards the close of the night, when three of us were happily dancing around, '*Two shillings for the special bus.*' Myself and Mary Carroll had funded our friend to go the dance as she was short of money, '*I can't ask Mam,*' she had said. The new man our friend was dancing with quickly piped up, '*I'm going on the bus,*' the understanding being that he would take care of her fare. '*Jesus, Mary and Joseph,*' Mary blurted out, '*what are we going to do?*' The last local bus was long since gone. By the time Mary and I got outside it was pitch dark and we were facing a walk of five miles. By the Grace of God, we caught sight of the Carey lads turning their car, having left George Carey's girlfriend home to Newcastle, so we very much appreciated that lift home. Another time I went to Saggart with Kathleen Hurrell and as usual, we waited for the last dance, then ran outside for the bus, but there was no sign. Some lads standing around realised our predicament, '*The bus is gone, it left early,*' they said. Out came two lads we knew from the dancehall to pick up their bikes. They kindly gave us a crossbar the five miles home, with one of them peppering in case his girlfriend ever got wind of it.

The community hall at Newcastle had a proper dancehall and people came from Rathcoole, Saggart, Lucan, Naas and Clondalkin and even further afield to dance there. Bands who played there included Billy Carter, Johnny Butler, Jimmy Dunney and Johnny Devlin.

There were about two or three big dances a year at Baldonnel and sometimes the hall was hired out – I remember Billy Carter's Band playing there. It was either the bike or the bus to get to Baldonnel. It was frequented by outsiders as well as Air Corps personnel.

Peggy Dell, a great pianist, started her working life selling records in Woolworth's before setting up her own band that played at The Slipper at Fox and

Fun night out. Back L-R, Mick Hurrell, Vincent McCurtin, Myles Matthews. Front L-R, Gert Small, Dolores Looney, Anne Bradley.

Party time - Annie Bradley, Dolores Looney and Gertrude Small.

Geese. Another man, Jimmy Dunny, was a foreman in CIE before setting up his own band.

Another place to go was to Ardclough Hall in Straffan but I only went once as you had to take a 'special' bus. Yet another place we went dancing on occasion was to the Garda Depot in the Phoenix Park, where you met lots of tall men with shiny shoes, some who were not Gardai.

The odd time, we'd get the bus to dances in town. Phil Murtagh played in the Metropole and it was upmarket, often frequented by models. Billy Watson played in Clery's, which was more down to earth. The Ballerina was known for its great dancers. The Crystal was a frequent venue for medical students and the National by nurses. Other places we frequented were the Ierne, the Olympic Ballroom or the Four Provinces. The only problem with town is that we had to

Dinner Dance. Back L-R, G. Hill, X, T. Reynolds, X, V. McCurtin, M. Matthews. Middle, R. Ryan, X, Gert Small. Front, A. Bradley, D. Looney, F. Ryan

leave in time for the last bus at 11.30 p.m., which meant missing the last hour of dancing. We used to dance on until the very last minute, then tear into a run down to the quays, panting when we managed to catch that last bus.

Most dance bands belonged to an 'association' which policed a set of rules regulating what bands could play in venues. Bands outside the association had to play outside Dublin, except for the Mansion House, which was open to them. As the dancehall at Islandbridge was not a member of that association, big dance bands from England often played there. I recall the dance bands of Billy Watson, Phil Murtagh, Johnny Devlin, Earl Gill, and Billy Carter, who played the violin.

It is hard now to imagine life without television but I do remember the earlier programmes when TV arrived in the 1960s including *Lincoln Vale and the Everglades*, the *High Chaparral*, *Get Smart* and the original version of *Hawaii-Five-O*, which starred Jack Lord in the lead role. I also remember the first continuity announcers, including Gay Byrne's wife, Kathleen Watkins.

Kathleen regaled us in a recent TV programme about the trials at Raidió Teilifís Eireann in the early days, when the reception went on the blink, a regular occurrence. During periods of disturbance, Kathleen was tasked to don another hat and entertain listeners by playing her harp which was always close to hand for this purpose.

Photograph of Heron by Mary Reynolds

29.
GHOSTLY TALES

Like all Irish places, Clondalkin was steeped with ghostly lore, often centred on dark and lonely places and most likely precipitated by a few drinks in local hostelries. As children, we used to say certain nearby places were haunted, then we'd scurry away. One of these was the big house at Sally Park, opposite Leinster Terrace.

Ballymount House was supposed to be haunted. At certain times of the year, a phosphorus light emitted from the marshy ground that surrounds it and at night time, light appeared to be in motion in the distance. People used to say it was a ghost walking around carrying a lantern. Many old people in the neighbourhood believed they saw lights moving and they called them, 'The Ballymount Lights.' After dark, we'd often look out our kitchen window and see a bright light flickering in the distance and say it was 'Will-o-the-Wisp.' It was probably the light of a car or motorbike in the Dublin Mountains. Sometimes, a mist can be seen rising from bogs, much the same thing.

As a schoolgirl in 1937, Sheila Nixon, of Yellow Meadows, Watery Lane, related a ghost story told to her by Bartholomew Butterley about Knockmitten. Back then, Knockmitten comprised a cluster of cottages, farmhouses and a church reached via a lane leading from the 7th Lock Road. The story goes that during Cromwell's invasion, the place had been burnt to the ground and the bishop killed and buried in the graveyard. People claim to have seen the ghost of the bishop standing at a gate leading to the old road.

Monastery Road is the location for several ghoulish stories. Not alone is Tully's Castle said to be haunted by the tragic Betty O'Tullach, but 'the hooded monk' is said to cross the road near Mount Saint Joseph. Several drivers re-counted how they had to jam on to let the apparition of a monk cross the road, but then saw nothing there.

Some people claimed to have seen the Banshee sitting on the Monastery Road in Clondalkin combing her hair. One local lady described a little old woman sitting in the middle of the road. I must confess to never having heard or seen a Banshee in my lifetime.

Miriam Hanlon of 'Drom Aoibhinn' on the Monastery Road recounted a story told to her by her father, John Hanlon, (listed as a 'lime-man and farmer') about the graveyard at the Carmelite Monastery, Mount Saint Joseph. Appar-ently, the study of anatomy became an absorbing interest with the establish-ment of medical schools in the 19th century, and with this interest came the need for a supply of human bodies. A reign of terror began with night-time stealing of newly buried corpses for sale to medical schools for dissection pur-poses, no questions asked. Freshly buried bodies were removed from graves, put into sacks and hoisted them onto the shoulders of some unfortunate passer-by who was obliged to carry the body for miles at gunpoint. These men were commonly known as *"Sack-em-ups."* As a result, the people of Clondalkin got permission from the Brothers to leave their dead in a vault in the graveyard which was guarded by relatives of the deceased. The vault is no longer in use but it is still visited by sightseers. The vault lies under the Monastery Road and its entrance is concealed under ivy that grows along the wall of the graveyard.

Opposite Raheen House, Moore's Lane led up to Clonburris House, which was said to be haunted.

A record in Thom's Almanac of 1882 shows, 'J. Moore, Esq., Clonburris House,' which is obviously how Moore's Lane got its name. Cecilia Loughlin of Leinster Terrace related a ghost story as part of the School's Folklore Collection about a young girl who worked in Clonburris House who was in love with a certain young man.

She did not know that this young man was a robber and would do anything to get money. She had money saved up, and this man knew if she died he would fall in for her money. One night as the girl was waiting for her lover to come, she climbed up into a tree. She saw the man coming but he was not alone, so the girl began to sing,

"One moonlit night as I sat high
I waited for one but two passed by
My heart did ache
and the leaves did shake
To see the hole the fox did make."

The man saw her and threw a lassoe over the tree. The other man helped him.
It is said that when they were taking her down from the tree, one of her hands
caught in it and the mark of the hand still remains. I have seen the tree myself,
but as it is very old and covered with ivy it is impossible to see the mark.

Cecilia also related a folklore tale for the Schools Collection about a young farmer, Tom Byrne, who passed a particular set of gate pillars at Greenhills. He had been told that if he said '*Key Hole Open*', one of the gate pillars would open. He pitched his fork into the ground and no sooner had he said the words than the pillar swung open and he was invited inside by people he believed to be human. After feasting, they detained him inside for twelve years, until he asked to leave. By the time he left, he was a withered old man.

Rita Graham of The Square in Lucan, who attended the local Presentation College, wrote a piece about fairies for the Schools Folklore Collection, recounting her mother's story. It was said that fairies lived in an underground passage between Clondalkin and the Hermitage in Lucan. The story goes that about half way between the two places, a fairy bush existed and at certain times of the year, the fairies used it as a ballroom. She also described how a man dressed in red walked from the Liffey Bridge to Esker and hid a sack of gold along the way but nobody could ever find it.

Yet another tale used to go around about a haunted former servant's room in Moyle Park College, where nobody would sleep. The story goes that the Catholic servant of the non-Catholic resident family was refused a priest in her dying hours. Apparently, the rector performed an exorcism and cut slits in the window to release the uneasy spirit and a Mass was said in that room on the anniversary of that date, with no further ghostly appearances.

The hills of Dublin, bordering the Wicklow mountains, have a long history of macabre tales and paranormal events, between stories of 1920s Civil War executions taking place on lonely roads, UFOs and no end of ghost stories. Our

Ruin of the Hell Fire Club, Dublin Mountains

relative proximity to the infamous Hell Fire Club, where card playing, drinking and carousing took place, brought forth all sort of stories like the appearance of the Devil, in human form, only identified by his cloven hoof. Founded in 1735 by the 1st Earl of Rosse, Richard Parsons, who was said to be '*a man of humour and frolic, alleged sorcerer and dabbler in black magic,*' the club used to meet in a hunting lodge built around 1725 by the Speaker of the Irish House of Commons, William Conolly (sic), on Mount Pelier Hill. Strangely, the building had all but one window facing the wrong way for the sun. It took the fancy of the public as 'the Hell Fire Club' and that remained its name forever after. A popular destination for a bicycle spin or a picnic, you were happy to visit during the day but never at night – reputedly, good people did not go there at night.

Given the remoteness of its location, the stories of wild behaviour, debauchery, occult practices and demonic manifestations became part of the lore over the years but could never be verified. A venue for non-stop drinking sessions, with young 'bucks,' supposedly devoting their time to the practice of unbridled hedonism, they swigged *'scultheen,'* a special mixture of whiskey and butter. It was said that a chair was left vacant at each gathering for the devil and they engaged in black masses, where defrocked priests performed parodies of the Catholic Mass and the sacrifice of black cats, such that mutterings of 'satanism' stuck in peoples' minds at any mention of the Hell Fire Club. In addition to the spectral cat, paranormal events were reported such as the apparitions of nuns, poltergeists, weird sounds such as bells with séances held there as a lark and talk of getting a priest to perform exorcisms. The club seemingly disbanded following Parson's death.

Some of the club's legendary visitors were said to include 'Buck' Whaley. He is said to have travelled to Jerusalem in 1789 for a bet of ten thousand pounds and played handball against the Wailing Wall amidst the protests of indignant rabbis. He eventually fled to the Isle of Man to escape financial embarrassment, allegedly after an encounter with the devil in St. Audeon's Church, near Christchurch in Dublin. Another was 'Tiger' Roche, was 'wanted' far and wide, in London, Canada, and Australia for 'duelling activities.' Another contemporary, 'Buck' English, was said to have once shot a sluggish waiter in an English inn and then had him put on the bill for £50.

A tale abounded of the late-night card games with strangers, typically ones who wandered in on a stormy night. A player drops a card under the table and when he stoops to pick it up, he notices that the visitor has a cloven hoof. This motif also pops up in connection with other haunted houses in Ireland. Today Mount Pelier Hill and much of the surrounding lands are owned by Coillte, the State forestry company, and are open to the public.

I never saw a ghost myself, but our Uncle Harold believed in ghosts and he was a great storyteller.

People from around Castleknock, claimed to have seen strange happenings near White's Gate, near the entrance to Farmleigh in the Phoenix Park. In particular, they claimed to have seen a black dog, much larger than normal, in the vicinity of these gates. My uncles, Harold and Eddie, often took a short cut along there and mentioned a strange incident as they cycled in towards town one night. A large shadowy creature ran between their bikes and they both remarked on the fact that they had seen a ghost. Suffice to say that neither of them were drinkers. Uncle Harold's tales often came to mind when walking home alone on a dark and windy night.

Blackberries by Monica Sproul (nee Small)

EPILOGUE

People can make or change a village. In Clondalkin, our family had a place in the community and a unique identity. As kids we learned everything we knew about nature there – how to catch fish, how to listen, how to trust your senses, your intuition, how families and communities can be affected by illness and tragedy. These things I kept with me always. My instincts were developed and built on for life, at a time when I knew not what lay ahead, good or bad. It is natural, however, that people break away bit by bit and many end up living between two worlds, their childhood home and their new life. Unlike many communities in Ireland, most of the children I grew up with were lucky enough to get work and remain in the greater Dublin area but many left and I never saw them again.

As time pushes on, change comes about, and so it did in Clondalkin. From the late 1940s, pockets of development started along Tower Road, Monastery Road, Newlands and in the Haggard field. Building burgeoned ahead relentlessly as farm after farm was sold on. Many of the former homes of grandee families in the area are now gone, demolished or in ruins. Corkagh House was unfortunately demolished along with the 'Hex,' the former playhouse but the estate is now an OPW property enjoyed by the public and Deansrath is still there, in the ownership of the OPW. The vicinity of our old place has become built up, but if you look across to the Dublin mountains, it still looks relatively pastoral.

While advances in mechanisation and technology and cars for all brought more comfortable times, a lot was lost, like neighbourliness and closeness to nature. I have no affinity with the multi-storey apartment blocks in Clondalkin nor do I know anybody in the new estates. As time goes on, I seem fated to be a stranger among strangers. The Clondalkin I knew has changed for good, vanished beyond recognition, but the old landscape is imprinted in my mind. While traversing the roads of life, I also traverse the roads of my youth in a different way to newcomers. I pass by a gate or a fence that has not altered and everything is preserved at once in my mind in its former outline, as if time had stood still. Every step I take, past certain places, and past the homes of people who lived there once brings back memories. Many are now gone but not forgotten.

I feel myself called back into the past, to my old life, showing me how far I have travelled and how remote that old way of life has become, but that sense of belonging creeps through me once more. I am once again the girl who took sheer pleasure skipping across the fields with others, heading for the Sandy Hole. All those familiar landmarks come to mind – the river below with its mucky bank from cattle going for a drink, the fading bracken and heath, the haggard, the Mill pond and the once-present Mill chimney. Sounds in my head carry me back; the Mill hooter, a ticking grandfather clock, or animal sounds. A particular memory I have of living at Raheen was on sunny Sunday mornings when all the windows were open and the stillness was broken by the chime of

Saying Goodbye to Raheen

church bells ringing out before Mass and church services. With the bells as a reminder of the time, there was no need to watch the clock.

Smells bring me back too; the scent of thickened foliage and farmyard smells. On a trip to New York, the smell of horse manure from the jarveys' horses operating around Central Park brought me back to our yard. As if it was yesterday, I remember going down the Nangor Road on my first day at school and yet eight decades of life have crept by.

What mostly comes to mind is the warm atmosphere in our home, the childhood I enjoyed, and the gatherings with family, relations, neighbours and friends, all those precious stored memories.

I think myself back to evenings when we sat around the table in the kitchen looking across to the Dublin mountains, watching the sun going down and the birds kicking up a rumpus before converging on a roosting spot for the night.

Roosting Birds by Monica Sproul (nee Small)

OTHER READING ABOUT THE GREATER CLONDALKIN AREA

Ball, F.E. 1995 (reproduced from 1906 lithograph), *A History of the County Dublin: The people, parishes and antiquities from the earliest times to the close of the eighteenth century.* Part Fourth. The HSP Library, Dublin.

Bolger, Dermot (editor), *County Lines, a portrait of life in South County Dublin.* Published by New Island 2006

Bunbury, Turtle, *CORKAGH - The Life & Times of a South Dublin Demesne 1650-1960,'* *published by South Dublin County Council in May 2018*

Byrne, Roy H.& Graham, Ann, *From Generation to Generation, Clondalkin Village, Parish & Neighbourhood,* by Brunswick Press Limited 1989

Corcoran, Bart, 23 Arran Quay, Printer, *A New Song Sheet adding a new song: The Powder Mills of Clondalkin .*

Cowell, John, *Dublin's Famous People, Dublin,* 1980, p24-5 (Bianconi.]

D'Alton, *History of County Dublin,* 1838.

Dix, E.R, *The Lesser Castles of the County Dublin,* 1897

Dowling, Eamon, *Families of Newlands, Co. Dublin,* by Genealogical Society of Ireland, 2001

Grose, Francis, *Antiquities of Ireland.*

Joyce, Weston St. John, 4th edition, 1939, *The Neighbourhood of Dublin: Its Topography, Antiquities and Historical Associations.* Dublin: M.H. Gill & Son, 1921. *Published by The Skellig Press, Dublin.* (first published 1912)

Kerr, John, *1992. Queen Victoria's Scottish Diaries. United Kingdom: Eric Dobby Publishing. pp. 146–159. ISBN 1-85882-018-9.* (1880 description of the Dirnanean estate)

MacCarthaigh, Deasmhumhan, *Gleanings from the District of Lucan.*

McNally, Mary, *South County Scrapbook*, History of South Dublin County, by Brunswick Press Limited, 1989

Lewis, Samuel, *A Topographical Dictionary of Ireland,* 1837. Extract, Clondalkin, a parish.

Other references:-

Duke of Leinster's press clippings, [PRONI D/3078/6/7; MIC 541/25], description by John Cowell from '*Dublin's Famous People*,' [Dublin, 1980, p24-5.]
'*Sharing Memories*' – extract from Clondalkin Historical magazine.
Clondalkin Historical Archives
Journal of the Royal Society of Antiquaries of Ireland, 1899

Helpful websites:-

www.duchas.ie (The Schools Folklore Collection)
www.niah.ie
https://irishwaterwayshistory.com/tag/castleknock/
www.fingalcoco.ie
https://www.gaa.ie/the-gaa/oral-history/members-roundtower-gaa-club-clondalkin.
www.thom'sdirectoryofireland.ie
http://www.dublin1850.com/porter1912/intro.html (Porter's Guide and Directory for County Dublin, 1912

www.askaboutireland.com (The Mills of South Dublin County)
Old Clondalkin and Surrounding Districts, Facebook site.

A final word relates to wonderful records everybody can share in, for free.

One is the National Inventory of Architectural Heritage (NIAH), which is part of the Department of Arts, Heritage, Regional, Rural and Gaeltacht Affairs, set up in 1990 for the establishment and maintenance of an inventory of monuments, as well as groups of buildings and sites to be protected, which serves as a central record for architectural heritage purposes. www.niah.ie.

A further resource is the local history collection at South Dublin County Council Library in Tallaght.

Another great record is the National Folklore Collection, in particular, The Schools Collection, a *collection* of *folklore,* old cures and history compiled by schoolchildren and written in their own handwriting in Ireland in the 1930s. The original records held at the Folklore Department in UCD are now available on-line: www.duchas.ie. The contributions from children in the locality are too numerous to include in this book but some may be interested to find handwritten contributions from their forebears. The following is a list of children who contributed while at local national schools in Clondalkin, but it must be noted that this list might not be exhaustive:-

Bracken, Vincent, Clondalkin
Doyle, Breeda, Main Street, Tallaght
Feighery, Lillie, Danesrath, Clondalkin
Flanagan, Sinead, Cornerpark, Newcastle
Galvin, Nora, Tower House, Clondalkin
Hanlon, Miriam, Monastery Road, Clondalkin
Loughlin, Cecilia, Leinster Terrace, Clondalkin
Murphy, Monica, Riverside Farm, Watery Lane, Clondalkin
McCreevy, Chris, 9th Lock House, Clondalkin
Nixon, Sheila, Yellow meadows, Clondalkin
Nolan, Kitty, Commons, Clondalkin

Nolan, Peggy, Commons, Clondalkin
O'Brien, Harry, 9th Lock, Clondalkin
O'Connor, George, Mill Yard, Clondalkin
Ryan, Maura, Drimnagh Road, Clondalkin
Tully, John, Collinstown Park, Clondalkin

ABOUT THE AUTHOR

Gertrude Reynolds (*née* Small) was born and raised on the Old Nangor Road in Clondalkin, where the Small family lived since the 1920s. Gertrude recalls the vibrant past of Clondalkin and surrounding areas from the time when much of it was farmland, dotted with grand houses. In this book, she meanders along its roads telling you who lived where and how the community intermingled, a blurring of lines between memoir and local history.